External Debt, Savings, and Growth in Latin America

External Debt, Savings, and Growth in Latin America

Edited by
Ana María Martirena-Mantel

Papers presented at a seminar sponsored by the International Monetary Fund and the Instituto Torcuato di Tella, held in Buenos Aires on October 13–16, 1986

International Monetary Fund, Washington, D.C.
Instituto Torcuato di Tella, Buenos Aires
1987

© International Monetary Fund, 1987

Library of Congress Cataloging-in-Publication Data

External debt, savings, and growth in Latin America.

  Includes bibliographies.
  1. Debts, External—Latin America—Congresses.
2. Saving and investment—Latin America—Congresses.
3. Latin America—Economic policy—Congresses.
I. Martirena-Mantel, Ana María. II. International
Monetary Fund. III. Instituto Torcuato Di Tella.
HJ8514.5.E984 1987   336.3'435'098   87–21422
ISBN 0–939934–95–7

Price: $12.00

Contents

Foreword ix

Acknowledgment xi

List of Participants xiii

Introduction and Overview 1
  Ana María Martirena-Mantel
World Economic Outlook and Prospects for Latin America
Impact on Debtor Countries of World Economic Conditions
Choice of Growth Strategy
Fiscal Policy, Growth, and Design of Stabilization Programs
Adjustment, Indebtedness, and Economic Growth
Savings in Brazil
Observations

World Economic Outlook and Prospects for Latin America 26
  Anthony Lanyi
Slow Growth in Industrial Countries
  Recent Developments
  Medium-Term Outlook
  Policy Issues
Debt Crisis and Its Consequences for Developing Countries
  Origins of Debt Crisis
  Recent Developments in Debt Crisis
  Medium-Term Outlook
  Policy Issues
Conclusions

Comments 51
  Carlos Bazdresch P.
  Winston Fritsch

Impact on Debtor Countries of World Economic Conditions   60
  Rudiger Dornbusch
A Conceptual Framework
  A Model
  Welfare
  Credit Rationing
  System-Wide Adjustment
  Foreign Demand
  Market Access and Creditor Country Policies
Real Exchange Rate and Inflation
Some Facts and Some Problems
  Commodities
  Interest Rates
  Private Sector Lending
  Investment
Solutions to Debt and Growth Problems?
  Debt-Equity Swaps
  Reversal of Capital Flight
  Debt Relief
References

Comments   87
        Vittorio Corbo
        Daniel Heymann

Choice of Growth Strategy: Trade Regimes and Export Promotion   95
        Julio Berlinski
The Problem
Devices of Trade Intervention
  Import Protection
  Export Taxation (Protection)
  Multilateral Trade Arrangements
  Exchange Rate Regulations
Bias Against Exports
  Sources of Bias
  Changes in Anti-Export Bias
Changes in Import Protection
  Initial Conditions
  On New Reform Proposals
Conclusions
Annex
References

Comments   114
>   *Sterie T. Beza*
>   *Germán Botero A.*

Fiscal Policy, Growth, and Design of Stabilization Programs   121
>   *Vito Tanzi*
Fiscal Policy and Design of Fund Programs
Stabilization Policy and Economic Growth
Concluding Remarks
References

Comments   141
>   *Luis Jorge Garay S.*
>   *Ricardo Hausmann*

**Adjustment, Indebtedness, and Economic Growth:
   Recent Experience   154**
>   *Guillermo Ortiz*
Debt Strategy: Implementation and Results
Financial Aspects
Adjustment Process
Indebtedness: Impact on Adjustment Program
   Exchange Depreciation
   Inflation and Fiscal Deficit
   Indebtedness and Capital Flight
Adjustment and Growth?
References

Comments   175
>   *Jorge Marcano*
>   *Leonidas Ortega*

Trends and Prospects for Savings in Brazil   180
>   *Carlos A. Longo*
Composition of Financial Savings
Savings in Decline
Increases in Investment
Financing the Deficit
Mobilization of Savings

Comments   195
>   *Aldo A. Arnaudo*
>   *Pedro A. Palma*

Foreword

Under its seminar program for nonofficials, the International Monetary Fund was privileged to have been joined by Instituto Torcuato di Tella of Argentina in sponsoring a seminar on "External Debt, Savings, and Growth in Latin America." The seminar, which was conducted in Spanish, was held at the Hindu Club, located in Don Torcuato, near Buenos Aires, in October 1986, and was attended by economists representing a wide range of views from universities, banks, research centers, and other nonofficial institutions in Argentina, Brazil, Colombia, Ecuador, Mexico, the United States, and Venezuela. Participants, who attended in a personal capacity, also included members of the staffs of the Fund, the Economic Commission for Latin America and the Caribbean, and the World Bank.

The relevance, indeed the urgency, of the topics discussed provided an opportunity to have a frank and constructive exchange of views and experiences which, I am convinced, has enriched the understanding of the issues and has contributed to focusing the search for appropriate solutions. This, of course, is a major objective of the seminar program, as well as the objectives of promoting a better understanding of the work of the Fund and of improving the Fund's knowledge of thinking in academic, business, and other nongovernmental circles.

This book represents the continuation of the Fund's effort to publish a wide variety of views about its role and activities in the developing world. While all the views expressed are not necessarily shared by the Fund, it is our hope that their dissemination can contribute to a more informed discussion of the issues.

MICHEL CAMDESSUS
Managing Director
International Monetary Fund

Acknowledgment

It is important to record the warm thanks of all the participants in this seminar to those who were responsible for its success.

I should begin by referring to the devoted and tireless organizational work of Hernán Puentes, of the External Relations Department of the International Monetary Fund in Washington, D.C., and Alberto Petrecolla, Director of the Instituto Torcuato di Tella in Buenos Aires, both of whom spared no effort to arrange this seminar.

My special thanks are due to Mónica Fiorini and Mercedes Vigliershio de Viña of the Instituto Torcuato di Tella, who with rare skill and efficiency overcame the many obstacles inherent in the operational details of holding such a seminar. I would also like to thank Jennie Lee Carter, Assistant Editor in the External Relations Department of the Fund, for expertly directing the volume from draft through publication, and the English Division of the Bureau of Language Services of the Fund, for translating papers from their original language.

Finally, in my capacity as moderator and editor, a mark of confidence placed in me by both institutions, I received great help from Javier Ortiz and Pablo Gómez through their patient, professional transcription of the seventeen hours of sessions.

ANA MARÍA MARTIRENA-MANTEL
*Senior Economist, Instituto Torcuato
di Tella, and Professor of
International Economics,
University of Buenos Aires*

List of Participants

Argentina

Aldo A. Arnaudo
Universidad de Córdoba

Julio Berlinski
Instituto Torcuato di Tella

Roque Fernández
Centro de Estudios Macroeconómicos de la Argentina

Daniel Heymann
Comisión Económica para América Latina y el Caribe

Brazil

Jose Luis Carvalho
Fundaçao Getulio Vargas

Winston Fritsch
Pontificia Universidade Católica do Rio de Janeiro

Antonio Kandir
Universidad de Campinas

Carlos A. Longo
Fundaçao Instituto de Pesquizas Económicas

Colombia

Germán Botero A.
Consultant

Javier Fernández
Consultant

Luis Jorge Garay S.
Ministerio de Hacienda

Armando Montenegro
Junta Monetaria

Ecuador

Antonio Acosta
Banco Pichincha

Leonidas Ortega
Banco Continental

Mexico

Carlos Bazdresch P.
Trimestre Económico

United States

Rudiger Dornbusch
Massachusetts Institute of Technology

Venezuela

Ricardo Hausmann
Instituto de Estudios de Administración

Jorge Marcano
Ministerio de Hacienda

Pedro A. Palma
Metroeconómica

Luis Supelano
Instituto Venezolano de Planificación

International Bank for Reconstruction and Development

Vittorio Corbo

International Monetary Fund

Sterie T. Beza
Anthony Lanyi
Guillermo Ortiz
Hernán Puentes
Vito Tanzi

Instituto Torcuato di Tella

Ana María Martirena-Mantel
Alberto Petrecolla

Observers

Ricardo Arriazu
Consultant

Alfredo Canavese
Instituto di Tella

Roberto Cortés
Instituto di Tella

Juan C. de Pablo
El Cronista Comercial

Guido di Tella
Instituto di Tella

Pablo Gerchunoff
Instituto di Tella

Adrián Guisarri
Bridas

Rolf Mantel
Centro de Estudios Macroeconómicos de la Argentina

Armando Ribas
Consultant

Carlos Rodríguez
Centro de Estudios Macroeconómicos de la Argentina

Osvaldo Schenone
Centro de Estudios Macroeconómicos de la Argentina

Introduction and Overview

Ana María Martirena-Mantel

The decision of the International Monetary Fund to hold seminars on a periodic basis in various countries gave rise, in the Buenos Aires seminar, to an event whose importance was particularly evident. During the two and a half days of exposition and debate, economists from the Fund, the World Bank, the Massachusetts Institute of Technology, and various Latin American countries (Argentina, Brazil, Colombia, Ecuador, Mexico, and Venezuela—from universities, banks, private financial organizations, central banks, ministries of finance, research institutes, planning institutes, etc.) met to share opinions and ideas put forward by colleagues representing diverse approaches to desirable economic policies. Nonetheless—and this is what makes these seminars attractive, in my view—the majority of the participants, in the final analysis, always revealed a significant degree of modesty, in that they did not claim to have the perfect answer of how to adjust without internal and external costs and in such a way as to bring about sustained growth without distortions.

Following is a summary of the main arguments advanced by each speaker, immediately followed by a synthesis of the comments of the discussants, and of the discussion that spontaneously occurred throughout the sessions. The section concludes with some final observations.

World Economic Outlook and Prospects for Latin America

The principal message contained in Anthony Lanyi's substantial paper is that in the past five years there has been a kind of awareness

1

among specialized public opinion—perhaps to a greater extent than in government departments—of a basic fact: the interdependence of the world economy. The developed countries and the developing countries are interdependent; the debt crisis among the latter endangers the financial stability of the former, while any growth crisis in the capital importing developing countries significantly affects employment in the developed countries. This is a reality, despite our "small country" assumptions so prevalent in the economic analysis of open economies, which can nonetheless be reinterpreted, as does the author, by assuming that the impact on the developing countries of events in developed countries is stronger than the opposite phenomenon.

The author distinguishes two major crises in the post-1982 period. The first of these, the growth crisis, began in the 1970s as a result of the slowing down of growth in the more developed countries; the second, the debt crisis, began at the end of the 1970s with the increase in the debt of countries that were seeking to increase their growth rate within the context of a slow-developing world economy.

The author devotes a good part of his paper to a factual analysis of both crises. He explains the slackening of growth in the developed economies (a) by using recent statistical data, (b) by quantifying a range of hypotheses that emphasize medium-term (1988–91) trends, which he calls "the IMF hypotheses," and (c) by discussing various aspects of the economic policies of these economies.

He next explains the causes of the debt crisis in the developing countries, dividing the latter into three main groups—those with and without recent debt problems and those of Latin America. For the developing economies, the author also explores (a) the origins of the debt crisis and recent data, (b) medium-term prospects (1987–91), and (c) some aspects of their economic policy.

Within this analytical framework the author asks a vital question, while at the same time establishing the limits of a possible answer: What can be done about the growth crisis without making the debt crisis worse?

The paper notes the lack of consensus in the developed countries regarding the underlying reasons for the slowdown of growth. However, various policy measures could help to rectify the situation, such as greater financial stability, a reduction in the proportion of resources absorbed by the public sector (despite the considerable ignorance that still exists concerning the long-term effects of this reduction), an attack on market rigidities, on which he observes correctly that market imperfections should not be regarded as unalterable facts of life; they can be impacted through specific programs, several of which are still at the experimental stage.

Regarding the developing countries, the author displays a notable intellectual balance in stressing that the debt crisis is the result not only of inappropriate policies in the developing countries (of which we are all aware) but also of exogenous factors in the international economy that hurt the developing countries, such as the increase in nominal interest rates in the major countries (1979–80), which affected the servicing of debt through variable interest rates; the increase in real interest rates as the world prices of primary products declined; the appreciation of the U.S. dollar (1981–84), reflected in the falling international prices of tradable goods; the increase in the price of oil for oil importing countries and for the non-oil exporting countries; and the reduction in external demand as a result of the recession in the major developed countries. The author also mentions the probable dangers for the developing countries of having to plan their economic policy in the context of the heavy burden of external indebtedness which include the assumption that there may be good prospects for a major increase in their foreign trade on the one hand and/or of obtaining significant official assistance for their development on the other.

This brings us to the central question of this paper: What can be done to solve the growth crisis without worsening the debt crisis? In the first place, Lanyi considers that there is wide scope for debt renegotiation, and, in the second place, he clearly and decisively rejects (a) any repudiation by the debtor countries of their debts and (b) the refusal of the developed countries to alleviate the debt situation.

The first commentary on Lanyi's work dealt with the diagnosis and the prognosis that clearly emerged from his analysis. Regarding the diagnosis, the commentator "saw" a prescription in the paper: the indebted countries have behaved badly and so must mend their ways and do things properly. In part, the commentator agreed; what they were seeing was the end of the import substitution model and of the idea of bringing about growth through rapid indebtedness. This was recognized and accepted in principle as a change in the right direction, but it had to be asked whether this change would actually occur. For it to happen some things had to alter, and the commentator asked why Latin America had adopted import substitution policies that were then backed up by borrowing. Certainly, mistakes had been made, including analytical errors, but in many developing countries social forces constrained policymakers, and there were social limits. It was not only productive resources and geography that mattered; one also had to consider the social characteristics of some of these economies, which identified them as naturally more *dirigiste,* a fact which could not be cured by economic policies alone. Raymond Aron said: "These are countries where the State builds the Nation and not the Nation the State." Since these structures could not easily be dismantled, it was not possible to apply general recipes; on the other hand, it was not possible to do nothing and just leave things as they were.

Regarding the prognosis, the commentator noted that Mr. Lanyi's paper said nothing about the probable evolution of the financial system, from which it could be inferred that everything would stay the same. If this happened, not everyone would be happy, and probably not the Fund either. It would be better for the creditors to recognize explicitly that they had lost part of their capital, because, even if they wished to do so, many debtor countries could not continue along the present path without a strong probability of facing bankruptcy and/or deep recession.

The commentator summed up with a plea for common sense, namely that more time should be given to the debtor countries, capital losses should be absorbed, and a new start should be made by making room for the necessary structural changes that respected the social constraints already mentioned.

Another commentator referred to the need to take capital losses into account in the projections in Lanyi's work. The explicit absence somewhat undermined the projections, in that it reduced the probability of their being fulfilled. Also, since these projections related to a scenario already so intrinsically uncertain, the question arose as to what contingency measures were envisaged and what was the role to be played by the international lending organizations in helping to promote the acceptance of these losses.

In some of the comments on this paper, the author was regarded as very concerned to point out the "faults" of the most indebted developing countries and the "virtues" of other, less-indebted developing countries. These speakers did not regard this as a very felicitous classification in view of the great structural diversity of the countries within each group, which contained countries as structurally different as the Republic of Korea, Bolivia, and Mexico. One commentator touched on a recurring theme of this seminar, namely that of defining the notion of structure in a developing country, along with the degree of its immutability or flexibility. In this sense, virtue or blame became functions of the structural characteristics of each economy, although it was clear that on occasions the policies of some developing countries left a great deal to be desired. However, it was noted that the structure of an economy, with which virtuous characteristics were frequently associated, is the direct result of the economic policies carried out by the authorities.

The structuralist theme closed with an important observation regarding general equilibrium, which identifies the initial structure of an economy as the sum of previous policies at $t = 0$, but also as a function of the institutional characteristics that clearly are independent of these policies. But if they are independent, there may be an initial sequence of mistaken policies, and the process of correcting these (the prerequisite of any structural reform) will necessarily take time, basically owing to our lack of knowledge concerning the complexity of this process of indebtedness, which is frequently at odds with stabilization policies, thereby making comparisons unilluminating.

The discussion on this paper ended with a reference to the need for a sensitivity analysis that quantified the influence of the economic policies of the countries of the Northern Hemisphere on the various debtor countries, broken down according to their structural characteristics. It would be desirable that a work of this nature should explore the prospects for greater coordination of macroeconomic policies by these countries and the role of the Fund in this context (a recurring theme throughout this seminar, which is taken up in the concluding observations).

Impact on Debtor Countries of World Economic Conditions

To investigate the impact that macroeconomic events in the developed countries have on the debtor countries, Rudiger Dornbusch presented two models, one real and one financial. The real model is a simple one of the Mundell-Fleming type, though expanded. It corresponds to a small country participating in the international capital and primary goods markets, though not in the nontraditional exports market. Three kinds of internationally tradable goods are distinguished: traditional exports, nontraditional manufactured exports (imperfect substitutes for similar goods of foreign origin), and competitive importable goods.

The real model can be reduced to a system of two independent equations that determine endogenous variables, real absorption capacity, and the terms of trade between nontraditional exports and competitive importable goods. The international interest rate, external indebtedness, and the international price of oil are taken as exogenous.

With this model the author undertakes various exercises. First, comparative static analysis is used to illustrate the effects of external shocks such as a rise in oil prices, an increase in the external interest rate (interpreted in the model as the intertemporal terms of the trade), and a reduction in the conventional exogenous terms of trade for traditional exports.

Second, the author examines social well-being by analyzing the process of adjustment to these external shocks, first by considering a distortion-free economy that maximizes the utility of households and firms, and is subjected to constraints between two periods. The author finds that even under these ideal conditions the external shocks that cause the terms of trade to deteriorate also affect levels of well-being adversely, since to go into debt to finance disequilibrium, rather than adjusting it, is a suboptimal option, except when the shocks are purely temporary. When capital market distortions or credit rationing are introduced, the endogenous terms of trade deteriorate (real depreciation of the exchange rate) because it becomes necessary to adjust to temporary shocks also, all of which intensify the effects of the initial shock on levels of well-being.

Other "special effects" analyzed by the author that increase the cost of adjustment and the impact on well-being of external shocks include, for example, simultaneous adjustment by various debtor countries seeking to expand their exports at the same time (which causes a deterioration in the terms of trade or real depreciation, both regarding manufactured exports and traditional exports), and ends in a worldwide glut of developing country exports.

The financial model contained in the second part of the work is used to discuss the relationship between the rate of inflation and the real exchange rate. It uses the so-called Oliveira-Tanzi effect, along the lines of the macroeconomic models with multiple equilibria recently developed by various Argentine economists studying hyperinflation (G. Escude, A. Canavese and A. Petrecolla, R. Fernandez, and R. Mantel) and also by M. Bruno and S. Fischer.

One crucial conclusion that emerges from this analysis is that debt service ends up being extremely inflationary in the countries that can least afford to allow this to happen (cf. the plus sign of the partial derivative of the fiscal deficit coefficient in relation to the real exchange rate). In other words, as the real exchange rate is depreciated in order to raise external competitiveness, negative financial effects appear in the form of an increase in the real value of payments to service a debt contracted in dollars, and hence in the coefficient of the fiscal deficit.

Professor Dornbusch's paper gave rise to a very lively discussion that focused both on the models and the conclusions. Regarding the former, one commentator referred to the disaggregation of the real sector of the economy with the two terms of trade, one endogenous and the other exogenous; this entails accepting the hypothesis of imperfect substitution between (nontraditional) manufactured exports and their substitutes of foreign origin for developing countries, which results in the real depreciation being identified with the decline in the terms of trade. Although this is a logical conclusion from the model, it is not a very useful result from the point of view of the actual experience of various small developing countries (such as the Republic of Korea or Turkey), where clearly this decline in relative prices was not necessary to enable them to penetrate the international markets for manufactured goods. Even if this deterioration in the relative price of nontraditional exports is accepted, it is followed by a possibly efficient expansion of the industries producing import substitutes, in view of the induced substitution effect.

Another conclusion that follows from the logic of the financial model, but whose significance in the real world was of some concern, was that relating to the increase in inflation brought about by any attempt to deregulate the financial markets as a result of the increase in the velocity of circulation and the decline in the demand for money.

A serious concern was also reflected in another commentary on Professor Dornbusch's work, involving the message received by the developing countries over time from the developed countries. In the 1970s, predictions were being made about movements in certain prices which did not in fact subsequently occur, such as an increase in commodity prices, a reduction in international exchange rates, and growth in the industrial countries. The message being received today is that of adjustment with growth, or, in blunter terms, pay your debt and open your economies. The speaker asked whether, leaving aside the internal policies of the developing countries themselves that may promote this growth, the international conditions existed for this outcome. In practice, the debt constituted a serious problem that was still not fully understood. It was serious because it was probable that the trade surpluses that were being achieved, very large in some cases, could not be sustained in the medium term. In other words, there was an incentive not to make the transfer implicit in these trade surpluses, which implied that current account surpluses and deficits should not be seen merely in terms of exports or imports but in terms of savings and investment. It was just as bad to achieve a trade surplus through a fall in investment as to increase the deficit through a fall in savings, since both undermined the long-term equilibrium of the economy. More specifically, the speaker identified a basic dilemma in querying the medium-term feasibility of the flow of domestic savings required to make the transfers entailed by adjustment, since very probably the public would reduce savings rather than consumption expenditure, which left very little room for growth.

Nonetheless, one now hears calls for structural changes in trade, fiscal policies, and exchange rate policies in the Latin American countries to help solve the debt problem. If Professor Dornbusch's financial model were accepted, the feasibility of this objective becomes doubtful, since there is a clear conflict from the financial point of view: trade liberalization requires depreciation of the real exchange rate, which increases the deficit! In turn, a higher real exchange rate may mean lower real wages in terms of exportable goods, as has frequently been the experience in some Latin American countries. Finally, the commentator pointed to the need, in a "perfect world," for certain contingency arrangements to be incorporated in the monitoring of the debt situation in order to offset shocks and facilitate adjustment. In other words, as various seminar participants had noted, contingency arrangements should be agreed between the parties involved in fixing targets (international institutions and the member countries) to take into account unforeseeable events that might make these targets impossible to maintain in absolute terms; there could be more general use, for example, of the contingency clauses in the recent agreement with Mexico, which linked debt service payments to oil prices.

Another aspect of Professor Dornbusch's paper that aroused comment was the negative impact of real depreciation on the deficit emerging from the model. Bearing in mind that export taxes are an important source of receipts in Latin America, it was necessary to take account of the possible positive net effect of an increase in exports as part of the adjustment process, an issue which should be examined in the light of the deterioration in the international prices of certain export items in Latin American countries.

Another comment saw the solution proposed by Dornbusch to the debt problem as being nothing more than palliatives. It was pointed out that we needed to know more about the contribution that each of the various proposals put forward, for example, "debt-equity swaps," Baker Plan, Bradley Proposal, and "debt-relief," could make to solving the problem.

Choice of Growth Strategy

Julio Berlinski began by recalculating for 98 countries the hypothesis put forward by Simon Kuznets in 1964 regarding the inverse relationship between the share of foreign trade in the gross national product (GNP) and the size of a country and the positive correlation between this ratio and the GNP per capita, taking the size factor into consideration. Taking this hypothesis as a starting point, the author presented an exhaustive survey of the principal tools used in Latin America to control imports and to promote exports, emphasizing their considerable variety, the lack of coordination between them, the major role played by tariff exemptions in Argentina and Brazil, and the role of nontariff restrictions (quantitative restrictions and surcharges on imports). One important aspect of this research is the theoretical and empirical analysis of the anti-export bias and its makeup, which could lead to the improvement and refinement of export promotion tools.

The paper discussed two principal kinds of anti-export bias. On the one hand, there is the absolute bias, measured by the negative effective rate of protection due to the high cost of tradable and nontradable inputs, which renders the export sector noncompetitive. On the other hand, there is the relative bias, which results from the fact that the nominal protection rewards sales of the same good differently, depending on whether these occur in the domestic or the international market. Hence the traditional attempts, for example, to offset the anti-export bias through subsidies basically involve an attack on the absolute rather than the relative bias.

To calculate these biases, the author divides tradable goods into three groups: agriculture or primary commodities, the agro-industries, and other industries. He finds that the last-named sector suffers the highest absolute bias as measured by the negative rate of effective protection, and that the agro-industries internalize the external competitiveness of primary product activities by receiving high positive rates of effective protection for their sales in the domestic market.

Berlinski's work ends with a proposal designed to improve this state of affairs as a response to the question as to how both kinds of bias can be reduced. To lessen the relative bias, he proposes, on the one hand, that account should be taken, at $t = 0$, of the institutional framework or initial conditions for the reform, and, on the other hand, that a compromise should be sought between the best policy from the point of view of the trained economist and a policy that is a function of the credibility that it possesses, and which can be embodied in stable, lasting rules by economic policymakers. To achieve an increase in exports he proposes a phased reform, designed to achieve a major initial expansion of exports (capable of "purchasing" credibility) by reducing the absolute bias through reimbursements and drawbacks, culminating in the full liberalization of imports which would eliminate the relative bias by introducing rationality into the incentives to domestic sales. The basic justification presented by the author for this first stage is that export promotion is a historical fact that already exists at the start of the process. Therefore, the aim must be to improve its application by reducing the relevant bias. For the author, credibility is a function of the sequential approach, which shortens the time required to achieve the long-term benefits brought about by the elimination of the above-mentioned double bias.

Many of the comments stimulated by this work focused on the sequential nature of the process of opening the economy, which the author proposes should be preceded by an expansion of exports. It is not clear why credibility requires this expansion in exports, when in reality it should be a function of the degree of compatibility of the various policies among themselves. It might happen that export subsidies would not produce the required structural change in production, such that resources are transferred from nonmarketable and import-substituting sectors to the sectors producing exportable goods. Furthermore, if these subsidies are high enough, the need to transfer resources could be avoided and goods could be exported that previously were import substitutes. Thus, a sequential process such as that proposed by the author might end up merely prolonging existing distortions, even leaving aside the problem that any export promotion policy entails for public finances, a problem which in fact requires that explicit attention be given to the linkages between commercial policy and financial policy.

Another commentator discussed the experience of twenty countries in a World Bank project that was capable of throwing some light on the optimum sequence for opening the economy on the terms suggested by the author. Reference was made to the Republic of Korea, where in the 1960s a very complex system of export subsidies was devised which in later studies by Larry Westphal was shown to be neutral at the margin. This neutrality indicated a lack of relative bias in the so-called Korean miracle. However, this aggressive subsidy policy would not be feasible today because of regulations of the General Agreement on

Tariffs and Trade, which leaves us with the real exchange rate as the crucial variable in implementing the process of opening the economy.

There was an interesting discussion on this point, during which it was pointed out that in practice Japan, the United States, Brazil, and even the Republic of Korea had industrialized with protectionist policies, but that it was impossible to draw any conclusions from these experiences regarding the notion of "intelligent protection" that could lead to it being possible to "pick the winner." Economists are very ignorant in this area, which frequently produces a situation in which political systems, which are responsible for the design of tariff regimes, end up by protecting every product at any price (as in Argentina). Therefore, it is not clear how providing export subsidies can put an end to internal distortions since, when these exist, the conditions of Lerner's theorem are not completely satisfied. The solution has to be simple: tackle the import substitution sector as soon as possible, reduce tariffs, and simultaneously allow the real exchange rate to rise to achieve external equilibrium. If this solution is not adopted, it is because the consequent dismantling of the tariffs around highly protected sectors undermines some very long-standing privileges.

Finally, it was noted that the financial cost of promoting exports through subsidies increases in line with the success of the policy, while the financial cost of tariff reductions declines with the success of the process of opening the economy. Therefore, in terms of the financial effects of the two policies for opening the economy, the tariff reduction strategy would be more credible because the treasury would not press for it to be abandoned.

Fiscal Policy, Growth, and Design of Stabilization Progams

The general objective of Vito Tanzi's paper was to respond to a common complaint by critics of the Fund that the countries faced with a situation such as the oil or debt crisis are obliged to follow stabilization policies that are incompatible with economic growth.

The author strongly challenged this criticism, setting out the general guidelines of what he called the "financial approach to the balance of payments" or the "financial approach to stabilization programs," while at the same time raising a series of questions for discussion. In general terms, these focused on the link between the short term and the long term in the approach taken by the Fund, which involved the recognition that growth without stability was not technically feasible in the long term and that stability without growth was not politically feasible except in the short term. The financial approach to the balance of payments had several simultaneous implications.

• In the first place, it involved the recognition that there is a macroeconomic approach and a microeconomic approach to stabilization policies. The former, which is that traditionally followed by the Fund, is based exclusively on demand-management policies that consist of setting financial targets or limits based on an implicit model (Polak and Robichek) linking the budget deficit and the balance of payments outturn. Then each country decides on the specific way in which it will meet the financial target; in other words, it decides which tax rates it will raise or which expenditures it will reduce, with the advice of the Fund. Under this approach it makes little difference whether the financial target is achieved by reducing productive expenditure or by raising taxes that generate major disincentives. The second, or microeconomic approach, involves the recognition that financial policy affects both aggregate demand and aggregate supply; in other words, it entails an examination of the specific financial measures adopted, since in the medium term these do make a difference in relation to the target of reducing a given financial deficit.

• The recognition of the crucial difference between these two approaches leads naturally to both a theorem and a corollary. The former tells us that the macroeconomic approach is a necessary but not sufficient condition for growth, which requires effective structural policies that attack the microeconomic distortions in the economy. The corollary points out that the greater the reaction of supply to the structural changes (microeconomic approach), the less the amount of demand regulation required; in other words, it will be that much less necessary to use the macroeconomic approach, with its concentration on variables such as the levels of saving and investment or the amounts of tax receipts. However, this does not necessarily mean accepting the existence of tradeoffs between greater microconditionality and greater flexibility in the macrotargets.

• In the author's view, the transition from the macroeconomic approach to the microeconomic approach, not yet complete, gives rise to several vital questions for the International Monetary Fund and for its member countries, questions that contain a double danger. Concerning the macro approach, the danger lies in attention being diverted from the basic objective of economic policy (lasting gains in the balance of payments, growth, and price stability) to the fulfillment of the targets for their own sake to establish the success of the program.

Concerning the micro approach, the danger lies in the increased conditionality (defined as the range of policies that the Fund expects member countries to follow to obtain access to the general resources of the Fund) that may be entailed if it is necessary to identify a core of structural policies on the supply side.

As was to be expected, this paper gave rise to a lengthy and animated exchange of views involving sixteen contributions, which are grouped under various headings and summarized below.

It was stated that the paper did not set out a theory of growth nor a specific model of growth, but that it nevertheless assumed that growth would be positive if distortions were eliminated through the microeconomic approach, that is, distortions that prevented relative prices from assigning productive resources efficiently. In the absence of a theory of growth, and since at present the sources of economic growth were not precisely known, it was difficult to define these new conditions objectively. The World Bank, for example, had an objective and practical standard of conditionality, namely, the rate of return; what was needed was a more practical criterion than that of "growth," which was perhaps too abstract. Although it was true that there was no theory of growth generally accepted among economists, it could nonetheless be agreed, without any need to adopt any of the many existing theories, that the paper pointed out the destimulating effects of many distortions whose removal would have positive effects on growth.

Another group of comments stressed the merit of the paper in spelling out some of the basic problems, both methodological and operational, revealed in Fund programs. It was because of these problems, which the author grouped under the name of the macroeconomic approach, that the paper essentially sought to extend conditionality to the allocation of resources, given the inability of aggregate financial targets to achieve the objectives of adjustment in a context of permanent growth. Therefore, the crucial issue in Mr. Tanzi's work was that of extended conditionality, since there was no need to prove that distortions existed in Latin America, whatever economic approach or economic model was used and accepted. These distortions are a reality in both the public and private sectors, and to remove them would unquestionably mean a movement toward the real limits of productive potential, a prerequisite for any lasting growth. However, it was also noted that extending conditionality was not a simple matter, in that, although there might be a consensus regarding the existence of distortions at the microeconomic level in many markets, there was no comparable consensus as to what was the best way of eliminating them; nor was there sufficient theoretical or empirical knowledge on which to base, with the appropriate precision, the proposed extension of conditionality, or double conditionality as it was termed by some participants, who expressed great concern on this issue. In their view, the elimination of these distortions should be a long-term task supported financially by the Fund in the meantime, since knowledge was still lacking regarding the function providing the precise link between the inputs of a policy decided by the authorities and the result of that policy (a problem common to both microeconomic and macroeconomic policies, although many people claim to see a one-to-one relationship between inputs and results).

In other words, several participants expressed their doubts as to the degree of objectivity attainable in the actual process of monitoring by the Fund of an extended conditionality oriented to growth and economic development policies. It was also made clear that the excessive emphasis placed by Fund programs on the macroeconomic aspects of stabilization totally ignored microeconomic structural aspects. If the former, although a necessary condition of adjustment, were conceived of as being independent of the latter, market distortions were left intact to act as permanent sources of many aggregate problems. It frequently happened that, because of the total absence of microeconomic conditionality, governments ended up taking decisions on political grounds at the expense of criteria of economic efficiency. For example, infrastructure was ignored and roads and highways left unrepaired, while unproductive expenditure that had direct political consequences was left untouched. Obviously this was a problem affecting any representative democracy, but it was also true that the effects increased exponentially with the degree of structural maladjustment in the economy. It was for precisely this reason that the extension of conditionality sought to influence in some way (although just how was not yet very clear) the microeconomic aspect of adjustment, through a close scrutiny of the kinds of investment to be reduced in countries that were called upon to place natural, endogenous limits on their financial deficit as a proportion of GNP. There was no doubt that these natural limits existed, since they were the result of the level of development of the domestic capital market, the size of the tax burden that the country could support, and/or the inflation tax, which was always neutralized by the consequent loss of receipts, given the current constraint on external borrowing in the light of the existing stocks of external debt. In scrutinizing the kind of expenditure to be reduced or the type of tax to be increased or introduced, or the structure of public service tariffs, et cetera, one would be helping to ensure that the latent problems did not remain untouched because only the symptoms of the disease had been attacked.

Some participants expressed concern that this issue could vitally affect the relations between the different international financial institutions, such as the International Monetary Fund and the World Bank, since the Bretton Woods Agreements created a clear division of labor between them. From the beginning it had been the World Bank's role to be concerned with the supply side in its impact on the growth of member countries, although recently the Bank had been moving toward structural adjustment loans. Nevertheless, it was regarded as a very positive sign that attention was no longer exclusively focused on the size of the financial deficit, in the light of the international reality of the 1970s and 1980s, which had produced so many exogenous supply-side shocks; these, when added to the internal problems of many economies, made it difficult to distinguish between short-term adjustment and medium- and long-term structural changes. Therefore the initial division of functions between the two international organizations ought to be regarded more as a matter of institutional history, now superseded by a new reality that required growing institutional cooperation to facilitate adjustment with structural change. In other words, for several participants, the real problem was not who would design the new conditionality, but how the specific conditionalities of the Bank and the Fund were to be reconciled when they made an agreement with a member country, in order to avoid differences of opinion in their respective recommendations.

Adjustment, Indebtedness, and Economic Growth

Guillermo Ortiz put forward his own views on some issues closely related to those discussed by Vito Tanzi. In broad outline, he dealt with the need to link adjustment to growth and consequently to the necessity for structural changes, a subject which, as the speaker acknowledged, has become rather fashionable.

He discussed these issues not only from the standpoint of what was necessary or desirable but also, and more fundamentally, from the standpoint of the practical problems actually created by the implementation of adjustment programs, in terms of their effects on growth. Hence the importance of the basic question put forward by the author as the title of the last section of the paper—"Adjustment and Growth?" This contained some valuable thoughts deriving from deep study of the experiences of the Fund in designing stabilization programs over a period of time.

In the author's opinion, it was necessary to make a crucial distinction between moderately indebted countries and highly indebted countries, which came down to differentiating, at $t = 0$, between countries with moderately unbalanced flows of funds and countries with enormous imbalances of all kinds, including large stocks of debt, resulting both from their economic structure and from inappropriate domestic policies.

What differences could be observed between these countries, as subsequently revealed in terms of the degree of success achieved by the stabilization programs agreed with the Fund? In practice, despite the tremendous efforts by the countries with enormous initial imbalances to solve their external problems, the Fund programs had not been successful either in reducing the rate of inflation or in re-establishing sustained growth. It seemed as if the countries that desired and attempted macroeconomic adjustment, with the concomitant real reduction in public and private sector debt, saw in the process of seeking this adjustment a new inherent dynamic that worked against the stabilization process itself. This phenomenon was not yet completely understood, but was reflected in practice in stabilization costs that were higher than the accepted doctrine on these matters suggested, since this doctrine had been developed exclusively from the Fund's experience with countries with moderate imbalances of flows, because prior to the 1980s external debt problems had not reached such proportions. The author suggested that the problem of the stock of debt was capable by itself of complicating the relationship between growth and inflation with a different dynamic from that incorporated in the current macroeconomic approach of the Fund's stabilization programs.

No doubt this line of argument went some way toward explaining the grave problems of countries like Mexico, Argentina, and Brazil. It could also, in the manner of a laboratory experiment, implicitly endorse the introduction of "shock" stabilization programs in Argentina (Plan Austral), Brazil (Plan Cruzado), and Israel, which included price controls; in other words, a laboratory experiment implicitly reflecting a basically different endogenous dynamic.

Those who commented on this paper, both the invited speakers and the other participants, were in general agreement on the analysis and description of current external indebtedness. The notion that Fund programs are successful in dealing with moderate inflation but not with higher levels of inflation was illustrated by Mexico's various stabilization programs, of which only that of 1954 was successful, with inflation then at some 15 to 20 percent. It was suggested that when inflation reaches 50 or 60 percent the programs fail, possibly because the Fund model does not include the concept of inertial inflation, independent of demand factors or expectations. Other participants noted that the existence of inertial inflation required greater automatic flexibility in interpreting the results of the macroeconomic targets in stabilization programs, going beyond the current waivers (used for minor, localized, and correctible deviations from stabilization program targets); that is, moving on from the current acceptance of major, general, and irreversible deviations (such as those produced by changes in exogenous variables, e.g., changes in the international prices of basic exportable commodities, which seriously affect the performance of the program) to accepting the possibility of changing the program in the light of uncertainties about the country's financial capabilities. There had been a number of changes in attitudes recently and these should be extended.

Various commentators pointed out the need for greater analytical precision in the kind of dynamic complication caused by the stocks of debt per se, and to illustrate this with further examples of actual adjustment experiences.

This paper gave rise to the most intensive discussion of the entire seminar regarding concrete solutions to the debt problem, with interventions not only from those who deplored the absence of this kind of debate, especially concerning politically viable solutions, but also by those who pointed to ways in which some of the Fund's action programs devised to deal with specific cases could be improved. The starting point for this discussion on concrete solutions was a kind of "devil's advocate" contribution, in the form of a very clear and candid triptych of diagnosis, objective, and tactics of the creditor banks and the international organizations regarding the external indebtedness of developing countries from 1982 onward.

In summary form, the diagnosis pointed to the origins of the debt in the problem of illiquidity, leading to a domino effect in Latin America initiated from outside by increases in international interest rates which aggravated a pervasive existing problem. The objective consisted in re-establishing normal financial flows to these countries. Finally, the tactics were based on two rules of the game that could not be broken and so far had not been broken: the "case-by-case" approach which did not create precedents (the system could not support massive bankruptcies) and the principle that concerted action must always prevail over any potential unilateral action. This logical scheme was disrupted only temporarily by the accident of the drastic fall in the prices of oil and other basic commodities, which hit most severely the "model" (in terms of the triptych) countries—Mexico, Venezuela, and Ecuador.

From this standpoint, it was, in the opinion of several participants, extremely unlikely that the seven or eight hundred private banks, governed by twenty or thirty different banking and financial systems, reflecting a wide range of attitudes, could in the aggregate be regarded as willing to "negotiate and compromise," as it was put during the seminar, and that all that was lacking were serious proposals by the debtor countries. More specifically, if the only realistic solution to the debt problem was a reduction in interest rates on the debt so as to make debt service payments possible, then the Fund and the World Bank should promote simulation studies that could identify, under various alternative economic growth scenarios for certain countries, feasible payments hypotheses in terms of the generation of trade surpluses.

Other commentators noted that sensible concrete proposals had indeed been made to the creditor banks. Mexico, for example, had proposed an automatic capitalization of interest on the debt, taking into account changes in oil prices and interest rates and involving constant amounts of repayment in real terms; this proposal had been rejected. In response to the observation that such proposals were rejected because they ran contrary to the philosophy of the bankers, since this implied converting the banks into forced partners of the country in question, the seminar was referred back to an important point raised during the debate on Professor Dornbusch's paper: the absence in the international legal system of the kind of machinery that governs firms in every country in any capitalist system; in other words, the possibility of calling a meeting of creditors. The absence of a higher international tribunal made it necessary to have recourse to a system of unilateral proposals, for example for converting debt into long-term, low-interest bonds, as an alternative to possible capitalization solutions, which would require a certain amount of across-the-board negotiations. However, the current bankers' cartel, in the form of advisory committees, and the case-by-case approach that entailed the prior approval of the Fund, penalized banks such as those in Europe, for example, that would be willing to negotiate on an individual basis but in the final analysis could not leave the cartel.

Some commentators anticipated the probable argument regarding the failure of the analytical model underlying the stabilization programs for countries with major imbalances and large initial stocks of debt; in their view, the model was correct, the failure being attributable rather to the countries that could not fulfill the commitments undertaken in the agreements because they lacked the political capability to do so. This naturally gave rise to the question as to why some countries undertake to perform something that they cannot perform, and indeed why they are asked to perform something beyond their power. The first question was answered in fairly direct terms: loans from the Fund are cheaper than loans from other sources, but it was also admitted, on the second point, that there could possibly be design problems in some stabilization programs, especially when a large number of such programs had to be concluded in a period of only three or four years.

Savings in Brazil

In this work, Carlos Longo reviewed recent developments in savings in Brazil (broken down into domestic, external, and public savings), and in the tools of financial intermediation, noting the orthodox but progressive policy of the Castelo Branco Government, which introduced structural changes through reforms in the banking system, the capital markets, and the tax system. The author was at pains to contrast this experience with the current need for in-depth institutional reforms in order to maintain the rate of growth, which had been significantly affected by problems associated with the mobilization of domestic savings.

The paper began by examining the changes in financial intermediation instruments in Brazil and went on to refer to the recent decline, as revealed in the national accounts, in domestic savings. After mentioning the main investment peaks, the author concluded by discussing the problems faced by the present government in financing its deficit (now stabilized at about 6 to 8 percent of gross domestic product) under the cruzado plan. The speaker questioned the medium-term and long-term potential of this plan, since it had to coexist with problems of maladjusted relative prices, excess demand, a growing generalization of currency margins, and shortages of goods and a deterioration in their quality in order to get round the price freeze imposed under this decidedly unorthodox plan.

The author concluded his paper by proposing a series of constructive measures to improve the currently difficult situation of Brazil's economy. The paper, although dealing entirely with Brazil's experience, gave rise to an animated discussion that frequently transcended the case study in order to raise general issues and experiences common to many developing countries, such as Argentina, Chile, and Venezuela, especially concerning the position of the financial markets in conditions of high and variable inflation, on the one hand, and low inflation, on the other. It also provoked much discussion about Brazil's economy in the recent past and the lessons to be drawn for the future; Brazilians present at the seminar expressed a range of different views about developments in their country's economy.

It was interesting to hear about the experience of Argentina and Brazil regarding institutional changes in their central banks and investment banks, the focus being on the issue of indexation of financial assets and its influence on the generation of private saving. Several commentators raised the important question of the design of a good financial system in a context of high and variable inflation, analyzing the alternatives of a free market with a floating interest rate or an indexed financial market. If the floating rate is abandoned under these conditions the result will be that experienced in both countries, reflecting the evolution of the market toward the short term (60 days in Brazil and 30 days in Argentina). If maturities are extended with a floating rate, the result is Argentina's terrible experience under Circular 1050, since the rates reflect inflationary expectations, so that the short-term volatility is extended into the long term, although the long-term market is intrinsically more stable. It would seem necessary, in countries with a long experience of high and unanticipated inflation, to accept the division of the capital markets into short term and long term, through some indexation of the financial system which increases long-term assets. However, this indexation requires that certain conditions be met, such as, for example, low or medium inflation rates (not exceeding 40 to 50 percent a year), otherwise the indexed financial assets will be established in current money, with the grave results experienced in Brazil and Argentina in 1975. The reason is that high inflation rates are associated with a high volatility of relative prices, and sooner or later it will be necessary to supplement the system with subsidies to the financial system, which then become extremely difficult to eliminate. Argentina's experience with indexation, unlike that of Brazil and its indexed treasury bills (ORTNs) since 1964, has been very bad, since the system was established in 1975 at a time when the rate of inflation was accelerating from 40 percent to 300 percent a year. It is also regrettable that neither the austral plan nor the cruzado plan makes provision for indexation, when inflation is not so low as to make this superfluous; its omission undermines long-term contracts in general. On the other hand, correct indexation of the financial system also requires an appropriately consistent macroeconomic framework that avoids large government deficits and the consequent "crowding-out" that gives rise to high interest rates.

It was noted that Chile's experience in the 1960s was interesting; an indexation system was introduced for housing loans made through private banks, which became very important in that they enabled Chile to create a capital market that lasted for fifteen years, enabling housing to be financed through the issue of obligations at real interest rates of 8 to 9 percent a year. The system collapsed in 1973, when the inflation rate reached 600 percent a year. People could not meet payments from their wages, and the government could find no better solution than to suspend indexation for a year. Another instructive experience from Chile concerned the consequences of the financial reform of 1975, when the commercial banks introduced medium-term and long-term indexed loans into the market that initially were not very popular. With the inflation rate at about 300 percent, people preferred to stay with nonindexed short-term loans, but when inflation fell to about 50 or 60 percent a year, these indexed instruments became much more widely used, although no institutional change occurred. However, when real annual interest rates climbed to 40 and 50 percent after the macroeconomic adjustment, the financial system could not withstand the consequences, and many loans became unrecoverable.

Another group of comments dealt specifically with Brazil's economy, the speakers questioning some of the author's hypotheses and conclusions regarding private and public investment, the generation of trade surpluses, and the evolution of the cruzado plan. These commentators were divided between optimists and pessimists. The former took heart from a recent survey which made it possible to quantify a widespread impression that private investment was increasing; breaking this down into investment for modernization and investment to increase installed capacity, it was clear that the latter was increasing much more rapidly than the former, having risen 243 percent between 1985 and 1986, much faster than demand. Furthermore, 60 percent of the firms surveyed had increased their investment since the introduction of the cruzado plan. Other speakers felt it was wrong to attribute recent investment gains to the cruzado plan, since investment had already been accelerating before the plan, which had already created a very damaging uncertainty regarding future relative prices, which could not be adjusted in the event of real shocks.

There was general agreement regarding the need to achieve a financial surplus to facilitate the recovery of public investment in Brazil as a means of maintaining the rate of growth from 1987 onward, given the significant effects on investment and private savings and the need to overcome bottlenecks in key sectors. Some speakers took a pessimistic view: even if the necessary adjustments were made in lagging public service tariffs, and fiscal reforms (made possible by a 5 percent reduction in the tax burden as compared to the 1970s) were carried out, this would not be enough to solve the financial problems of the public sector. The possible crisis in the external sector would require transfers overseas to be reduced, not only through an adjustment of flows but also by attacking the problem of the stock of debt, because of the concentration of external indebtedness in the public sector. In the author's view, on the other hand, internal adjustment had to be undertaken first, which was not necessarily very orthodox if the budget deficit was large.

Concerning the short-term consequences of the cruzado plan, the optimistic speakers sought to discount the comments of the more alarmist commentators (the majority) by pointing out that an examination of overall demand did not appear to indicate that the shortage of goods was getting worse. They pointed out in this regard that at the beginning of the cruzado plan (1) while stocks held by households and firms were very low, the process of replenishing them would tend to lose impetus as time passed, (2) people had anticipated their requirements to take advantage of the price freeze while it lasted, and (3) there had been a kind of monetary illusion that had led to the disappearance of many savings accounts. It would therefore be dangerous, against this background, to attempt drastic adjustments in demand through a restrictive monetary and fiscal policy that could cause problems for the cruzado plan, which had been implemented in the context of pre-existing imbalances among relative prices, aggravated by the rapid expansion of demand. The discussion ended in the conclusion that controls on demand should be lifted as part of a movement to a system of administered prices to enable the cruzado plan to function; some of the other Brazilian participants thought that this process would lead to the disappearance of the private sector from Brazil's economy.

Observations

The three issues referred to in the title of this seminar—external debt, savings, and growth—have proved to be closely linked in their application to Latin America. The adjustment entailed by the existence of external indebtedness, and reflected in the need to generate current account surpluses, if considered from the standpoint that the required transfer of resources can only be sustained in a context of growth (F. Machlup in modern guise) requires the generation of an adequate level of savings. Alternatively, if these transfers are achieved at the expense of investment, growth and hence future generations will suffer. These are the core issues justifying the title and subject matter of this seminar, which were approached with total frankness and freedom by the participants, not with the objective of achieving immediate results in economic policy, but rather with the far-reaching aim of raising and reflecting productively on issues of great relevance to the countries of Latin America and the world economy in general.

One recurring theme in the discussion of the various papers presented at the seminar concerned the need to bring consistency and coordination to the macroeconomic policies pursued by the more developed countries, and the effects that their present absence is having on the world economy and especially on the less developed countries. If these policies have a decisive impact on the international economic environment, which in turn governs the possibility of correcting the external imbalances of the developing countries, with the assistance of the International Monetary Fund, the question then arises whether the international organizations can influence the policies of the largest countries with a view to their overall optimization.

The debate showed that this is an issue of profound concern, not only to the economists from the less developed countries who were present at the seminar, but also to international institutions such as the Fund and the World Bank. The Fund has recently embarked on a more intensive use of economic indicators (such as those published in the latest *World Economic Outlook*), which point to the need for a reduction in the U.S. budget deficit and for expansion in the Federal Republic of Germany and Japan. However, it is important to remember that, while these indicators are useful tools, they cannot automatically bring about changes in current policy, and it would be premature to express a view about their results. It was also noted that the 1986 Annual Report of the World Bank called attention to the fact that without a reduction in the U.S. budget deficit, without an expansion in Germany or Japan, without a reduction in the real rate of interest in conjunction with the reduction of taxation in the United States (to the extent that this would not occur automatically through the consequent reduction in "crowding-out"), then the future growth of the world economy would be seriously affected, particularly in the less developed countries. Nonetheless, it was also accepted that the specific problem of the debt would not be solved per se by the recovery of the industrial economies; the developing countries had a long way to go in their domestic policies for stabilization, but they also had to be given access to the international market for loan funds and the possibility of selling their exports.

The discussions on these points ranged widely, and it is possible to distinguish the following points of view: (1) those who believed that the current inconsistency in financial policy objectives in the largest countries is the principal cause of the economic crisis that exploded in August 1982, and who pointed to the need for the Fund to do something about it; and (2) those who asserted that the Fund's surveillance power is asymmetrical, since, although it can exert influence over the policies of member countries who use its resources, it has little power over the policies of countries that do not use these resources and even less over the most important countries, despite the many initiatives put forward in the Fund's Executive Board on this question.

Another much-discussed issue, going beyond the specific papers in which it was raised, was that of the possible extension of Fund conditionality, which might involve moving from the traditional macroeconomic approach of stabilization programs (which concentrate on the size of the budget deficit) to the microeconomic approach (with its possible trade-offs with the former). The latter approach, in analyzing the quality of the specific policies adopted by the countries implementing adjustment, also attaches importance to the removal of distortions in the resource allocation process that are capable of affecting growth.

Concurring with these arguments were also (1) those who were concerned that the extension of conditionality would affect the division of labor between the Fund and the World Bank, and who referred to the need for compatible conditionality in the agreements made between the two organizations and specific member countries, and (2) those who, accepting the fact of the distortions, were concerned about the extension of conditionality in a context where there was no professional consensus about the best way of eliminating them, an issue which highlighted the current lack of knowledge about the precise functional relationship between policy inputs and obtainable results. Dispelling the ignorance about these functional relationships was a complicated matter, particularly because of the problems resulting from the fact that accumulated stocks of debt had proved capable by themselves of introducing into the relationship between growth and inflation a different dynamic from that built into the macroeconomic approach.

Both major groups of issues—among many other possible themes that will occur to the interested reader of the discussions—made it clear once again that achieving the desirable adjustment with growth will require a combination of domestic efforts by the various countries involved and an international context markedly more favorable to these efforts than that existing at the end of 1986.

World Economic Outlook and Prospects for Latin America

Anthony Lanyi

Since 1982, the international debt situation has been a chief focus of the International Monetary Fund's *World Economic Outlook,* as well as of the general economic surveys published by other institutions and of numerous books and articles by academic economists. Out of this bewildering mass of data and analyses, one central truth has clearly emerged: the world economy has been facing not only a "debt crisis" but also a "growth crisis," and that these crises are closely interrelated. The growth crisis emerged initially as the result of the slowdown in economic growth experienced by most industrial countries since the early 1970s. The debt crisis, while resulting from the conjunction of various developments in the late 1970s and early 1980s, can be seen broadly as the result of a number of developing countries attempting to maintain high rates of growth in a slowly growing, and therefore increasingly competitive, world economy. The excessive debt burdens that accumulated became themselves a further impediment to growth in the indebted countries, and to some extent in the entire world economy. At the same time, slow growth has extended and deepened the debt crisis by weakening the ability of indebted countries to meet their debt service obligations and thereby has postponed a return of confidence on the part of both domestic and foreign investors.

The medium-term outlook crucially depends, therefore, on the success with which the governments of industrial and developing countries alike implement policies to promote growth. Growth in the industrial countries is the major stimulus to the expansion of world trade, which in turn is a necessary condition for a satisfactory growth performance in the developing countries. But strong, effective economic

26

management in the indebted countries is also a necessary condition, because the wasteful use of foreign and domestic savings, which itself was a major original cause of the debt crisis, will only weaken incentives for inflows of foreign capital, as well as the repatriation of residents' holdings abroad. Moreover, merely to respond to foreign demand without an adequate expansion of domestic productive capacity will inevitably lead to a recurrence of pressures on the price level and the balance of payments. These points, while true for all developing countries, are especially pertinent to the heavily indebted and inflation-prone countries of the Latin American region.

This paper, which is based closely on recent work of the Fund staff,[1] is divided into two parts. The first part deals with the slowdown of growth in industrial countries, giving a sketch of recent developments, followed by a summary of the medium-term outlook and major policy issues. The discussion will also touch on aspects of policies in those countries that are relevant to the economic environment faced by the indebted developing countries. The second part of the paper will concentrate on the latter countries themselves, first discussing the relative roles of world economic environment and domestic economic management in the evolution of the debt crisis and then reviewing the medium-term prospects, especially for those developing countries with a heavy external debt burden, and the policy choices faced by those countries.

Slow Growth in Industrial Countries

Recent Developments

The deep recession from which the world economy is still recovering was superimposed on a longer-term slowdown in economic growth that dates from the early 1970s. The compound average growth rate of real gross national product (GNP) in industrial countries was about 4½ percent from 1963 to 1973 and just under 2½ percent from 1973 to 1985. The sources of this slowdown are complex and not completely understood, and an analysis of them would be beyond the scope of this paper. It is fairly clear, however, that the slow economic growth was associated with a slower rate of growth of productivity per worker (rather than, for example, a slower growth rate of the labor force), and this in turn was to some extent associated with

---

[1] In particular, International Monetary Fund, *World Economic Outlook: A Survey by the Staff of the International Monetary Fund* (Washington, April 1986).

a slowdown in the pace of capital-deepening. There are indications, however, that other causes—not all of them easily measured—were involved. For example, the rise in energy costs is generally thought to have had a negative impact on worker productivity; other hypothesized factors include the completion of the process of "catching up" in Europe and Japan to technological innovations first introduced in the United States and the growing relative size of the service sector (with its slower measured increase in productivity).[2]

Superimposed on these long-term trends was the recession of the early 1980s, which had an especially severe impact on developing countries because of the unusual conjunction of high interest rates and (after 1982) limited availability of external finance. The subsequent economic recovery since 1983 has also had unusual features, such as a declining rate of inflation and falling prices of primary commodities. While the recovery of demand and lower nominal interest rates have benefited the indebted developing countries, these benefits have been more or less offset by the sluggish prices in commodity markets and the fact that real interest rates are still high. As the recovery proceeded in 1983–84, it was believed by many observers that its unusual features would be of a sort to ensure continued sustained growth for the remainder of the decade, since low inflation and nominal interest rates, supported by expected fiscal adjustments in the United States, could be expected to stimulate a resurgence of private investment, construction, and household consumption.

Against this background, economic developments in 1985 and in the first half of 1986 were disappointing in a number of respects. Expansion was less than expected in the industrial world, the volume of world trade increased only modestly, and primary commodity prices weakened. As a result, economic growth in the developing countries, which had rebounded in 1984, slowed, and their real export earnings stagnated, which in turn worsened the outlook for the restoration of general creditworthiness, impeded progress in reduction of the relative size of the debt burden, and made it more difficult for many countries to resume a satisfactory growth performance.

Despite these developments, it is the assessment of the Fund staff that economic performance of the industrial countries, and therefore of the world economy as a whole, will tend to improve in the latter part of 1986 and in 1987, since a significant part of the expected benefits from lower interest rates and energy prices has yet to be felt in final

---

[2] For a discussion of these factors, see International Monetary Fund, *World Economic Outlook* (cited in footnote 1), pp. 163–71.

demand in industrial countries. Nevertheless, significant uncertainties remain with respect to the impact of major changes taking place in the world economy, including not only the reductions in interest rates and energy prices already mentioned but also the large shift in the pattern of exchange rates and the planned improvement in the U.S. fiscal position. On balance, therefore, the most likely outcome would appear to be a continuation in 1986 and 1987 of the approximately 3 percent growth of GNP achieved for the industrial countries in 1985. This outcome, however, assumes the implementation of the policy intentions of major countries, in particular a substantial cut in the U.S. fiscal deficit that has been the declared intention of both the executive and legislative branches of that country's government, together with continuation of the somewhat greater monetary accommodation recently in evidence in the United States and some other countries, as well as the supply-side policies discussed below.

Medium-Term Outlook

To assess the correct policies for dealing with the continuing debt crisis of Latin American countries, it is necessary to form a judgment as to the likely medium-term consequences of alternative policies. The medium-term scenario prepared by the Fund staff represents an attempt to come up with such a judgment. The scenario should thus not be interpreted as a *forecast* of medium-term developments but rather as a set of quantified assumptions aimed at assessing the implications of current trends and analyzing the constraints facing developing countries.

The starting point of this medium-term scenario is to focus on developments in the industrial countries and to treat these developments, for the sake of simplicity, as exogenous to those in the developing countries—that is, it is assumed that industrial countries are essentially unaffected by economic trends in the developing countries. This is admittedly unrealistic, and indeed it is clear that the depression of economic activity in many capital importing countries, including some of the largest ones, has had a significant dampening effect on the industrial economies. Nonetheless, since the influence of economic trends in the industrial countries on the economies of the developing countries is many times more powerful than the influence in the reverse direction, it seems broadly reasonable, and a great deal simpler, to proceed with first constructing a global economic "environment" depending on developments within the industrial countries, and then analyze the impact of this environment on the developing countries.

With regard to the industrial countries, the staff has estimated the growth of productive potential in line with the growth of labor, capital, and productivity in recent years, and it is assumed that output over the medium term (1988–91) will grow at approximately its estimated potential rate in the United States and Japan and slightly faster than potential in most of the other major industrial countries. These assumptions result in an average economic growth rate of 3 percent for all industrial countries throughout this period. Underlying this scenario is the assumption that the governments of European countries will succeed in alleviating some of the structural rigidities that have led to high unemployment rates through implementation of policies discussed in the next subsection.

The Fund staff has assumed that monetary growth will be such as to stabilize inflation in 1988–91 at close to the rates prevailing in 1987. There can be expected to be, in line with this development, a stabilizing of the terms of trade for primary commodities, whose prices after 1986 can be expected to rise in line with, or even slightly faster than, those of manufactures. An improvement in the U.S. current account, and some deterioration in the current accounts of the Federal Republic of Germany and Japan, is projected over the medium term in this scenario, resulting in part from the very sizable exchange rate movements that have occurred over the past year and a half, and in part from the expected improvements in the U.S. fiscal position. Over the medium term, also, the current account deficits of the major industrial countries as a group will tend to grow, mainly because the initial improvements arising from the sharp drop in oil prices will gradually be offset as the volume of oil imports rises in response to lower prices and as the oil exporting countries cut back on their imports. Another important influence on the underlying payments positions of industrial countries is the further accumulation of indebtedness by the United States. The cost of servicing this debt will become a growing element in the U.S. payments position and a reason for the United States to continue to experience a sizable, if smaller, current account deficit, despite recent dollar depreciation and the expected fiscal adjustment.

Policy Issues

From a Latin American standpoint, the principal interest in policies in industrial countries is with regard to what measures might be taken to strengthen their economic growth performance. The fact that mildly optimistic assumptions, such as those employed in the Fund's medium-term scenario, nevertheless produce a rate of growth substantially below that enjoyed in the 1960s and early 1970s is itself a matter for concern. The concern stems not only from the direct linkages between growth of GNP in industrial countries and the demand for exports from developing countries but also from the well-established fact that low growth and high unemployment in industrial countries has long been associated with protectionist trade and agricultural policies. In this connection, the scenario envisages only modest reductions in unemployment in most European countries over the next five years. While the situation in Japan and the United States is assumed to be more favorable in this respect, a greater openness of markets in these countries is impeded by long-entrenched policies favoring agriculture and certain problem industries.

As stated earlier, the reasons for the long-term slowdown of growth in the industrial countries since the early 1970s is still in large part a matter for conjecture. For that reason, while there is no lack of proposals for stimulating growth, it would also be fair to say that there is no clear consensus in this regard. In most industrial countries, the policy stance has for some years been based on the notion that improved growth performance requires an environment of financial stability and increased flexibility in the functioning of markets. In line with this underlying concept, governments have sought to reduce the share of resources absorbed by the public sector, to bring down inflation and inflationary expectations through deceleration of monetary growth rates, and to reduce structural rigidities in the operation of markets.

One of the major uncertainties in the world economic environment is whether the impact of reducing fiscal deficits, which in the short run may be deflationary, can be offset by incentives to promote an upsurge of private investment activity and private consumption. The disappointingly weak level of economic activity in the first half of 1986 has given special urgency to this question. Nonetheless, the Fund staff has not concluded that there is a case for changing the present strategy of fiscal policy. First, it seems too early to conclude that the industrial economies have encountered a cyclical downswing. Second, there seem to have been lags in the positive response that might be expected both to lower oil prices (on the part of oil importing sectors and countries) and to lower interest rates; this positive response, however, could be negated if the United States (in particular) fails to assure market participants that its fiscal imbalance is being brought under control.

Fiscal policy is, however, not the whole story, and it is not the same story in all countries. Countries such as the Federal Republic of Germany and Japan, where a strong fiscal position has already been achieved, are in (or may soon be in) a position to stimulate demand, either through tax reduction or, as in Japan, through increases in public expenditure. The choices here are based on factors special to each country: for instance, on public judgments as to the current adequacy of the social infrastructure. In these countries, but especially in countries that must implement further fiscal retrenchment, other policies are needed to help ensure that the desired "crowding-in" of private sources of expenditure actually occurs. Continuation of a flexible approach to monetary policy, to permit the needed decline in nominal interest rates in line with the lower rate of inflation, is an important element of the strategy. Another concerns the structure of government revenues and expenditure. The tax reform measures passed by the U.S. Congress are one example of measures to induce a greater supply of effort by both businesses and individuals, as well as to improve savings. Another area for possible improvement is in the allocation of government expenditure: clearly, some types of expenditure help more to increase productivity in the economy than do others, although choices here are complicated by the presence of other legitimate objectives of public sector activities.

While there is considerable public debate in industrial countries about the optimum reduction in public spending and the desirability of privatizing certain activities, there is a degree of consensus that improvement of market processes is necessary to improve economic performance. One area where rigidities have long been prominent is labor markets. While attempting to preserve social goals that continue to be valid, it also needs to be recognized that the price of factors of production must be flexible in the face of changes in supply and demand. Such flexibility would limit losses of employment in declining industries or during general economic downturns. Flexibility would be assisted by provision of facilities for retraining and relocating displaced workers. In developing modalities for making wages (and perhaps also hours) more flexible, one has the impression that the industrial world is presently only at the beginning of a period of experimentation. It is a positive sign that in some countries, at least, labor unions have accepted the need for new ideas in this area.

Although the imperfections of labor markets are perhaps the best publicized of structural problems in industrial countries, there are other rigidities whose alleviation or elimination would improve economic performance. One area in which action has been taken in several countries, notably in the United States and Japan, is that of financial market deregulation. Other areas include the curtailment of subsidies used to maintain uneconomic activities, deregulation when the cost of regulation clearly outweighs benefits, antimonopoly legislation, the sale of publicly owned enterprises, when the latter have not been meeting the test of domestic and foreign competition, and, as mentioned earlier, tax reforms.

It may be wondered why, in a paper for a conference devoted to Latin American problems, so much space should be given to policies in industrial countries. The justification is not only that adequate growth in industrial countries is a sine qua non for resolving both the debt crisis and the growth crisis in developing countries. Also, the solution of the structural problems just discussed is a necessary condition for carrying out the large reallocations of resources in industrial countries that would eventually be involved if their markets were to be opened up to both agricultural commodities and manufactured goods from Latin America and other developing regions.

In addition, it may be noted that such structural problems are also relevant to analyzing the economies in a number of Latin American countries, especially the more urbanized and industrialized ones. Despite the convenient and politically sanctioned division of the world into "industrial" and "developing" countries, it is clear that differences among developing countries—that is, between "middle-income" and "low-income" countries—or between the advanced and the backward regions within the same country, can be much greater than those between the more industrialized developing countries and the less wealthy industrial countries. Just as many of the economic institutions in developing countries have been modeled on those of industrial countries, there is also considerable scope for learning from the efforts of industrial countries to remedy previous mistakes in policies, at a time when, as will be discussed in more detail below, many developing countries must themselves undertake substantial policy reforms.

The Debt Crisis and Its Consequences for Developing Countries

Origins of Debt Crisis

There is a long historical precedent for countries in the early and middle stages of their development to engage in international borrowing in order to raise their rates of economic growth. However, failure to control adequately the growth, structure, and terms of external borrowing can lead to balance of payments difficulties and ultimately set back the pace of economic development. Thus, while all develop-

ing countries were affected by the various shocks to the global economy that occurred in the late 1970s and early 1980s, many countries
were able to avoid serious liquidity problems and large setbacks to
their growth process, while many others were hit by the crisis, with
whose features we are all by now familiar. Perhaps a useful way of
briefly sketching the profile of the debt crisis is to indicate the differences between those countries that experienced debt-servicing problems—defined for this purpose as those which incurred external
payments arrears during 1983–84 or which rescheduled their debt
during the period from end-1982 to mid-1985—and countries that
avoided such problems.[3]

It is well known that a protracted tendency for external indebtedness to grow more rapidly than GDP leads to a solvency problem,
namely, an inability to service debt out of current national income;
that a growing ratio of debt to exports, while sustainable in some
circumstances for specified periods, will eventually lead to a liquidity
problem, namely, the inability to generate sufficient foreign exchange
to pay for both scheduled debt service and essential imports; and that
a persistently negative difference between the rate of growth of exports and the average interest rate on debt implies added debt-
servicing difficulties. Such difficulties may also be exacerbated by a
rising proportion of debt at commercial terms, a fall in the average
maturity of the debt, an increase in the share of total debt at variable
interest rates (during periods when interest rates in world financial
markets are rising), and a rise in the share of short-term debt in the
total.

Table 1 shows that a number of these danger signs were strongly in
evidence for the vulnerable groups, namely the broad group of countries with recent debt-servicing problems and the group of "Western
Hemisphere" countries as defined in the *World Economic Outlook*;[4] the
latter group will also be referred to as "Latin American countries." For
those countries, the emergence of danger signs was even more striking
than for the broader group of debt-problem countries. For countries
that did not encounter debt-servicing problems, however, the four
indicators shown in Table 1 were consistently at far lower initial levels,
and as a consequence the rise in debt burden (shown as debt and debt
service as ratios of exports) was less rapid.

---

[3] This discussion is based on the Fund's April 1986 *World Economic Outlook* (cited in
footnote 1), Chapter V. For definitions of the two groups of capital importing countries, see
the Statistical Appendix of that publication, p. 174.

[4] In the *World Economic Outlook* (see footnote 1), the Western Hemisphere group com-
prises all countries in the hemisphere except the United States and Canada.

Table 1. Capital Importing Developing Countries: Selected Indicators of External Debt Developments, 1973–85

Period averages; in percent

	1973–74	1975–78	1979–80	1981–82	1983–85
External debt (as a percentage of exports of goods and services)					
Capital importing countries	95.8	119.4	115.5	137.5	161.2
Countries with recent debt-servicing problems	112.0	153.8	156.9	210.3	254.6
Countries without recent debt-servicing problems	80.8	90.3	80.9	84.2	100.3
Western Hemisphere	139.8	188.1	190.3	241.7	287.3
Debt service payments (as a percentage of exports of goods and services)					
Capital importing countries	13.0	16.9	18.1	22.7	23.2
Countries with recent debt-servicing problems	17.0	24.7	26.4	35.6	34.9
Countries without recent debt-servicing problems	9.2	10.2	11.1	13.2	15.5
Western Hemisphere	22.3	34.0	36.6	45.9	41.1
Share of total debt at floating interest rates					
Capital importing countries	21.1	34.7	44.7	51.1	53.6
Countries with recent debt-servicing problems	29.6	42.4	53.5	59.8	62.8
Countries without recent debt-servicing problems	10.2	23.7	30.4	35.2	37.9
Western Hemisphere	34.2	51.3	66.3	71.6	72.3
Share of short-term debt in total debt					
Capital importing countries	6.8	13.7	18.4	20.7	16.5
Countries with recent debt-servicing problems	9.1	14.3	20.1	23.3	17.0
Countries without recent debt-servicing problems	3.8	12.9	15.6	15.9	15.5
Western Hemisphere	6.3	13.1	21.5	24.6	15.4

What lay behind these divergent trends was a variety of factors, of differing importance from country to country. One prominent difference between the groups of countries with and without debt-servicing problems was the fact that for the former group there was a sharp fall in gross saving as a proportion of gross domestic product (GDP) between 1977 and 1982, so that net foreign borrowing seems to have been used largely to prevent an equally sharp fall in investment (which did decline somewhat nevertheless). For the countries that avoided debt problems, gross saving actually increased slightly between 1977 and 1982, reflecting in part active adjustment policies undertaken at the onset of the second round of petroleum price increases. It is also significant that, for the debt-problem countries, adjustment since 1982 has entailed a further substantial drop in the investment ratio, while for the other group, which has also reduced its current account deficit, the investment ratio fell only slightly. (The relevant data, presented in Table 2, must be regarded in light of the caveat that saving and investment estimates in many developing countries are subject to a wide range of possible error.) While GDP in the groups of countries with and without debt-servicing problems grew at roughly comparable compound annual rates in 1973–80 (about 5 percent and 5¾ percent, respectively), their growth performance in 1982–85 diverged substantially (0.7 percent and 5.7 percent, respectively). This divergence was related in large part to the amount of investment undertaken, but also to the fact that the countries without debt-

Table 2. Capital Importing Developing Countries: Gross Savings and Capital Formation, 1973–86

In percent of GDP

	Average 1973–77	Average 1978–80	Average 1981–82	1983	1984	1985	1986
Gross capital formation							
Capital importing							
developing countries	23.9	25.7	24.3	21.4	20.0	19.4	19.9
Countries with debt-							
servicing problems	24.1	25.0	21.8	17.9	16.1	15.3	16.8
Countries without debt-							
servicing problems	23.7	27.3	26.6	26.9	23.8	22.9	22.8
Western Hemisphere	23.2	24.4	21.7	19.4	17.7	16.8	17.0
Gross savings							
Capital importing							
developing countries	16.8	25.7	13.0	13.0	15.2	15.2	16.2
Countries with debt-							
servicing problems	19.2	25.0	11.4	12.7	14.4	13.0	14.6
Countries without debt-							
servicing problems	13.7	27.3	14.3	14.2	15.9	17.5	19.7
Western Hemisphere	19.8	24.4	11.6	12.2	14.5	14.3	15.1

NOTE: Each figure represents the median value for the indicated group of countries.

servicing problems tended to show significantly lower incremental capital-output ratios than the debt-problem group.

Another important factor contributing to the accumulation of external debt has been capital flight. For capital importing countries as a whole, external financing requirements were increased by about two thirds during the late 1970s and early 1980s by outflows of resident capital. For countries in the Western Hemisphere, foreign borrowing needs were almost doubled in this manner, unlike in some regions, such as Asia and the Middle East, where capital outflows represented in large part the prudential accumulation of official reserves and the extension of export-promoting trade credits.

A further factor in the development of debt-servicing problems for some of the capital importing countries was the extent to which borrowed funds were used to increase the economy's capacity to generate foreign exchange earnings. For countries that avoided debt-servicing problems, export volumes grew by a compound average rate of 4¾ percent between 1973 and 1982, while for debt-problem countries the growth rate was less than ¾ of 1 percent. While this divergent export performance reflected in part different export compositions—which in turn partly resulted from different resource bases and overall levels of economic development—it was to a considerable extent also due to a policy stance favoring the maintenance of international competitiveness and productivity improvements in countries with better export performance. Indeed, the export diversification that often accompanied stronger export growth was typically the result of a sustained policy strategy.

While it would be an oversimplification to say that domestic policies were the main cause of the deteriorating external position of countries with debt-servicing problems, or that policies of other countries were beyond criticism, there does seem to have been a tendency to greater policy weakness in the former group. In particular, in many of these countries, policies were either initiated or continued during the 1970s and early 1980s that included an expansionary fiscal and monetary stance, accompanied by a set of pricing, interest rate, and exchange rate policies, as well as trade and exchange restrictions, that tended to reduce domestic savings and the efficiency of investment, encourage capital flight, and discourage the growth and diversification of exports. By contrast, many of the countries that avoided serious debt problems pursued policies that were at least somewhat more successful at encouraging the domestic mobilization of savings, the efficient use of investable resources, and export growth and diversification. Weaknesses in demand-management and supply-side policies in the debt-problem countries were at times also accompanied by short-comings in external debt management. For instance, as the need for external finance increased, the greater tended to be the relative amount of reliance on commercial and short-term borrowing; and the inadequate monitoring of external debt prevailing in a number of countries enhanced the danger that the debt and debt service would grow to unsustainable magnitudes before the authorities had the op-portunity to perceive the situation and put the necessary adjustment measures in place.

The emphasis in this discussion has thus far been placed on the policies carried out by capital importing countries as a cause of exter-nal debt difficulties, rather than the more commonly stressed exogen-ous developments in the world economy that had an impact on these countries. This has been done partly to right the balance of prevailing views, but also because the undeniable effects of exogenous develop-ments were felt alike by countries with and without debt problems and were superimposed on trends of debt accumulation and export per-formance that had already become evident over the preceding decade.

The only factor that has clearly hurt countries in widely differing degrees has been the movement of primary commodity prices. First, the series of oil price increases in 1979–80 clearly set back oil im-porting countries. Nevertheless, some oil exporters—notably, Mexico, Nigeria, and Venezuela—experienced serious debt-servicing prob-lems by the early 1980s because of expansionary spending programs that were financed by rapid increases in the level of outstanding for-eign borrowing and that included domestic investments, the timing of whose prospective returns was mismatched with the schedule of amortization payments on the corresponding financing. The balance was tipped for these countries by the weakening of oil prices, begin-ning in 1982. For countries exporting non-oil primary commodities, the combination of weak prices and lower export volumes resulting from the 1980–82 recession led to falls in the purchasing power of exports, and the continued weakness of those prices since 1982 has made it difficult for those countries with a large overhang of external debt to recoup their external position.

The sharp increase in nominal interest rates in industrial countries in 1979–80 fed through to interest payments on external debt es-pecially quickly for Latin American countries because of the large proportion of their debts that was at variable interest rates. Since the increase in nominal interest rates occurred just before the U.S. dollar price of internationally traded goods began to fall, real interest rates rose sharply in 1980, and between 1978 and 1984 the ratio of interest payments to exports more than doubled for countries with debt-servicing problems.

Similarly, the strong appreciation of the U.S. dollar over the period 1981–84 had the effect of depressing the dollar prices of internationally traded goods without a corresponding effect on the U.S. dollar magnitude of external debt (about 80 percent of which is estimated to have been denominated in dollars). Thus, for these countries, about two fifths of the rise in debt ratios between 1979 and 1983 is estimated to have resulted from the U.S. dollar appreciation.

Recent Developments in Debt Crisis

Since the beginning of the debt crisis, the growth of total debt has rapidly decelerated in U.S. dollar terms, although continuing to edge upward as a percentage of exports of goods and services. For capital importing countries as a whole, debt in nominal terms has grown from $761 billion at the end of 1982 to $914 billion (an increase of 20 percent overall) at the end 1985; another $50 billion increase is expected during 1986. For the Western Hemisphere, the increase during this period was from $333 billion to $369 billion, an increase of only 11 percent, with $382 billion projected for the end of 1986. Because of the weakness in commodity prices during this period, even these relatively modest increases in the stock of debt in nominal terms translate into increases in the ratios of debt to exports: from 151 percent in 1982 to 180 in 1986 for all capital importing countries, and from 273 percent to 332 percent in the Western Hemisphere. Nevertheless, debt service ratios improved substantially for countries with debt-servicing problems, partly because of the fall in interest rates but in considerable degree also because of large-scale debt restructurings carried out by both official and private creditors. In the April 1986 *World Economic Outlook* the Fund staff estimated that market borrowers rescheduled over $80 billion of debt service due during 1982–85, and new or prospective arrangements in 1986–87 would defer another $52 billion. One notable aspect of these arrangements was that the proportion of short-term debt in the total was greatly reduced.

The improvements in the debt situation have been brought about in part through strenuous adjustment efforts, which have brought current account deficits down substantially for virtually all categories of developing countries. For Western Hemisphere countries, deficits declined from −33.4 percent of exports in 1982 to −3.4 percent in 1985. Larger current account deficits are projected for 1986—for capital importing countries as a whole and for Western Hemisphere countries among them, mainly as a result of the decline in primary product prices, especially the price of petroleum.

The weakness of commodity prices throughout the period of adjustment for countries with debt problems has meant that much of the adjustment has had to come about through a compression of imports. The volume of these countries' imports fell by about 15 percent in each of the years 1982 and 1983. From 1983 to 1986, imports are projected to have risen by only 1 to 1½ percent. In Western Hemisphere countries, the volume of imports was cut by a cumulative 36 percent in 1981–83, with a recovery of about 5 percent from 1983 to 1986. The growth in real GDP of these countries, however, was a great deal stronger than might be adduced by supposing a tight link between imports and output. In the Western Hemisphere, for example, there were falls of 1 percent and 3 percent in output in 1982 and 1983, respectively, but increases of 3 percent and 3¾ percent in 1984 and 1985, despite a level of imports that remained far lower than in the years immediately preceding 1982. The apparent reduction in import-dependence of growth during this period may be due to a number of factors, such as the fall in investment ratios (investment expenditure probably tends to be more import-intensive than other types of expenditure) and in aggregate demand (leading to a reduction in consumer goods imports); undoubtedly another contributing factor has been the depreciation in real effective exchange rates in most countries carrying out major adjustments, which would have had the effect of raising import prices relative to prices of domestic goods and therefore of encouraging both direct import substitution, as well as a switch from traded to nontraded goods in the consumption expenditure as a whole.

Two views are possible of the recent performance of the debt-problem countries in general and Latin American countries in particular. An optimistic view would stress the fact that, despite an extremely unfavorable external economic environment, declines in the levels of economic activity in these countries were limited to relatively small magnitudes, thanks in part to the efforts of the Fund and private creditors to provide debt relief and some new financing, and in part to strong adjustment efforts by the countries themselves, which, inter alia, tended to maintain the volume of exports. As a result of all these efforts, and the recent decline in interest rates, debt service ratios have fallen significantly, and for a number of countries that experienced debt problems the situation has become more manageable than it appeared a few years ago. Indeed, for a number of these countries, an acceleration in the momentum of economic growth appears to be underway.

A more pessimistic view would stress the fact that per capita income for developing countries as a whole has been virtually stagnant since 1979, and for some important groups of countries—for instance, in Africa and in the Western Hemisphere—has actually fallen; for these groups, even the most optimistic projections would not foresee re-attainment of the per capita income levels of the late 1970s until 1990. Furthermore, the poor performance of commodity prices since 1981 has offset efforts to reduce the debt-export ratio. For this and other reasons, many countries face years of further adjustment efforts before being assured the commercial external financing that they con-sider necessary for resumption of their growth efforts. Until that time, they face as well a depressed domestic economic outlook, which has a discouraging effect on private investment.

Both these views capture key elements in the outlook for Latin American, as well as for other, indebted countries. They have been taken into account in the medium-term scenario for capital importing developing countries prepared by the Fund staff, a description of which now follows.

Medium-Term Outlook

The baseline medium-term scenario just referred to is grounded in the assumptions regarding economic developments in the industrial countries which were described above (pp. 29–30). The key assump-tions and results of the scenario are summarized in Table 3.[5] Basically, the picture given by these assumptions is one of sustained growth in those countries at rates that are relatively modest compared with those attained in the 1960s and early 1970s. These growth rates would be accompanied by equally modest rates of inflation. The real depreci-ation of the U.S. dollar that took place in 1985 and 1986 would form the basis for the structure of rates assumed to be in effect for the remainder of the decade. The oil price decreases occurring early in 1986 would not be reversed, but oil prices would rise in tandem with the prices of other goods in world trade after 1987; for non-oil pri-mary commodities, the deterioration in prices that occurred in 1982–86 would be partially offset by these prices rising somewhat more rapidly than oil and manufactures prices over the period 1988–91.

Underlying this scenario, also, is an important set of assumptions

---

[5] The figures in Table 3 are based in general on those that appeared in the April 1986 *World Economic Outlook* (see footnote 1) but were updated in September.

Table 3. Summary Results of Baseline Medium-Term Scenario, 1977–91

In percent

	Average 1977–81[1]	1982	1983	1984	1985	1986	1987	Average 1988–91[1]
Industrial countries								
Growth of real GNP	2.8	-0.4	2.6	4.8	3.0	2.7	3.1	3.0
Real six-month LIBOR[2]	3.0	6.7	5.9	7.1	5.1	3.9	3.0	3.3
Increase in GNP deflator	8.3	7.2	4.9	4.2	3.8	3.3	3.1	3.3
World economy								
Change in world price of manufactures[3]	8.4	-2.3	-3.1	-3.3	1.0	17.5	6.5	3.0
Change in world price of oil[3]	23.6	-4.3	-11.4	-2.4	-4.3	-45.7	3.4	3.0
Change in world price of non-oil primary commodities[3]	4.6	-10.1	7.1	3.7	-12.2	-1.5	-1.5	4.0
Growth of total external credit to capital importing countries[3,4]								
Private	19.0	12.6	5.1	2.2	2.3	2.8	2.2	1.6
Official	15.4	14.0	14.2	11.7	6.3	6.1	6.8	7.2
Capital importing developing countries								
Growth of real GDP	4.9	2.0	1.7	4.8	4.1	3.2	3.4	4.8
Growth of import volume	7.1	-6.4	-2.1	4.2	2.5	-0.5	2.3	5.2
Growth of export volume	5.0	-1.6	7.9	10.9	2.6	4.4	5.4	4.8
Countries with recent debt-servicing problems								
Growth of real GDP	4.0	-0.1	-2.5	2.6	2.9	2.3	2.9	4.3
Growth of import volume	5.1	-14.3	-15.0	1.8	-1.4	-3.2	4.6	5.1
Growth of export volume	3.2	-4.8	5.8	7.5	0.1	1.0	4.2	4.2
Western Hemisphere								
Growth of real GDP	4.3	-1.0	-3.1	3.2	3.7	2.7	3.5	4.6
Growth of import volume	6.7	-17.7	-22.3	3.0	-0.6	0.0	7.9	5.3
Growth of export volume	5.5	-2.5	8.5	8.6	-1.7	-0.1	5.7	4.2

As ratio of goods and services to exports

	Average 1977–81	1982	1983	1984	1985	1986	1987	1989	1991
Capital importing developing countries									
Current account balance	-14.2	-18.0	-9.8	-4.0	-3.8	-7.0	-6.0	-4.8	-4.8
Total external debt	122.5	151.3	160.7	154.0	168.8	179.5	173.0	159.4	147.1
Debt service payments	18.5	24.7	22.3	23.2	24.0	25.5	24.1	23.1	20.9
Interest payments	8.1	14.2	13.5	13.6	13.6	13.0	11.7	9.6	8.8
Amortization payments	10.3	10.4	8.8	9.5	10.4	12.4	12.4	13.6	12.2
Countries with recent debt-servicing problems									
Current account balance	-20.8	-30.5	-10.8	-3.9	-1.5	-9.0	-8.6	-6.0	-4.7
Total external debt	167.5	238.6	254.0	245.0	264.7	292.8	281.8	256.8	233.4
Debt service payments	27.4	39.9	34.3	35.2	35.2	40.6	38.3	37.3	31.9
Interest payments	11.8	24.3	23.2	23.2	23.0	23.1	20.2	16.6	15.0
Amortization payments	15.6	15.5	11.1	12.0	12.2	17.5	18.1	20.7	16.9
Western Hemisphere									
Current account balance	-24.3	-34.4	-9.1	-2.3	-3.7	-11.2	-10.1	-8.7	-6.9
Total external debt	200.4	273.1	290.4	275.2	296.2	331.3	316.3	292.9	270.6
Debt service payments	37.1	50.6	41.9	41.1	40.3	46.0	43.2	44.1	37.5
Interest payments	16.8	32.0	30.6	29.6	28.9	27.7	23.9	20.2	18.8
Amortization payments	20.3	18.6	11.3	11.5	11.3	18.3	19.3	23.9	18.7

NOTE: Based on results published in International Monetary Fund, *World Economic Outlook: A Survey by the Staff of the International Monetary Fund* (Washington, April 1986).

[1] Compound annual rates of change.

[2] London interbank offered rate on six-month U.S. dollar deposits, deflated by the U.S. GNP deflator.

[3] In U.S. dollars.

[4] Includes trade financing.

concerning the availability of external financing for developing countries as a whole. This assumption constitutes a kind of constraint for
the entire scenario exercise, as it specifies maximum flows of financing
available to all developing countries but does not specify projections
for individual countries or groups of countries; these were carried out
by the economists who prepared the projections for individual countries upon which the first round of the scenario exercise was based.
Thus, only if the sum of individual assumptions exceeds the assumption of total financing for all capital importing developing countries is
any adjustment made to the projections aggregated from individual
country estimates. For the group of capital importing developing
countries as a whole, then, it is assumed that flows of official development assistance will remain approximately constant in real terms and
that foreign direct investment will rise roughly in step with real GDP
in host countries, while trade credits rise pari passu with imports.
Private lending (in terms of U.S. dollars) is assumed to rise at an
annual average rate of about 2 percent over the period 1988–91,
reflecting continued caution on the part of commercial banks with
regard to non-trade-related private lending. Nevertheless, the sum of
the financing assumptions imply continued growth of external indebtedness in real terms.

A final set of assumptions underlying the medium-term scenario
relates to the policies followed by the capital importing countries
themselves. Fund desk economists were asked to describe, and to build
their baseline projections on, the policies most likely to be pursued by
each country's authorities over the scenario period. The resulting
projections reflect the fact that external circumstances will be continuing to compel the authorities in many countries to follow policies
directed toward reducing internal and external imbalances. These
policies account in large part for specific features of the scenario
outcome, which is summarized in Table 3 (which also shows recent
developments and the short-term outlook). For instance, the declining
current account balances of the capital importing countries, and especially those with debt-servicing problems, are policy related, as is the
fact that import volumes, as already pointed out, have grown less
rapidly than output during the period of adjustment (1982–85) and
are projected to grow at approximately the same rate as output over
the medium term, in sharp contrast to the period before 1982, when
imports grew substantially more rapidly than GDP. These developments stem in considerable part from strong demand-management
and exchange rate policies, although also to some extent from imposition of trade and exchange restrictions.

Notwithstanding the generally weak growth performance of the countries with debt-servicing problems since 1982, their growth is expected to pick up substantially after 1986. This is due to two principal factors. First, the fall in commodity prices has apparently bottomed out; the terms of trade for non-oil commodities should undergo a slow improvement from 1988 to 1991, while the price of oil is also likely to keep pace, at the very least, with prices of other traded goods. (With regard to oil prices, the staff estimate is probably on the conservative side, since the repercussions of the recent fall in petroleum prices on world demand and supply have not had time to work themselves through.) Assuming that there is no tightening of protectionist restrictions in either industrial or developing economies, the growth of export revenues should both stimulate and facilitate the achievement of higher rates of growth of demand and investment, supported by higher rates of growth of imports. Second, the short-term deflationary effects of the adjustment policies that have been carried out over the past four years have dominated longer-term benefits for the allocation of resources, which can be expected to show their full impact over the next several years. Admittedly, however, the results of the scenario may also depend to some extent on a shift of emphasis in policies in the debt-problem countries, which is discussed in the succeeding subsection.

The steady growth of exports, combined with import growth that is only slightly faster than that of output, will enable these countries to maintain current account balances (relative to exports of goods and services) that remain low by historical standards, although the sharp rise in current account deficits of countries exporting petroleum and non-oil primary commodities has raised substantially the overall current account ratios of capital importing countries (and subgroups, like the Western Hemisphere countries) from the ratios achieved in 1984–85. Thus, the accumulation of external debt will proceed at a relatively modest pace, while the improved growth of export revenues projected, together with the lower interest rates expected to prevail in world financial markets, will also contribute to a steady reduction in the ratios of debt and debt service to exports of goods and services (see Table 3).

The scenario results for the Western Hemisphere countries, also shown in Table 3, reveal trends similar to those for the broader groups of capital importing and debt-problem countries; the difference is that for Latin American economies the starting points for debt and debt service are very much higher, and therefore the overall external position much more vulnerable. While the Fund staff considers the projections presented here as a feasible possibility, there is admittedly room for discussion of whether the rates of economic growth projected for the Western Hemisphere countries would in practice be achievable without greater net capital inflows; such inflows, however, if taking the form of financial borrowing at commercial terms, would add to stocks of such debt that are already intolerably high. This issue, as well as related questions, is considered in the following subsection.

Policy Issues

The developments in industrial countries, reviewed above, are the major determinants of the external economic environment facing the developing countries. The conclusion to be drawn from that discussion is that effective, well-coordinated policies among the industrial countries can be expected to result in a sustained rate of economic growth of about 3 percent, which is considerably lower than that attained during the years between the post-World War II recovery and the first oil shock. While it is possible that strong supply-side policies, accompanied by an upsurge of confidence in the private sector, could result in a better growth performance, our limited understanding of the reasons for the decline in growth in the 1970s gives little ground for firmly linking specific policies with an improvement in this regard. Not only does this outlook limit the potential growth of demand for exports of developing countries, it also renders uncertain the progress that is likely to be made in opening up markets in industrial countries and in increasing flows of official concessional assistance. At the same time, continuing limited growth and heavy debt burdens in many of the capital importing countries suggest that future increases in commercial lending and direct foreign investment are unlikely to proceed at a rapid pace, and in any event both the governments of debtor countries and the international financial community will continue to perceive a need to reduce debt ratios, and therefore to maintain relatively low current account ratios.

One must conclude, therefore, that the governments of countries with debt problems must confront the task of achieving satisfactory rates of economic growth—in broader terms, meeting their long-term development objectives—in the face of a relatively unsatisfactory world economic environment. This is not to say that the international community should not seek to press for enlightened policies of national governments that would improve that environment—for instance, more liberal trade policies that would improve long-term growth prospects in both countries where import protection is reduced and those whose exports thereby benefit. Nonetheless, it would be imprudent to base domestic policies of indebted countries on the expectation of dramatic improvements in foreign trade opportunities or in official development assistance in the foreseeable future.

The fundamental question, then, is how to deal with what has earlier been termed the growth crisis without at the same time worsening, or failing to deal effectively with, the debt crisis. Acknowledging that there is ample scope for creditors to restructure outstanding debt and improve terms—and as mentioned earlier, such steps have already been taken in many instances—it must also be said that the unilateral repudiation of debts or limitation of debt-service payments by debtors is as short-sighted as would be the refusal of creditors to contemplate any form of debt relief, because such a unilateral action would increase the reluctance of creditors to extend any new financing in the future. Similarly, it is shortsighted to undertake domestic policies that lead to temporary increases in domestic demand and output at the expense of future improvements in the efficiency of resource allocation, in growth potential, and in international competitiveness.

As usual, the Fund finds itself in the role of having to deliver a message that is not universally popular. The fact that it must play this role is often mistaken for a lack of concern about the immense problems of poverty in many countries, even in those countries in Latin America that can be regarded as semi-industrialized and relatively advanced. The Fund never ceases to call for greater flows of concessional assistance to those countries that are in need of it and can demonstrate that they can use it effectively. But its chief function is to advise members on how to achieve the best possible results on the basis of admittedly unsatisfactory circumstances.

In this context, chief emphasis must be put on improved policies in the debtor countries themselves. In most instances, the scope for improvement is substantial. By the early 1980s, many countries had come to depend, as a matter of routine, on the inflationary financing of government deficits, with the result that inflation—with all its attendant distortions of prices and investment incentives—had become engrained in both the expectations of the private sector and the decision-making machinery of the government. A necessary, if not always sufficient, condition for eliminating such inflation was the reduction of the combined demands of the government and private sector for credit so that aggregate demand would be brought into line with supply, given a real net capital inflow that represented a sustainable increase in external indebtedness. Success in undertaking such initial measures, however, has often been at the expense of the level of

economic activity and at the same time has not always been sufficient
to reduce inflation to manageable rates. The initial success of the
recent policy experiments in Argentina and Brazil suggests that extraordinary measures may be necessary in the face of long-entrenched
high inflation, although what is the most effective sequencing of such
measures with the conventional instruments of demand management
is still an open question, as the rather different approach taken in
Bolivia suggests.

More seriously, however, the recent experience in Latin America
also suggests that growth is inhibited not just by inflationary distortions but by problems typically called "structural," a blanket term
covering both the way in which resources and investment are allocated
and the pattern of incentives faced by producers in both the private
and the public sectors. A possible interpretation of developments in
recent years is that in a buoyant world economy there was more room
for wasteful investment and misallocation of existing resources than
during a period of stringency, so that only since 1982 have certain
deep-seated problems inhibiting growth in many economies become
fully clear. A somewhat different interpretation would stress the fact
that many of the structural problems are part and parcel of under-
development itself, and getting out of them would require the massive
investment in both physical and human infrastructure that is in considerable part excluded by the constraints presently posed by both the
fiscal situation and the scarcity of external financing.

Despite these constraints, however, considerable improvements are
possible both with regard to the allocation of public expenditure and
the operation of markets. Such policies will serve to increase domestic
saving and to stimulate more efficient investment decisions, in part by
facing investors with the true economic cost of capital and of foreign
exchange. Improvements on the fiscal side are covered thoroughly in
the paper presented to this seminar by Vito Tanzi and therefore
require no further treatment here. In addition, there exists a wide
range of possible actions to promote savings, investment, and efficient
choices within the private sector. Such policies include the correction
of misaligned exchange rates and interest rates; removing other price
distortions created by government action; and freeing individual
productive units, whether private or state-owned, from inefficient,
burdensome, and often inconsistent government controls over their
activities; and liberalizing restrictions on foreign trade and payments.

This is not to say, of course, that the government does not itself play
an important role in directly fostering productive activities in the

private sector. Its role is perhaps even more crucial, in some respects, in developing than in industrial countries, for instance with regard to the provision of "human" infrastructure. It is also necessary at times for the government to sponsor the creation of new private economic institutions, as is sometimes true, for example, with regard to the reform of financial institutions. Agriculture is also an area in which government infrastructural and technical assistance often plays a crucial role, especially when agricultural production is dominated by small-scale producers.

In the types of policies outlined above, as well as those discussed in Mr. Tanzi's paper, the more efficient operation of market forces can contribute not only to the promotion of exports (especially by maintaining a realistic exchange rate and liberalizing imports) but also to efficient import substitution. An example of this is food production, which is often subject to negative biases through official price controls; and the proper pricing of foreign exchange may also stimulate other types of import-substituting production, for example, of basic consumer goods. There is a danger, however, that unfavorable developments in the world economy, leading to poor export prospects and inadequate external financing for indebted developing economies, will induce some countries to undertake a strategy of import substitution that is based on restrictions and controls rather than on comparative advantage. Such policies are self-defeating, since they tend to undermine export performance and create import-intensive industries, while reducing the scope for long-term economic growth. Moreover, such policies encourage heightened protectionism in other countries, thereby further dampening the growth of world trade.

It goes without saying that a policy strategy of improving growth and maintaining a strong current account performance (because of continued scarcity of external financing) requires strong macroeconomic policies, especially because of the need to mobilize domestic savings and to discourage capital flight, as well as to create a favorable climate for private investment. Fiscal and monetary restraint are required to keep inflation under control and limit the share of saving captured by the government.

Conclusions

The world economic events of the past half-decade have brought about a significantly heightened perception of global economic interdependence. The facts, for example, that an economic crisis in large

Latin American countries could threaten financial stability in industrial countries, or that a sharp cutback of Latin American imports has
a significant impact on North American jobs, represent new insights
for the noneconomist. Recent issues of the Fund's *World Economic
Outlook* have emphasized, to take another example, that creating more
dynamic economies in the industrial world is not only an important
goal for its own sake but perhaps even more important for its implications for the developing countries. While it would be naive to suppose
that these considerations have become dominant ones for governments in industrial countries, the perceptions of these interconnec-
tions have become far more widespread, and are far more often mentioned, in public discussions.

This fact, admittedly, is at this point cold comfort for the governments and people of Latin America, faced with difficult decisions and
little prospective relief from recent cutbacks in living standards. In
this setting, one hopeful sign is the redoubled effort of international
institutions, especially the World Bank and other multilateral aid institutions, to expand flows of assistance. The Fund has proceeded on
several fronts to give assistance. Indirectly, it is hoped that efforts by
industrial countries, assisted by technical inputs from the Fund, to
better coordinate macroeconomic policies, will nurture sustained
growth of the world economy. In addition, the Fund continues its role
of policy advisor and catalyst for external financing for countries with
debt problems, and it has repeatedly urged all parties concerned to
increase private and official financial flows to countries that can use
them effectively. In particular, there is a great need for additional
resources to be channeled to low-income countries in forms that do
not lead to unsustainable increases in debt burdens. The Fund has also
repeatedly called for efforts to liberalize world trade, which would be
of special importance for Latin American countries, many of whom
have substantial industrial sectors and have a chance to increase their
exports of manufactures. This would require a combination of domestic reforms in these countries, together with new trade agreements
under the General Agreement on Tariffs and Trade and a rolling back
of trade restrictions introduced during the past several years. There
is also scope for expansion of certain types of agricultural exports,
whose volume is presently limited by protectionist agricultural policies
in a number of industrial countries.

Comments

Carlos Bazdresch P.

Mr. Lanyi's paper is undoubtedly a work of great interest. It coherently combines a good deal of the thinking and the research efforts of the International Monetary Fund staff. It is a paper that we can all benefit from reading, both because of Lanyi's efforts to form a coherent whole and because of its informed speculation as to the future.

I agree with Lanyi that current data suggest that the medium-term scenario for the industrial countries is that they will on average grow at a relatively slow annual rate of about 3 percent. This is neither the time nor the place to discuss this prediction. I will only say that the same prediction is being made in places very different from the Fund, such as ECLA, although there the most widely accepted prediction is of an even lower growth rate. This fact undoubtedly adds some plausibility to Lanyi's forecast. It is not an optimistic prediction to give us cause for celebration, but neither is it a pessimistic forecast foreshadowing some disaster. It is, I would say, rather a melancholic prediction, heaped with nostalgia for the good old postwar days.

I also concur with Lanyi that it is not easy to foresee from this scenario any sizable increase in official funds to finance growth in the developing countries. It is equally difficult to foresee the industrial countries reducing their protectionism, not even—or perhaps even less so—their agricultural protectionism. From this, Lanyi's assertion that "... it would be imprudent to base ... policies of indebted countries on the expectation of dramatic improvements in foreign trade opportunities or in official development assistance in the foreseeable future" would appear to be valid. What is more, in terms of the scenario Lanyi describes, this statement is optimistic.

As Lanyi indicates, we deduce from this that the countries that are currently experiencing difficulties because of the size of their external debt have to make some changes—which we are now supposed to call "structural"—to increase their savings ratio, the productivity of their economies, and their export capacity as fast as possible. Once again—this time, it would seem, definitive—the death of the import substitution "model" has been announced.

Despite all these points of agreement with Lanyi's paper and many others that I could mention, I note that it lacks any reference to a number of important issues.

In the first place it should be noted that, although the scenario described by Lanyi is currently the most widely accepted, it assumes that the confrontation between the two international blocks does not generate any inflationary pressures or large-scale violence. Let us hope this is so. But like Sombart, we must remember that expenditure on weaponry has always been a driving force behind economic growth, so that if the confrontation does not abate, the situation, unfortunately, could become quite different. No less strange is the prediction of slow growth in the capitalist world at a point in time when technological change not only seems to be accelerating but has taken root in so many different places at once. This dissemination, no longer just of new technology but of the ability to copy technology from other places and generate new technology autonomously, would encourage a follower of Schumpeter to forecast that economic growth in the capitalist world will accelerate rather than slow down. Perhaps Lanyi believes that this is a "metaphysical" view. He is probably right.

A second point concerns the tendency noted by Lanyi to protectionism in the developed countries. I do not deny that the evidence so far supports Lanyi's statement. However, it should be noted that, because of the very fact that there is a crisis, such protectionism will be ever more expensive for the countries that practice it. The point here is that by lowering real wages in the developing countries the competitiveness of their agriculture will very rapidly increase, especially with regard to products with high specific value such as flowers, fruits, vegetables, and so on. The same would apply to already standardized manufactured goods. Consequently, protectionist barriers in the developed world will perhaps have to increase. This may occur, but in that case the high cost of such barriers will become increasingly obvious to consumers as well as to efficient production sectors in the industrial countries. Why does Lanyi believe that these sectors will not act to defend their interests?

A third comment relates to the need of the developing—particularly the overindebted—countries to create export capacity. In my opinion, this need is inescapable. However, like Lewis,[1] we must remember that this capacity should not be achieved at any price or by sacrificing import substitution policies too hastily. The problem is that, if all the low-wage developing countries try to export manufactured goods, it is most likely that they will be faced once again with a sharp decline in

---

[1] See W. Arthur Lewis, *The Evolution of the International Economic Order* (Princeton, New Jersey: Princeton University Press, 1978).

their terms of trade. Consequently, the correct policy needs to be thought through carefully.

But what is most noteworthy in Lanyi's paper is the lack of any discussion of what could happen to the financial system, and, particularly, of what could happen on the external debt front of the Latin American countries. The absence of any such discussion would seem to imply that Lanyi believes that things will continue more or less as now, or at least that whatever changes do occur on this front will not affect the other variables very much. It seems to me, however, that it will be difficult for things to continue the same in the future and, it also seems to me that, although for the world as a whole Latin American debt may not seem to be very important, for our countries—Argentina, Brazil, Peru, and Mexico—what might happen on this front is indeed of great importance.

It is possible, but not probable, that the present answer to the excessive indebtedness of some countries, outstanding among which, of course, is Mexico—based on involuntary commercial bank lending and "continuous" adjustment by the debtor country—will last for much longer. One of the several reasons for this is that practically none of the participants are happy with this solution.

The agreement between Mexico and the Fund drawn up in August 1986 was an appropriate and indeed an imaginative one. It cannot be denied that to reach this solution was an achievement in international cooperation. The Mexican authorities have expressed their appreciation for the support the Fund and the authorities of some of the creditor countries gave them. This support was the key to their reaching such a solution. It is obvious, however, that even with all its good points this agreement offers Mexico no more than the minimum, as it granted barely enough funds to enable Mexico's economy to grow at a very moderate pace in 1987–88. Mexico, with a labor force that grows by just under one million persons a year, has to boost its growth rate significantly if it does not wish to confront a vast structural crisis a few years down the road. Furthermore, while the above-mentioned negotiations succeeded in providing financing to cover needs in 1987 and perhaps also for 1988, the bare minimum financing for subsequent years was not found. This undoubtedly creates uncertainty in the private sector, which may again translate into pressure on the capital account. Thus, I think it very probable, if there is no substantial recovery in oil prices, that in the future—maybe in 1989—there will have to be another great negotiation process. This means that, despite the amount of financing and the advantages and new concessions that Mexico succeeded in obtaining in the 1986 agreement, by not having insured that the "net" transfer that Mexico will have to support in the next several years is consistent with the maintenance of a reasonable growth rate, the opportunity to achieve a lasting solution was missed.

It seems obvious to me that this agreement did not satisfy the creditor banks either, because they have pointed on many occasions to the undesirability, from their point of view, of increasing their exposure by acquiring more Mexican debt. Nor do I believe that the international financial authorities or those of the creditor countries are very happy to have to make such strenuous efforts to convince many commercial banks to take part in financing the agreement with Mexico.

In these circumstances, who is happy? If few—or none—are, the situation will probably change. What form might this change take?

There is one form this change will not take: the excessively indebted countries, with their inefficient productive infrastructures, will not turn into major exporters overnight thanks to some miraculous structural change, which indeed should not take place too swiftly, as it would then be unlikely to be a lasting one. Thus, for example, while I am quite sure that the Mexican Government will do its level best to comply with its side of the 1986 agreement, I am also sure that time will inevitably be required for these changes to mature—time that Mexico will also need in order to make a lasting recovery in its ability to pay.

Furthermore, I wonder whether in the relatively near future it will be more or less inevitable for the major creditor banks to have to increase the pace at which they are absorbing the loss of capital associated with the liquidity of the Mexican debt. Of course, considerable reserves have already been set up for this purpose, and perhaps there would be some way for this to take place in an orderly fashion. Both the multilateral institutions and the governments of the creditor countries can contribute to this process. As a matter of fact, as we all know, many solutions have been proposed to allow this absorption to take place in an orderly fashion, thus providing a foundation for an increase in the growth rate of the debtor countries.

The fact that this process may be taking place in an orderly fashion could help solve the debt problem, in that there would not be—as there has been until now—a threat of the debtors having to confront a new balance of payments crisis in the immediate future. This was on the point of being achieved in the 1986 Mexican agreement, but the issue was not yet ripe; perhaps it will become so at some time in the future.

These ideas suggest two scenarios different from those put forward by Lanyi:

In the first, the banks would continue to fail to absorb their capital losses and the governments would continue not to help them to do so. What would most probably happen then is that there would be an attempt to continue imposing the solution of involuntary lending and almost continuous stagnation in the creditor countries—especially if the latter do not behave properly. In this case, the creditors' united front would possibly split, with some banks finding themselves in serious difficulties, while some debtor countries would move ahead and others would declare an official or unofficial moratorium on their debt service.

The second scenario would follow from a decision to help banks absorb capital losses and to help debtor countries agree to a lasting solution to their external debt problem by trying, through adopting some of the many formulas that exist for this purpose, to make the debt service burden compatible with the achievement of a reasonable growth rate. This growth would allow time for the so-called structural change to mature so that the economies that are now excessively indebted could regain their ability to pay.

Hence I conclude that it is likely that the outlook for growth in Latin America will be either more pessimistic or more optimistic than in the scenario Lanyi offers us.

Winston Fritsch

Anthony Lanyi's paper is divided into two parts. The first analyzes the prospects for growth and the interaction of macroeconomic policies in the North and, consequently, the economic environment for the debtor countries. As was clear from his presentation, the analysis is conveniently divided into the short term, that is, until 1987, and the medium term, until the end of the decade.

The indebted economies are analyzed in the second substantive part of the paper. There is a brief overview of the situation since the 1982 crisis, and the outlook for the indebted economies is discussed in the scenarios outlined during the previous session.

I will organize my comments along the same lines as the paper itself. Thus, regarding the first part, I will start by commenting on the short-term scenarios. Mr. Lanyi rightly notes that events of 1985–86 are "discouraging": the sluggishness of the OECD economies and the abrupt worsening of the terms of trade of the indebted countries are factors that explain this. But he is optimistic about the near future, as the Fund, in the estimates on which it bases its forecasts, believes that the industrial economies will recover, as a result of lower interest rates and lower oil prices, and concludes that growth will be maintained at 3 percent, if—he says—the United States budget deficit is brought down and monetary policies remain flexible.

I think these forecasts need further elucidation. In the first place, I think that the main—because it is the surest—factor in the buoyancy of the world economy over the next eighteen months, is the effect of the real exchange rate adjustment of the dollar, and this is not referred to explicitly. The depreciation of the dollar will bring about an improvement of some US$30 billion in the U.S. trade deficit, which should add something like 0.75 percent to the growth rate of the United States.

As to the effects of the lower interest rates and oil prices, there is not the same certainty as there was when the Fund staff made the forecasts published in the *World Economic Outlook* early in the second quarter of 1986.

There are two effects connected with interest rates: first, I do not much believe in the estimates of the overall effects of monetary and fiscal impulses derived from the linkage models in the context of flexible exchange rates, because their variability is very large. The assertion by the author as to the possibility of an interest rate decline implies an optimistic view of the current flexibility of monetary policy implementation in the North, particularly in Europe and Japan. Interest rates in the main financial markets very probably will not continue to decline in a coordinated fashion. The recent comments by Mr. Pöhl, not to mention Mr. Stoltenberg, are not very encouraging in this respect, and if the Japanese were more explicit in discussing their monetary beliefs, they would be saying the same thing.

As to the effects of the decline in oil prices, it is interesting to note that when the Fund's *World Economic Outlook* was drafted there was more optimism about the positive effects of the decline in oil prices on demand in the OECD countries. But now we have seen that the oil collapse had a very perverse effect on the investment rate in the oil industry and other energy sectors as well as on imports by the major oil producers. The net effect on demand in the OECD countries is uncertain.

But as the author notes, the Fund's optimism is more apparent in its medium-term projections. In these projections, the methodology takes into account almost exclusively supply-side factors: these are mainly estimates of growth in the potential output of the major economies on the basis of forecast growth of productivity and factor endowment. Today's gigantic demand-management and coordination problems are assumed to have been solved. Thus, for example, it is assumed that money management will stabilize inflation and, more interestingly, that an improvement in the U.S. current account will take place in parallel with a reduction in the U.S. fiscal deficit. This scenario is clearly an extremely optimistic one. What would guarantee this happening is not discussed by the author. Note, for example, that if only the current account improves in the United States and the public deficit is not reduced, the revival in the level of activity and the consequent reduction of net saving in the private sector will certainly trigger a new interest rate hike, as happened in 1984.

In addition, there are the worrying questions related to the potential instability of international financial asset markets caused by the U.S. debt crisis; that is, by the accelerated growth of U.S. debt. As the United States changed from a net receiver of interest in the order of US$20 billion in 1982 to a payer of almost US$40 billion in the projected trade account for 1987 and the following year, it can be estimated that the U.S. external debt may reach about US$500 billion in 1989 and US$1 trillion in the first half of the 1990s. In this scenario, with a more or less stable exchange rate, if what we know about portfolio behavior is correct, I do not see how we are going to avoid an interest rate hike in dollar assets. This is not touched on in the paper.

And even in this medium-term scenario, looking at it optimistically, I think that with sustained 3 percent growth in the North, as predicted in the paper, the projection regarding the behavior of primary product prices, excluding oil, is a little conservative. I think that if the projections are made on the basis of the price equations derived from Chu and Morrison's research undertaken in the Fund, we would obtain more optimistic results. I wonder if there are implicit pessimistic hypotheses on the supply side that would explain the low price growth projected.

But allow me to turn now to the second substantive part of the paper, in which the author discusses the effects of these scenarios in the North on the indebted countries. Here I believe that the paper is too much concerned to demonstrate that the crises in the Western Hemisphere countries are to a large extent the fruit of their own *policy mistakes*, when compared with the performance of that other, "virtuous," group of developing countries—although these virtues are not exactly dwelt on in the paper. I think this kind of exercise is not very fruitful; by which I mean that there is little sense in separating and comparing a group of "sinful debtors," heterogeneous and all roughly comparable in size, on the one hand, with another group of "virtuous debtors." This is because there is a considerable variation in structure between the two groups, the virtuous and the sinful. For example, what sense is there in comparing the performance of a country like the Republic of Korea, which experiences an improvement in its terms of trade when the prices of raw materials collapse, whose export structure responds very positively to real devaluations, and which continues to turn to the banks for voluntary finance, with a country like Bolivia or even Mexico?

This "virtue" is to a large extent a product of the structural characteristics of their economies. Obviously the policies followed in Latin America were not exactly the best in every case, but it would have been more thought-provoking if this section had also discussed the mechanisms by which the shocks and fluctuations in the North are transmitted to the South. In this respect, today's discussion will only be complete after Professor Dornbusch's paper is presented this afternoon.

However, to have a proper view of this problem, it would be interesting to have something like a sensitivity analysis to quantify how it is that probable variations of such basic parameters as interest rates or GDP growth in the OECD affect the various groups of debtors in different ways. I think that the paper suffers a little, as do the Fund's estimates, from not making an appropriate disaggregation among the various groups of indebted countries. For, in fact, there are great differences between the indebted countries in terms of the effects of various world economic scenarios in relation to given variables. For example, Argentina, which has a very high debt/export ratio, is very sensitive to interest rates. Mexico, obviously, is very sensitive to oil price changes, and so on.

In conclusion, I would like to comment on two general points. First, there is a problem which in my view is now central to the future of our economies: the likelihood of more or less coordination of macroeconomic policies in the North and how it relates to the potential stability of the world economy. In this context, I would like to hear the ideas of the members of the Fund staff here today as to what role the Fund can play in promoting greater international economic coordination. I believe that at the most recent summit meeting in Tokyo last May, the Fund was informally given the task of designing objective indicators and surveillance mechanisms to enhance coordination. But nothing seems to have come of it so far.

Second, I would also like to have your comments on a point I think is crucial today for the debt problem. I think it is obvious that what Mr. Lanyi called the "growth crisis"—basically a problem created by the lack of savings to support medium-term growth, given a more or less fixed capital/output ratio, and the fact that there was an abrupt fall in the investment ratios in these economics after 1980—is a problem which, in addition to the effort to increase domestic savings, clearly calls for a reduction in real transfers abroad, and an end to the uncertainty inhibiting the growth of private investment. So I am asking you if you feel that the most likely medium-term scenarios will lead to these two favorable results that will help our countries overcome this savings/investment restriction.

Impact on Debtor Countries of World Economic Conditions

Rudiger Dornbusch

This paper addresses the impact on debtor countries of the world economic environment. It asks how external disturbances impinge on growth and on welfare.

The paper is organized in four parts. We start out with a conceptual framework which shows the relevance of world interest rates and the terms of trade for a debtor country's welfare. Several special linkages to the world economy, including credit rationing, are also considered. In the following section we investigate the linkages between external shocks and the rate of inflation. The analysis highlights that real depreciation increases inflation, the more so the larger the external debt. A discussion of facts and special problems of debtor countries follows in the third section. Here we draw particular attention to the implications for debtors of alternative monetary-fiscal policy mixes pursued by the industrial countries. The paper concludes with a discussion of external remedies for debtor countries, specifically debt-equity swaps, debt relief, and a reversal of capital flight.

A Conceptual Framework

In this section we set out a simple aggregative framework that describes the principal interactions between a debtor country and the rest of the world. The most direct effects are the following two:
- interest rates in world markets that determine the cost of existing debt service and represent the intertemporal terms of trade;
- the conventional terms of trade or relative price of exportables and importables.

We first set out the model and highlight the role of interest rates and the terms of trade. Then we turn to several more specialized linkages.

A Model

The model is a simple one of the debtor country, which produces only two goods: domestic manufactures and traditional goods. The latter are perfect substitutes for primary commodities traded in world markets. Home manufactures are consumed at home and also exported. They are an imperfect substitute for manufactures produced in the rest of the world and imported. In addition, we separate out oil as an importable or exportable with a price given in the world market.

Let P_x, P_t, and P_m be the prices in home currency of the three commodity groups. The home country takes as given the real price of traditional exportables in terms of importables, $p_t = P_t/P_m$. The world price of oil in terms of imported manufactures is denoted by p_0. Finally, the relative price of home manufactures in terms of foreign imported manufactures is denoted $p_x = P_x/P_m$.

The analysis now concentrates on the terms of trade between manufactures, exportables, and importables and the level of domestic absorption, A. Figure 1 shows internal balance along II and current account balance along EE. These schedules are drawn for given real interest rates in the world market, a given external debt, and a given real price of traditional exports and of oil.[1] The market equilibrium condition is

$$I(p_x, p_t, p_0, A) = 0. \tag{1}$$

The II schedule is upward sloping on the assumption that substitution effects dominate. A rise in the real price of exportables or a terms of trade improvement creates substitution effects against domestic goods on the demand side while raising supply. Furthermore, given the level of absorption measured in terms of importables, A, the purchasing power of spending in terms of exportables declines. The net effect of an increased real price of exportables thus is an excess supply. Hence, spending must rise to restore internal balance. Points to the right of and below II thus correspond to a boom and points to the left to unemployment. External balance equilibrium requires

$$E(p_x, p_t, p_0, r^*d, A) = 0, \tag{2}$$

where r^* is the world interest rate and d is the external debt.

---

[1] Throughout we assume that a country exports commodities or agricultural products—the traditional exports in our model. But the model is easily adapted to where the home country is a net importer of these goods.

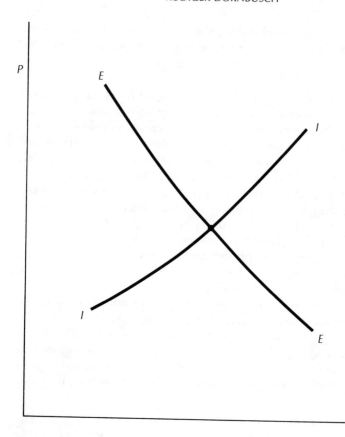

P

Absorption

Figure 1

The *EE* schedule is assumed to be negatively sloped: an increase in the real price of exportables through substitution effects worsens the external balance. But the decline in the real value of spending, for a given *A*, will improve the external balance. The net effect is ambiguous and we assume that substitution effects dominate. Thus, a spending cut is required to maintain the current account in equilibrium when p_x increases. Points above and to the left of *EE* correspond to a surplus and points below and to the right to a deficit.

This framework can now be used to investigate questions of comparative statics and of welfare economics. The analysis of external disturbances is straightforward:

• A rise in the real price of oil reduces real income and worsens the external balance. A decline in the real price of domestic manufactures is required to restore internal and external balance. Thus, a terms of trade deterioration, because of increased oil prices, carries with it a further worsening in the terms of trade. This is so because of the reduction in the real price of domestic manufactures relative to those imported that is required to restore external balance. The adjustment in the equilibrium real price of domestic manufactures is larger the smaller the share in marginal spending and the less substitutable are home and foreign manufactures.

In policy terms, an oil price shock worsens the external balance and the country responds by restoring current account balance via a corrective real depreciation. A policy of sustaining the relative price would require an increase in absorption. Such a policy would, of course, worsen the external balance further. This is not optimal for permanent disturbances, since ultimately the adjustment needs to be made and households, other things being equal, prefer a smooth consumption profile. But it is clear that failure of timely adjustment to relatively permanent disturbances is one of the explanations for the extreme adjustments that were ultimately required in Latin America.

• A rise in the real interest rate exerts two effects. First it reduces real disposable income by increasing debt service. To the extent that capital markets are tightly linked and consumers optimize inter-temporally, it also affects the preferred time profile of consumption, raising future relative to current consumption. The dominant effect, though, is likely to be the increased cost of debt service. If this is not automatically financed by the budget and by "new money," there will be a reduction in absorption and the need for a corrective real depreciation. Thus, increased debt service brings with it a worsening of the manufacturing terms of trade. This secondary cost is larger, the larger the share of manufactures in the marginal spending pattern. It is also smaller, the less substitutable home and foreign manufactures and the less substitutable resources are between manufacturing and traditional sectors. Only in traditional exportables can production for the world markets expand without the risk of terms of trade losses.

• A decline in the real price of traditional exports in terms of world manufactures reduces real income and demand for all goods. The excess supply of manufactures once again brings about a reduction in the equilibrium real price of exportable manufactures. Thus there is, just as in an oil price fall, a secondary burden stemming from an amplified terms of trade loss.

Welfare

The welfare economics of external shocks require an explicit welfare-theoretic framework of analysis. A minimal model was explored in Dornbusch (1985a). It was shown there that in a two-period utility-maximizing model the terms of trade and world interest rates appear as key determinants of welfare. A worsening of the terms of trade worsens welfare as does for a debtor a rise in the world real interest rate. The cost of a terms of trade deterioration is proportional to the (present value) of imports. The cost of increased interest rates is proportional to the stock of debt.

The welfare economics approach forces one to focus on the intertemporal aspects of adjustment to external shocks. Borrowing abroad to finance rather than adjust an imbalance is always possible but rarely optimal. Only when disturbances are transitory or optimal resource movements, because of adjustment costs, ought to be gradual does it pay to borrow abroad to finance current account imbalances. Of course, these exceptions may be very important. It is certainly conceivable that adjustment to higher interest rates requires expanding an exportable sector and that this in turn requires investment. Some of the investment may have to be financed by a cut in spending over and above the fall in real income implied by the shock. But naturally a good share of the resources should come from abroad. The mistake is not to leave a current account imbalance, but rather the failure to adjust consumption.

We now turn to a number of special effects that amplify the welfare and adjustments costs of external shocks.

Credit Rationing

The model of unrestricted optimization leaves no room for distortions arising from credit rationing. The costs of credit rationing, when effective, arise in two ways. The first is that the current account imbalance is smaller than it would optimally be. That means consumption smoothing is limited and/or investment is too low. These are the conventional costs associated with illiquidity, and it is apparent that a relaxation of effective credit constraints enhances welfare while a further restriction of an already effective constraint reduces welfare.

The second cost of credit constraints comes in the interaction with adverse external shocks. Since an effective constraint implies that at the margin there is no leeway for consumption smoothing or extra investment that does not come from a suboptimal cut in consumption, credit rationing reinforces the welfare cost of adverse shocks. It does so by forcing adjustment to stay off an optimal path.

A third and highly significant cost associated with the combination of adverse shocks and credit rationing is the induced adjustment in the terms of trade. Since an effective credit constraint implies that even transitory disturbances must be fully adjusted to, rather than being financed, a real depreciation is required, which further adds to the welfare costs of the initial disturbance.

System-Wide Adjustment

A second complication comes from looking at the costs of external shocks when many debtor countries jointly experience the same shock and adjust to it in the same manner. The attempt to secure extra exports to balance the current account via a real depreciation is pursued by each of the countries jointly. They compete with each other and as a result worsen their terms of trade.

The worsening of the terms of trade occurs both in respect to manufactures and traditional exports. It arises as a result of the cut in absorption required in adjusting countries. That cut in absorption directly frees resources for sale abroad, and it does so indirectly as real depreciation is used to shift resources from the home goods sector into traditional and nontraditional exports. The result is a world glut of developing country exportables and hence a decline in their real price.

As each debtor country cuts the wage in dollars and cuts its own absorption, the supply of manufactures and commodities from developing countries in the markets of creditor countries is increased and hence their real prices will decline. For commodities, the adjustment effort of debtor countries implies that prices are in fact not given but respond to the system-wide effort to earn foreign exchange by pushing traditional exports. With demand elasticities very low, the real price declines sharply. For manufactures, each country finds that the world demand curve it faces is shifting inward as a result of other countries' competitive depreciation. Where a given x percent depreciation relative to the dollar in a particular country might have been expected to yield a 10 percent increase in export revenue, it turns out to be only 5 percent because all debtor-country competitors follow the same adjustment strategy.[2]

The interaction with credit rationing is quite apparent. The more intense credit rationing, the larger will be the competitive adjustment effort of debtor countries in response to a common shock and hence the larger the excess cost forced upon them by a lack of credit. Credit rationing in the context of a shock thus becomes a fire sale after the

---

[2] These system-wide effects have been studied by Goldstein (1986), who documents their importance.

great fire. We return to this point below in interpreting the decline in the real price of commodities and exports of developing country manufactures in world markets.

It is interesting to note in this context the apparent resistance of the Fund to an interest rate facility. The lack of such a facility increases the adjustment burden and transfers benefits to creditor countries over and above their gains as lenders. The systemic redistribution implied by opposition to an interest rate facility has no foundation in welfare economics.

Foreign Demand

For a perfectly competitive economy, the level of foreign demand is of no interest except insofar as it affects the exogenous real prices of commodities or oil, or the world real interest rate. But when the export sector is less than perfectly competitive, foreign demand does matter. At the margin there is a discrepancy between marginal cost and price, and hence, at the margin, there are excess returns from an expansion in output. Increased foreign demand allows a widening of the profit margin or increased sales at going profit margins and thus they promote an increase in welfare.

The level of foreign demand and its stability and growth are also relevant in the context of scale economies. If manufacturing has scale economies, then production for the world market is a significant part of the profitability of an industry. A world recession means losses and a world boom implies profits.

Market Access and Creditor Country Policies

The adjustment problems of debtor countries to their individual and aggregate attempt to secure foreign exchange are often aggravated by the policies of the creditor countries. Two examples particularly come to mind. The agricultural policies of virtually all creditors lead to a worldwide glut in agricultural products. Particular debtor countries who would be expected to earn their way out of a debt crisis by an expansion of traditional exports find that in fact the world market for these commodities is collapsing under the weight of exports from inefficient producers.

The other vital issue is market access. As debtor countries seek expansion of their exports and contract imports, they face growing conflicts with creditors. Their export expansion runs into actual trade obstacles or, if that is not the case, at least into enough doubt about long-term market access so as to stand in the way of an effective adjustment program.

A peculiar variation on market access comes in a reverse way: developed countries have persuaded themselves that debtors should liberalize their imports. There is no question that many debtor countries, for example Argentina, have wildly inefficient industries and would be far ahead if they had never embarked on these investments. But it is doubtful that a period of external balance crisis offers the best opportunity to increase imports. One would have thought the opposite, except when there is a shortage of resources or an implicit tax on exports. For some countries, specifically Brazil, one would have to believe that import liberalization, for example of Mercedes or BMW imports as is widely claimed, would be an outright policy mistake. The same applies perhaps even more strongly to liberalization in areas where an infant industry case can be made. There is little doubt that Japan, the United States, the Republic of Korea, and Brazil have achieved their spectacular industrialization under the cover of protection. The argument that they would have done even better without rings hollow.

These same issues come up in a very striking form when free trade in high-technology products is claimed precisely to avoid the establishment of infants that could ultimately be efficient suppliers of the home market and even exporters. This argument applies not only to manufactures but, of course, also to services. Some of the Baker-Plan conditionality may therefore be viewed as a pre-emptive policy of securing markets for creditor country oligopoly profits. Resistance by debtors rightly emphasizes that when oligopoly is at stake there is something to be shared. None of this is to say that Argentina should have a car industry and an airplane industry; but it does say that Brazil might well be right in having a computer industry, and the Republic of Korea has already demonstrated that point.

Real Exchange Rate and Inflation

In this section we explore an important linkage that runs from the real exchange rate to the inflation process. Specifically, we want to argue that abrupt real depreciation, as may be associated with the news of involuntary debt service, will inevitably bring about a significant rise in the inflation rate.[3]

The model we use for this purpose is highly simplified. Suppose the

---

[3] This kind of model is explored in Bruno and Fischer (1985), Cardoso (1986a, 1986b), and Dornbusch (1985a). The fiscal side goes back to Keynes and Harberger and Tanzi (1977, 1978) and Oliveira (1967).

government finances a budget deficit by money creation. The deficit, measured as a fraction of gross national product (GNP), is denoted g:

$$g = g(p,R); \quad g_1, g_2 > 0, \tag{3}$$

where p is the rate of inflation and R the real exchange rate. The inflation rate affects the deficit ratio because higher inflation means that lags in tax collection erode the real value of taxes, the more so the longer the lags and the less taxes are indexed. This equation is shown in Figure 2 as the O-T schedule and is referred to as the Oliveira-Tanzi schedule. The real exchange rate appears as a determinant of the deficit ratio, because the real value of the service of an external debt contracted in dollars will increase when the real exchange rate depreciates.

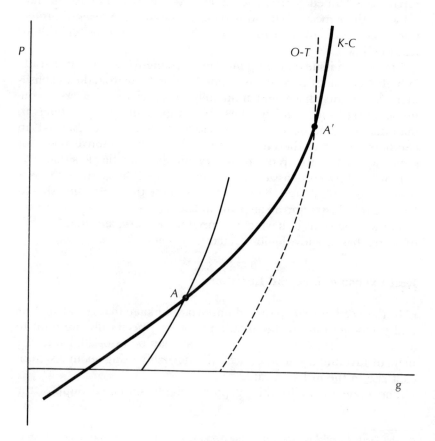

Figure 2

The government budget constraint states that the revenue from money creation must equal the deficit:

$$\dot{M}/P = gY \tag{4}$$

or

$$m = gV, \tag{4a}$$

where $V = PY/M$ is velocity and m is the growth rate of nominal money.

Let velocity be a linear function of the alternative cost of holding money:

$$V = a + bp. \tag{5}$$

Finally, we impose long-run monetary equilibrium so that nominal money growth is equal to the rate of inflation plus the rate of growth of output, y:[4]

$$m = p + y. \tag{6}$$

Combining equations (4a), (5), and (6) we obtain a relation between the inflation rate, the budget deficit ratio, and the structural parameters determining the inflation tax and the growth rate of output. We can refer to this schedule in Figure 2 as the Keynes-Cagan or K-C curve.

$$p = \frac{ag - y}{1 - bg}; \quad 1 > bg. \tag{7}$$

Note that because of nonlinearity the inflation response to shocks is extremely sensitive to the level of the inflation rate. Figure 2 shows how the deficit function and the inflation function jointly determine the deficit and the rate of inflation. We have consciously picked the case where the Oliveira-Tanzi schedule cuts the Keynes-Cagan schedule from below so that there is a unique equilibrium. Issues of multiple equilibrium, the dynamics, and comparative statics have occupied fully justified attention in recent analyses.

Five points can be inferred from this model:

• An increase in the deficit ratio, given R and p, will increase inflation. This is the conventional deficit-finance view, which is, of course, totally correct.

---

[4] This is the steady-state form. In the transition, allowance must be made for changes in velocity. It is easy to see from the model developed below that it affords the ingredients for hyperinflation processes where the interaction of accelerating inflation, real depreciation, and fiscal lags produces ever-growing deficits, money creation, and inflation.

• Financial deregulation, by raising velocity, raises inflation. (In terms of equation (7) the parameters a and/or b increase.) Deregulation may take the form of dollarization, interest-bearing deposits, reduction of restrictions on the liquidity of deposits, et cetera.

• A reduction in the growth rate of output will increase inflation.

• Other things being equal (tax structure and noninterest public spending), the inflation rate is higher the higher is the debt as a fraction of income and the higher is the real interest rate paid on external debt.

• A real depreciation, shown as a shift of the $O\text{-}T$ schedule out and to the right, raises the equilibrium rate of inflation from A to A'. This view is called the "balance of payments theory of inflation" in the history of monetary thought. It invariably dominates the "quantity theory school" by telling a richer and politically more satisfying story of why there is inflation.[5]

A summary point is suggested by this model: debt service is immensely inflationary in a country that cannot afford it. Blaming inflation on budget deficits is not wrong but misses the point that when the resources for debt service without recourse to money creation are not available then they must come out of the inflation tax. Needless to say, the inflation tax is highly regressive, so that in the end debt service is either financed by cuts in social spending, increased social security taxes, or increased seignorage. One way or the other, debt service is primarily a poor people's privilege. It is worth emphasizing this point to understand the solidarity, say in Argentina, between the domestic financial community and international creditors on the issue of debt service. This position contrasts sharply with Brazil, where the taxation system is less scandalous.

Some Facts and Some Problems[6]

Table 1 shows in summary fashion the key macroeconomic variables of interest to debtor countries. The table highlights the early 1970s when the world economy was booming, with negative real interest rates and rising real commodity prices and strong growth. By contrast, in 1980–82 real interest rates were exorbitantly high and the world economy moved into stagnation. Where the first period enhanced

---

[5] On a discussion of these issues, see especially Rist (1940).

[6] For a thorough review of the empirical evidence on linkages, see International Monetary Fund (1986), pp. 150–95.

Table 1. Key Macroeconomic Variables for World Economy

Annual averages

	LIBOR	Inflation[1]		OECD Growth
		Manufactures	Commodities	
1970–73	7.6	12.4	14.4	5.9
1980–82	14.7	−2.4	−13.3	0.9
1983–85	9.7	−0.9	−0.6	3.3

Source: International Monetary Fund (1986).
[1] Inflation rates in world trade.

creditworthiness and encouraged borrowing, the second period tested the vulnerability of excessive borrowing and produced the debt crisis.

The experience since 1983 has certainly not provided a world economic environment that unambiguously eased debt service. Real interest rates remained high, even though nominal rates declined. The reason for high real rates was, of course, the continuing decline of prices in world trade. Growth of industrial countries was above the magic 3 percent mark that had figured importantly in discussions of liquidity versus solvency, but it was not sufficiently strong to bring about export booms or terms of trade improvements.

The discussion following in the immediate aftermath of the debt crisis focused on the question whether the world economy would make a significant contribution toward a solution of the debt problem. In particular, it was argued that strong recoveries in the member countries of the Organization for Economic Cooperation and Development, the terms of trade gains associated with strong growth, and the decline in the U.S. dollar would combine to ease debt burdens significantly and help to restore creditworthiness.

Leaving aside the impact of the oil price decline, for which there are winners like Brazil and losers like Mexico, this prediction has by and large not come true. Most of the adjustment has been accomplished by a sharp cut in imports and increased export volume. The terms of trade gain between 1982 and 1985 remained roughly unchanged. The value of Latin American imports declined by 26 percent, while export revenue over the period 1982–85 remained unchanged.

Commodities

Declining commodity prices were matched by falling prices of manufactures in world trade, thus leaving the terms of trade roughly unchanged. Figure 3 shows the purchasing power of the World Bank index of 33 commodities in terms of the prices of their manufactures

Figure 3. Real Commodity Prices

Index, 1977–79 = 100

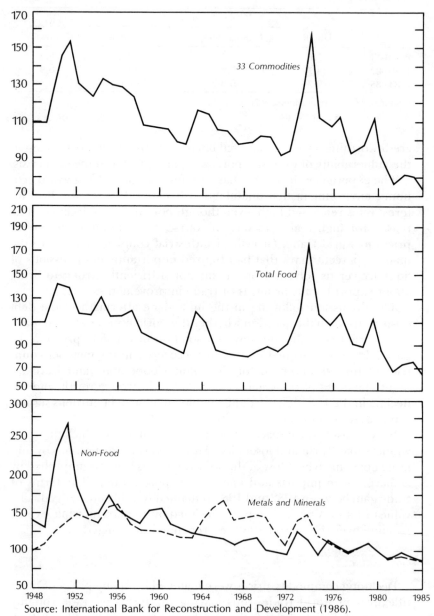

Source: International Bank for Reconstruction and Development (1986).

imports. The purchasing power declined sharply in 1980–82, but has remained nearly constant since then.

It comes as a surprise that the real prices of commodities should not have reacted more strongly to the dollar depreciation of 1985–86. The theoretical framework developed in Dornbusch (1985a) suggests that a real depreciation of the U.S. dollar (in terms of industrial countries' relative value-added deflators in manufacturing) will cause a rise in the price of commodities in dollars and a decline in price in terms of foreign currencies. But dollar depreciation and expansion in industrial activity notwithstanding, a significant recovery of commodity prices has failed to materialize.

The reason for the failure of commodity prices to rise must be seen in four facts. First, for agricultural commodities there is an obvious policy-induced glut, reflecting subsidization by industrial countries of their inefficient agriculture and sale in world markets at any price of the resulting surplus. The second reason is the world oversupply resulting from capacity expansion and substitution toward material-saving technology or consumption patterns. Examples that come to mind are smaller (lighter) cars that reduce steel demand, or substitution of optic fibers for copper in long-distance transmission. The third reason is the increased supply in world markets that comes from retrenched demand and real depreciation in the commodity-producing countries. Finally, the continuing high level of real interest rates keeps inventory demand depressed. The four reasons combine to more than offset the anticipated real commodity price recovery normally associated with expansion and dollar depreciation.

Interest Rates

Real interest rates remain high in all industrial countries. In the United States, they stand at a record high even after two years of relatively rapid money growth and declining nominal interest rates. Table 2 shows the U.S. real interest rate measured in terms of consumer prices for various subperiods. It is clear that the present interest rate experience is altogether unusual by historical standards. The same point is brought out by the annual average of real interest rates shown in Figure 4.

It is true that there have been previous episodes of positive real interest rates, for example in the 1960s. But the 1960s was a period of sustained growth, which makes it easier to live with high real rates than in a period where growth is declining and expected to falter. Adjusted

Table 2. Real Interest Rates in United States

Percent per year

Period	Real Rate	Period	Real Rate
1926–80	−0.1	1970–80	−1.1
1950–80	−0.1	1980–85	3.5
1960–70	1.3	1985–86	3.7

Source: For 1926–80, data are from Ibbotson and Sinquefield (1982) and for later years calculations are by the author.

NOTE: The real interest rate is the Treasury bill rate adjusted for the rate of consumer price inflation.

for growth expectations, the current real interest rate experience is therefore quite out of the ordinary.

There is considerable controversy on how to measure appropriately the real interest rate for developing country borrowers. The question is whether export or import price inflation should be used, either or both. But there is little question, whatever the exact measure, that real interest rates for debtor countries have been even higher than those for the United States. The issue then arises why real rates are so high.

One interpretation of the high real interest rates is the large U.S. budget deficit. The budget deficit as a fraction of gross national product (GNP) averaged almost zero in 1955–64 and less than 1 percent in 1965–72. In the 1975–84 period, it increased to 3 percent of GNP and in 1985–86 had already reached 5.2 percent. This large deficit is seen as absorbing an extremely large portion of world saving, thereby crowding out competing demands for funds by increasing the level of world interest rates.

This interpretation suggests that if the United States were to cut the deficit interest rates would decline. This is surely the case. The reason is that the resulting world recession would inevitably reduce money demand and hence interest rates. But it is clear that simply cutting the U.S. deficit need not necessarily help debtor countries. The resulting recession might further reduce real commodity prices and hurt the prospects for exports of manufactures from developing countries.

An alternative interpretation of the high real interest rates focuses on the typical aftermath of an inflation stabilization. When inflation disappears the demand for real balances rises. Unless the central bank accommodates the rise in real money demand by sharply increased monetary expansion (for a while), nominal interest rates will be slow to decline and real interest rates will remain high. Of course, the Federal Reserve has allowed money to grow quite rapidly, and as a result real interest rates have come down from their peak levels. But

Figure 4. U.S. Real Interest Rate

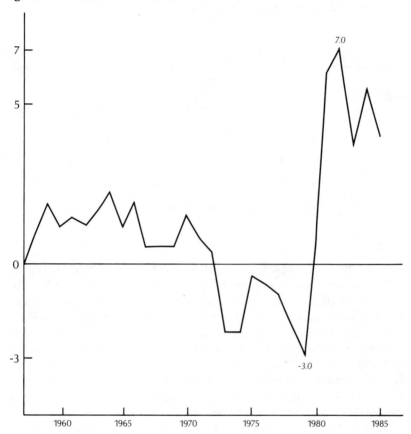

the monetization went in large measure to satisfy increased demand for real balances rather than creating a reliquification of the economy.

If this latter interpretation is correct, and it is certainly borne out by the fact that real interest rates have softened even as deficits are growing, then the correct policy advice is pushing further monetization on a worldwide scale. This would also be in the interest of debtors, except if it should risk an inflation so large that it invites a 1980–82-style tight money crunch. If the fiscal interpretation is correct, the implication for debtors is much less favorable. First, budget correction will be immensely slow and hence real interest rates are bound to stay quite high. Second, as budget correction occurs it will slow down aggregate demand and thus provide an offset to the benefits of lower interest rates.

Table 3. Gramm-Rudman Budget Amendment with Alternative Monetary Accommodation

	United States 1987–89		Fed. Rep. of Germany 1987–89		Japan 1987–89	
	No monetary accommodation					
Real GNP (percent)	−2.3	−1.9	−0.9	−1.4	−1.5	−2.2
Interest Rate	−2.3	−3.4	−0.8	−1.2	−0.4	−0.6
	U.S. and foreign monetary accommodation					
Real GNP (percent)	−1.0	0.7	−0.1	0.3	−0.3	1.8
Interest Rate	−4.5	−4.7	−3.0	−3.5	−2.8	−3.0

Source: Edison and Tryon (1986).
NOTE: All numbers represent deviation from baseline.

Many observers hope for a middle course where budget correction does take place and is supported by an accommodating Federal Reserve policy of easy money. In that scenario, growth is sustained by reduced interest rates. For the time being that scenario is unlikely, since budget correction has gone out of the express lane. But even so, it is interesting to explore the alternative routes of budget correction. A recent study by Edison and Tryon (1986) simulates in the Federal Reserve Board's multicountry model the effect of the Gramm-Rudman budget correction under alternative assumptions about U.S. and foreign monetary accommodation.

Table 3 shows the impact on U.S., German, and Japanese output and on interest rates for the two scenarios. In one case the Gramm-Rudman budget cuts take place without any monetary accommodation. In the other case the U.S. money stock is allowed to increase cumulatively by 4.5 percent above the baseline projection, and in the Federal Republic of Germany and Japan money growth is increased sufficiently to maintain constant the real exchange rate relative to the United States. For each of the scenarios we show the impact on levels of target variables in 1987 and in 1989.

The table shows the impact on the level of real GNP and on the level of interest rates. The soft-landing solution is the one where monetary accommodation takes place so that there is no large impact on the path of real output. In that case interest rate reductions are very sizable. This would be the scenario that would be of very significant assistance

Table 4. Latin America: Current Account
Imbalances and Financing, 1978–85

In billions of U.S. dollars

| | Current Account | Borrowing | |
		Official Creditors[1]	Private Creditors
1978	19.4	2.2	25.8
1979	21.8	2.7	27.4
1980	30.2	6.1	35.9
1981	43.3	6.5	54.1
1982	42.0	14.6	28.8
1983	11.4	17.7	2.0
1984	4.9	10.7	7.0
1985	5.9	5.1	−0.6

Source: International Monetary Fund (1986).
[1] Including reserve-related liabilities.

in solving the debt problem.[7] By contrast, budget reduction without monetary accommodation does lead to lower interest rates, but also to a steep reduction in activity.

Private Sector Lending

In the aftermath of the debt problem, lending by the private sector became involuntary, as did debt service by the debtor countries. The debtor countries produced sharp reductions in their current account imbalances, more than making up for the increased interest burden. This adjustment was forced on debtor countries by the lack of access to significant new money. Table 4 shows the shifts in the current account and in financing for Latin America.

The striking fact in this table is the large adjustment in the debtors' current account and the disappearance of private market financing. There is little doubt that the vigor of the adjustment programs was forced by the lack of access to new money. Of course, the question must also be asked whether there is anything wrong with the massive adjustment. If in fact overborrowing did take place, and if the debt is to be serviced, it can be argued that adjustment was essential. But that,

[7] It is worth noting that even in the case of monetary accommodation U.S. inflation slows down moderately as a result of the Gramm-Rudman budget correction.

of course, presupposes that debt service should be maintained. Many consider this latter question today primarily a political question.

Investment

The external balance adjustment in Latin America has been achieved largely at the expense of investment. This point is apparent by looking at Table 5, which shows the ratio of gross investment to gross domestic product (GDP) and the noninterest surplus, likewise measured as a fraction of GDP.

The shift in gross investment is approximately of the same size and is in the same direction as that in investment. Thus, effectively Latin America is accomplishing the improvement in debt service by cutting down on investment. There are several channels through which the current process of debt collection makes this almost inevitable. Perhaps the most significant is the fact that involuntary debt service forces on the government budget stringency that is most easily met by postponing or simply giving up investment. This effect is quite apparent in any of the debtor countries where public sector investment has declined dramatically. For example, in Mexico public sector investment has declined by 5 percent of GDP (Dornbusch, 1986c).

A second channel through which investment is adversely affected is, of course, the recession in economic activity in debtor countries, combined with the very high cost of capital.

The fact that investment is sacrificed, rather than consumption, is entirely appropriate when disturbances are short-lived. But a serious issue of misallocation arises when, as is the case now, the postponement lasts several years and is expected to continue. The growing labor force is not being equipped with expanding job opportunities and, as a result, emphasis is on wage cutting rather than on rising real wages.

The failure on the part of industrial country policymakers to recognize this anti-investment bias of current programs must be considered

Table 5. Latin America: Investment and the External Noninterest Surplus

Change, in percent of gross domestic product

	1977–82	1983–85
Gross Investment	24.3	18.5
Noninterest External Surplus	−0.6	4.7

Source: International Monetary Fund.

the most serious shortcoming of the adjustment strategy and a criticism of Fund supervision of adjustment programs.

Solutions to Debt and Growth Problems?

The ordinary aftermath of imprudent borrowing and adverse international conditions, as in the 1920s and 1930s most recently, is to bring about default on the part of debtors. Debts are normally written down, or simply not serviced for many years, and when service is resumed this occurs without full payment of arrears and often at reduced interest rates. The major differences in the present debt crisis are two. The first is that commercial banks and governments, rather than bondholders, are the main creditors. More significant is the fact that the major industrial countries have insisted on debt service and have managed a system, with the Fund as the chief coordinating agent, of debt collection. The system avoids illiquidity by making available essential "new money" at profitable spreads over the cost of funds to banks, and it enforces the debts by behind-the-scenes political pressure. The creditors are efficiently organized in this case-by-case approach, while debtors have been unable to put up a united front.

Latin America's problem is to gain debt relief so as to free resources for investment and develop speculation in support of the governments' ability to develop growth without financial instability. Tax reform and improved tax enforcement is certainly the overriding instrument. Improved efficiency in the public sector is important, but measures to attract capital or secure relief on the external debt seem the most desirable or practicable. We review here three directions: debt-equity swaps, reversal of capital flight, and Bradley-style debt relief.

Debt-Equity Swaps[8]

In the summer of 1986 debt-equity swaps were at the center of financial attention as an attractive part of a solution to the debt problem. Clearly not *the* solution, but a sound contribution. A short story may help to introduce the necessary cynicism.[9]

A man had bought an extraordinary, fantastic dog. How much had

---

[8] This section draws on editorials published in *Folha de São Paulo* and in *Cronista Comercial* (Argentina).

[9] For a strong statement of support for debt-equity swaps, see Morgan Guaranty Trust (September 1986).

he paid? Embarrassed silence, then the confession—half a million dollars. His friends were startled. Surely that was crazy, no dog could be worth that much, he should go back and sell the dog. Next day, when they met again, the dog owner was all smiles. Yes, he sold the dog; yes, he got a great deal. He had traded the dog for two cats. That is very much the essence of debt-equity swaps.

Developing country debts are traded at deep discounts in the secondhand market, ranging between 60 and 75 cents on the dollar for Brazil, Mexico, or Argentina. The discounts and the obvious problems in keeping Mexico afloat have shifted the creditors' attention to ways of liquidating debts without taking outright and open losses on the entire portfolio of developing country debts. Debt-equity swaps provide the answer: A bank holding, say, Brazilian Government debt sells these bonds at a discount to a U.S. firm. The U.S. firm in turn presents the debt to the Banco Central do Brasil to be paid in cruzados. The proceeds are used for foreign investment in Brazil. It seems that everybody gains: the bank has found a way of selling some of its illiquid portfolio; the investing firm gains the advantage of buying cruzados at a discount, and Brazil gains because the Government can pay its debt in local currency rather than in dollars. Moreover, much-needed investment takes place.

So why does the government drag its feet on this scheme rather than flying into the arms of foreign investors who bring this extraordinary deal? Anytime foreign banks and investors show indecent anxiety to conclude a deal, one must suspect something is rotten. This is, indeed, the case with debt-equity swaps. At best they bring little advantage, and more likely they are a complicated squandering of national assets.

The pressure on debtor countries to free the way for the scheme makes it important to look much more carefully at what is involved. The first step is to recognize that the government will have to finance somehow the repurchase of its debt from the foreign investor. It is obvious that it is impossible to simply print money to pay off the debt. In fact, the government would issue domestic debt and use the proceeds to buy back its foreign debt as it is presented by the foreign investor. Hence, when everything is done, the government has an increased internal debt and a reduced foreign debt. The country owns less of its capital stock, since the foreign investor will have bought some, and in return the country would have redeemed some of its debt. Thus the country swaps bad debt for good capital and the government swaps low interest (i.e., foreign debt) for expensive domestic debt.

Is there any advantage for the budget? In the budget there will now be reduced interest payments on external debt offset by increased domestic debt service. Whether there is a net reduction in interest depends on two issues: at what discount the external debt is traded and by how much domestic interest rates exceed the rate on external debt plus exchange depreciation. One would expect the net effect to be an increase in debt service. This would most definitely be the case if the government does not appropriate most of the discount at which the external debt now trades. Hence, for a country with a budget problem this would seem to be a quite awful idea.

Is this an advantage for the balance of payments? Here the debt-equity swap seems to be good news: foreign debt is reduced and as a result interest payments on the debt also come down. But, of course, there is an offset: the reduced interest payments on external debt are offset, at least potentially, by increased remittances of dividends or profits of the new foreign owners of the national capital stock. Hence, for the balance of payments, too, the trick will not do much good.

In fact, it is easy to paint a picture where things become much worse. Imagine a scenario where the ability to service the debt—domestic and foreign—deteriorates sharply, say because of a terms of trade deterioration or because of populism. Interest rates on the domestic debt will rise sharply and hence the budget deteriorates, foreign firms remit profits before the exchange rate is depreciated, or transactions become regulated. All this would happen even if no debt-equity swaps had taken place. The only difference is that now the scope for damage is much larger because the domestic debt is increased and capital has passed into foreign hands and thus benefits from a right to remit profits. In the absence of a debt-equity swap the creditor banks could be forced into increased provision of new money at extra-low rates, or into write-offs. Hence, when things go really bad the fact of having gone through debt-equity swaps makes them much worse. That, of course, accounts for the interest of the creditors, who are on the other side of the deal.

But is there not some sense in which more resources become available for investment, even if there are no net benefits for the budget or for the balance of payments? Once more the answer is "no." Debt-equity swaps are primarily and almost exclusively a balance sheet operation, selling good assets (why else would foreigners buy them?) for bad assets (why else would some creditor banks sell them at a discount?).

One might argue that the government could regulate things so that deals will be less a transaction in existing assets and rather be directed toward new, extra investment. But that is doubtful. More likely, fi-

nancial intermediaries will look for firms, domestic or foreign, who
are investing. They will approach them with a new kind of financing
package involving debt-equity swap, which, because of an implicit
subsidy by the government, turns out to be less costly than alternative
sources of finance.

Thus debt-equity swaps will finance investment, but they finance
investment that would have taken place anyway. Moreover, they do so
at the budget cost of a subsidy. Perhaps there may be the odd investment which becomes profitable just as a result of the implied subsidy,
but that will be the exception. The dominant effect is to give away
budget resources to the financial system that organizes the swaps.
Debt-equity swaps, in the end, will simply become a way of financing,
not an investment lever. To promote investment there are better and
more directly targeted means. Balance sheet tricks are not a substitute
for gaining extra real resources for investment as a result of genuine
foreign saving or an improved budget position.

Reversal of Capital Flight

The wishful thinking turns to the $100 billion or more of Latin
American assets that have fled from financial instability and taxation
to the industrial countries, especially the United States. Reversing
these capital flights, especially for Mexico or Argentina, would make
it almost possible to pay off the external debt. The reason is that much
of the debt was incurred in the first place to finance the exodus of
private capital.

Table 6 shows estimates of capital flight for various periods arrived
at by various procedures. Whatever the precise number for capital
flight, there is no question that it took place on an extraordinary scale
in Argentina, Mexico, and Venezuela—hence, the suggestion that reversing the mammoth outflow could help pay off the debt without
tears.

The idea that private capital could be the main solution, or at least
an important one, is naive. There is little or indeed no historical
precedent for a major reflow, and when it does happen, it is the last
wagon of the train. Einaudi once observed that savers "have the
memory of an elephant, the heart of a lamb, and the legs of a hare."
Capital will wait until the problems have been solved; it won't be part
of the solution.

It is often argued that if only countries adopted policies conducive
to guaranteeing savers stable positive real rates of interest the capital

Table 6. Capital Flight from Latin America

In billions of U.S. dollars

	World Bank 1979–82	Dornbusch (1985b) 1978–82	Khan and Ul Haque 1974–82	Morgan Guaranty 1976–82
Argentina	19.2	23.4	15.3	27
Brazil	3.5	1.9	0.2	3
Chile	n.a.	1.4	−1.9	0
Mexico	26.5	n.a.	32.7	36
Venezuela	22.0	n.a.	10.8	25

flight problem would not be an issue. But that argument is not very operational in three respects. First, in the context of adjustment programs it is unavoidable to devalue. Compensating savers for the loss they would have avoided by holding dollar assets would place a fantastic burden on the budget, which in turn would breed financial instability. Second, practicing high, positive real interest rates poses a serious risk to public finance. The public debt, which carries these high real rates, snowballs, and that in turn is a source of instability. Third, it is a very bad habit indeed to raise the return on paper assets above the prospective return on real capital. That is terrible supply-side economics, which ultimately erodes the tax base and deteriorates the financial system by souring loans. A country in trouble simply cannot opt to make its chief priority keeping the bondholders in place.

Capital controls, where feasible, are an essential part of a strategy to bring public finance in order rather than to paper over extreme difficulties for a while by extraordinarily high real interest rates. The latter strategy was, indeed, at the very source of the extreme mess in Argentina under Martinez de Hoz or in Mexico today.

It is also worth recognizing that the capital flight problem is to a large extent of our own doing. The U.S. administration, in an effort to fund our own deficits at low cost, has promoted international tax fraud on an unprecedented scale. The only purpose one can imagine for the elimination of the withholding tax on nonresident asset holdings in the United States is to make it possible for foreigners to use the U.S. financial system as a tax haven. To compete with the tax-free U.S. return, anyone investing in Mexico and actually paying taxes there would need a yield differential, not counting depreciation and other risk, of quite a few extra percentage points.

There is much talk about the problems of banks putting in new money only to see it spent by debtors like Mexico on capital flight. The fact is that the large banks are the chief vehicles for and beneficiaries of the capital flight. This system on all accounts enhances the political explosiveness of the debt crises by placing on workers in the developing countries an even more serious adjustment burden. The treatment of capital flight by the banking community, with these ideas in mind, is not only outright cynical but also shortsighted.

Debt Relief

Debtor countries have failed to form an effective cartel that could impose debt relief in the form of a write-down, sharply reduced interest rates or generous grace periods, and consolidation of debt into perpetuities. On the contrary, debtor countries have competed with each other and, as a result, have wound up with poor terms and a short leash.

There were only two attempts so far to turn debt service into a major political issue. One is the case of Peru; the other is the Mexican move of the spring of 1986. In each case the extreme domestic costs of debt service and the destructive effects on investment, inflation, and growth potential led the governments to try to limit the damage. It is hard to believe that Peru got very far, but it is certain that Mexico initiated an important change in policies and procedures. The Mexican success suggests that with enough determination debtors can in fact secure reduced spreads, contingency funds, and even an underwriting of growth.

At the same time the debt problem is starting to become a U.S. political issue. This is true in part for reasons of foreign policy. But another important motivation is that the poor U.S. trade performance is seen as a reflection of the debtor countries' need to earn foreign exchange for debt service. The most important initiative so far is that of Senator Bradley (1986a,b). The Bradley plan emphasizes the need to create a vehicle for trade-debt discussions. Focusing explicitly on the link between debtor-country trade concessions and targeted, limited debt relief, this approach makes debt consciously a political issue. Besides facilitating the regulatory system to make it easier to effect write-downs, the proposal also calls for reduced interest payments, extra money, and debt write-downs.

There are three kinds of unfavorable reaction to the Bradley plan. One reaction is to argue that the particular details—say the annual debt summit—are implausible, complicated, or undesirable. In the same vein, the write-downs are not insufficiently conditioned on performance of the debtor countries and hence not worth making.

Another criticism is much more basic. It amounts to the assertion that any and all kind of debt relief deteriorates or even destroys the beneficiaries' ultimate chances of renewed access to the international capital market. Countries who accept debt relief, it is argued, will be tainted. Only those who service humbly will see the day of voluntary lending. Historical precedent for all of Latin America would suggest the opposite.

Political solutions to the debt problem are likely to lie in the neighborhood of what Mexico secured and, unfortunately, far away from the ambitious Bradley plan. It is clear that gradually the resistance to write-downs will soften and terms will become more flexible. But it is also likely to be the case that the debt problem will remain an overwhelming burden on the growth prospects of Latin America. Taxpayers are unwilling to underwrite Latin American growth, and politicians are unwilling to underwrite the banks. Growth in Latin America will therefore depend in equal parts on a solution of the U.S. deficit problem with generous monetary accommodation and on the introduction of reasonable public finance in the debtor countries. With these two conditions in hand, and excepting extreme episodes such as the 1986 Mexican oil decline, growth can start again, although the losses of the 1980s will not be made up.

Solutions to the debt crisis involving debt relief encounter one apparently overwhelming counterargument: Latin America's debt reflects to a large extent mismanagement and capital flight. Giving debt relief in this case, and not for countries where management was more careful, amounts to rewarding poor policy performance and thus invites repetition. But this moral-hazard argument can also with equal justification be made in two other directions. First, not giving debt relief means that creditor countries enforce bad loans. They thus encourage poor lending policies on the part of commercial banks, who expect to be able to rely on governments to collect for them even the poorest sovereign loans. Second, in the context of capital flight, it is frequently argued that amnesty for tax fraud and illegal capital transfers is an effective and desirable policy for encouraging a reflow. Of course, the same moral-hazard argument applies here because of the undermining of future tax morality. Finally, the major weakness of the moral-hazard argument in cases such as Mexico and Argentina results from the very fact of capital flight: those who pay are primarily workers whose real wages are cut. Owners of external assets are rewarded by capital gains and thus turn out to be net beneficiaries of the debt crisis. The moral-hazard issue is as much an argument for debt relief as it is against such a measure.

References

Bradley, Bill (1986a), "A Proposal for Third World Debt Management," paper presented in Zürich, Switzerland, June 29, 1986.

——— (1986b), "Defusing the Latin Debt Bomb," *Washington Post*, October 5, 1986, p. C2.

Bruno, M., and Stanley Fischer, "Inflation and Expectations" (unpublished; Massachusetts Institute of Technology, Cambridge, and Falk Institute, Jerusalem, 1985).

Cardoso, Eliana A. (1986a), *Inflation, Growth and the Real Exchange Rate: Essays on Economic History in Brazil and Latin America, 1850-1983* (Garland, forthcoming).

——— (1986b), "Inflation and Seignorage in Latin America" (unpublished; Fletcher School, Tufts University, 1986).

Dornbusch, Rudiger (1985a), "Policy and Performance Links between LDC Debtors and Industrial Nations," *Brookings Papers on Economic Activity: 2* (1985), The Brookings Institution (Washington), pp. 303–68.

——— (1985b), "External Debt, Budget Deficits, and Disequilibrium Exchange Rates," in *International Debt and Developing Countries*, ed. by John D. Cuddington and Gordon W. Smith (Washington: World Bank, 1985), pp. 213–35; reprinted in *Dollars, Debts, and Deficits* (Cambridge, Massachusetts: MIT Press).

——— (1986a), "Inflation, Exchange Rates and Stabilization," *Princeton Essays in International Finance*, No. 165 (Princeton, New Jersey: Princeton University Press, October 1986).

——— (1986b), "Stopping Hyperinflation: Lessons from the German Experience in the 1920s," in *Macroeconomics and Finance: Essays in Honor of Franco Modigliani*, ed. by Rudiger Dornbusch, J. Bossons, and Stanley Fischer (Cambridge, Massachusetts: MIT Press, 1987).

——— (1986c), "Mexico and the IMF" (unpublished; Cambridge: Massachusetts Institute of Technology, 1986).

———, and Mario Henrique Simonsen, *Inflation Stabilization with Incomes Policy Support: A Review of the Experience in Argentina, Brazil and Israel* (New York: Group of Thirty, forthcoming).

Edison, Hali J., and Ralph Tryon, "An Empirical Analysis of Policy Coordination in the United States, Japan and Europe," Board of Governors of the Federal Reserve System, International Finance Discussion Papers, No. 286 (Washington, July 1986).

Goldsbrough, David, and Iqbal Zaidi, "Transmission of Economic Influences from Industrial to Developing Countries," in *Staff Studies for the World Economic Outlook*, World Economic and Financial Surveys, International Monetary Fund (Washington, July 1986).

Goldstein, Morris, *The Global Effects of Fund-Supported Adjustment Programs*, Occasional Paper No. 42, International Monetary Fund (Washington, 1986).

Ibbotson, R., and R. Sinquefield, *Stocks, Bonds, Bills, and Inflation: The Past and the Future* (Charlottesville, Virginia: Financial Analysts Foundation, 1982).

International Bank for Reconstruction and Development (World Bank), *World Development Report* (Washington, various issues).

———, *Commodity Trade and Price Trends* (Washington, April 1986).

International Monetary Fund, *Staff Studies for the World Economic Outlook,* World Economic and Financial Surveys (Washington, July 1986).

Khan, Mohsin H., and Nadeem Ul Haque, "Foreign Borrowing and Capital Flight," *Staff Papers,* International Monetary Fund (Washington), Vol. 32 (December 1985), pp. 606–28.

Melnick, Rafi, and Meir Sokoler, "Government's Revenue from Money Creation and the Inflationary Effects of a Decline in the Rate of Growth of G.N.P.," *Journal of Monetary Economics* (Amsterdam), Vol. 13 (March 1984), pp. 225–36.

Morgan Guaranty Trust, *World Financial Markets* (New York, March and September 1986).

Oliveira, Julio H.G., "Money, Prices and Fiscal Lags: A Note on the Dynamics of Inflation," Banca Nazionale del Lavoro, *Quarterly Review* (Rome), Vol. 20 (September 1967), pp. 258–67.

Rist, Charles, *History of Monetary and Credit Theory from John Law to the Present Day* (New York: Macmillan, 1940).

Tanzi, Vito, "Inflation, Lags in Collection, and the Real Value of Tax Revenue," *Staff Papers,* International Monetary Fund (Washington), Vol. 24 (March 1977), pp. 154–67.

———,"Inflation, Real Tax Revenue, and the Case for Inflationary Finance: Theory with an Application to Argentina," *Staff Papers,* International Monetary Fund (Washington), Vol. 25 (September 1978), pp. 417–51.

Comments

Vittorio Corbo

Professor Dornbusch has given us an excellent discussion of the effects of external conditions on Latin American debtor countries. He has also provided a helpful evaluation of different options for the solution of the debt and growth problems. Although I agree with most of the points in his paper, I would like to elaborate on four points: (1) the conceptual framework used to describe the principal interactions between a debtor country and the rest of the world, (2) the system-wide effects of many countries reducing anti-export biases in their trade regimes, (3) the relation between debt service, the fiscal deficit, and inflation, and (4) debt-equity swaps. I will discuss each of these points in turn.

Conceptual Framework

Professor Dornbusch's conceptual framework is based on a four-good model: domestic exportable manufactures, which are imperfect substitutes for goods produced abroad; domestic traditional goods, which are perfect substitutes for primary commodities traded in international markets; importable manufactures, which are perfect substitutes for manufactures produced domestically; and oil, which is treated as a separate commodity. He then analyzes the adjustment process under alternative external shocks (i.e., a rise in the real price of oil, a rise in the real interest rate, a decline in the real price of traditional goods in terms of importable manufactures, credit rationing, and system-wide export expansion).

In Dornbusch's model, the key relationship that has to bear most of the burden of adjustment to external shocks is the relative price between exportable manufactures and importable manufactures. Not surprisingly, both a rise in the real price of oil for an oil importing country and a rise in the real interest rate for an indebted country, if not automatically financed, will result in a reduction in absorption and a real depreciation. But this result is simply a strong implication of the model. An alternative model, and one that might be closer to reality, is one that assumes that exportable manufactures are perfect substitutes in world trade. In this type of model, relative prices will adjust through real devaluation rather than through a deterioration in the terms of trade. Recent empirical evidence from the Republic of Korea and Turkey, two countries that have adjusted quite successfully to external shocks, shows that adjustment took place even with an overall improvement in the terms of trade. In both cases the main contribution to the adjustment was a real devaluation. Even in Brazil, noncoffee terms of trade improved between 1981 and 1985, with a large turnaround in net exports (which reached a record level of US$12.5 billion in 1985).

System-Wide Effect of Many Countries Simultaneously Reducing Anti-Export Biases in Their Trade Regimes

In Professor Dornbusch's analysis, if countries jointly experience the same unfavorable external shock and adjust to it by trying to increase exports by devaluing in real terms, they will compete with each other and worsen their terms of trade. I would like to raise two points here. First, even if Professor Dornbusch's conjecture is correct, the relevant question is what would have happened if the countries had not devalued. Under such a scenario, most of the adjustment would have had to take the form of a cut in absorption, compression of imports, and ultimately a reduction in output. From a welfare point of view, this is probably a worse outcome than the combination of a real devaluation and a deterioration in the terms of trade.

Second, and more important, the share of developing countries in the markets for manufactures in most developed countries is still very small. In fact, the aggregate share of manufactured exports from developing countries in the consumption of manufactures in the developed countries is just over 2 percent. There is also great potential for intra-industry trade, as the experience of the European Communities has clearly shown. Indeed, the prime motivation for exporting in the highly indebted countries is the need to earn foreign exchange, so as to pay for badly needed imports of capital goods and raw materials and then to increase actual and potential output. Thus, there is substantial room for significant expansion of trade among developing countries and between them and developed countries.

Relation Between Debt Service, the Fiscal Deficit, and Inflation

I think that Professor Dornbusch is correct in emphasizing the fiscal implications of debt servicing. Clearly, rising official debt—often stemming from the fact that the public sector has been forced to assume responsibility for servicing the private debt—has made debt service an important component of total expenditures.[1] If no room is made in the budget for this source of extra expenditure, for example by reductions in other types of expenditures and/or increases in revenues, then domestic debt will increase: the result will be to crowd out other borrowers or, if the expenditures are financed by printing money, to accelerate inflation. Thus, the fiscal effects of debt servicing should be given much more consideration in the discussion of adjustment programs. Moreover, the fiscal consequences of a real currency depreciation, which will depend on the net effects on government revenues and expenses, needs to be taken into account if the depreciation is going to be successful.

---

[1] "The Latin American Transfer Problem in Historical Perspective," in *Latin America and the Caribbean and the OECD*, Organization for Economic Cooperation and Development (Paris, 1986).

Debt-Equity Swaps

Professor Dornbusch offers a negative assessment of the role that debt-equity swaps play (or could play) in the management of a debt crisis. He is especially concerned about the fact that commercial banks are promoting these schemes, which he argues cannot be desirable. If this is true, should any trade promotion activity be seen as bad? On a more serious note, a debt-equity swap is a transaction like any other; one should be concerned with the terms of trade of any transaction before making a judgment on the fairness of the activity as such. Debt-equity swaps raise three main issues, the first of which relates to the optimal level of debt. Even for a country that is planning to service its debt fully, to pay now when you can postpone the payment until tomorrow is not necessarily the best course. In the final analysis, the decision will depend on a comparison of the opportunity cost of the resources and the interest rate on a debt whose market value is below the book value. If the latter is higher than the opportunity cost, then a debt-equity swap where debt and equity are priced at *market values* will be welfare-enhancing. Professor Dornbusch is right that the conversion of debt into equity when the equity is not in a public asset still requires the issue of *domestic* public debt to pay for the debt instrument. In this case, the public sector has substituted the servicing of domestic debt for the servicing of foreign debt.

On the balance of payments side, there is an intertemporal substitution of interest payments today for uncertain dividends tomorrow. If enough postponement is introduced into the payment of dividends, this could be an important source of transitional financing, which could in turn allow the country to finance investment and thus to perform adjustment with growth. Finally, much can be learned about specific issues of implementation from the Chilean debt-equity swap legislation. I still think that debt-equity swaps, if done properly, can make a small (but positive) contribution to the overall effort of designing a strategy that will allow highly indebted countries to restore domestic growth and eventually external creditworthiness.

Daniel Heymann

Dornbusch's paper deals with three classes of subjects: the economic evolution of the industrial countries, the mechanisms by means of which the indebted economies adapt to external influences, and the problems and outlook regarding debt. These comments concentrate on the last two questions.

Dornbusch refers to the effect of rationing international credit and the restrictions imposed by industrial countries on access to their markets. In fact, external conditions, together with the economic policies of the Latin American countries themselves, seem to have been consistently procyclical in recent years, whereas, in the past, the international supply of funds and exchange policies tended to promote and accentuate disequilibria, with the subsequent cutback in credit, together with high interest rates and the fall in primary commodity prices, combining to impose a sharp and very severe adjustment.

The paper uses a model to analyze the characteristics of this adjustment. The model is probably better suited to some economies than others, particularly because the assumption that local industrial goods are (imperfect) substitutes for foreign manufactures is seemingly not universally valid. In some cases, industry operates as an uncompetitive sector. In such circumstances, nontraditional exports do not respond elastically to the real change rate, and an increase in the trade balance would be brought about by a contraction in activity (through fewer purchases of inputs) and a stronger reduction in absorption than when significant substitution effects are present. That is, the impression seems to be that means of adjustment depend on the overall structure of the economy, and particularly its foreign trade.

On the other hand, debt causes some additional complications not contemplated in the model. If the adjustment is contractionary, there may be an induced reduction in the expected return on investment. The existence of debt also introduces various uncertainty factors, particularly when servicing and new financing terms depend on volatile circumstances and frequent renegotiations. The economy faces an unpredictable liquidity restraint (which affects forecasts for relative prices and the viability of various activities), and the need to meet payments calls for hefty transfers of resources between domestic sectors, which are generally not defined "once and for all." The effect of such instability is probably to reduce demand for assets in the country.

The distributive element of debt is also an inflationary factor. Dornbusch mentions various effects of debt on the public sector deficit, apart from its direct impact; in particular, an increase in the real exchange rate makes total interest payments grow in terms of domestic goods. The net effect of the real exchange rate on government finances seems to depend on the characteristics of the tax system: a higher exchange rate undoubtedly increases the burden of interest, but it can increase collections of taxes on foreign trade, particularly when they are concentrated on exports; on the other hand, if the real devaluation is recessionary, revenue from taxes on domestic activity will decline. At all events, the conclusion will stand: debt significantly contributes to increasing inflation, especially in countries with small capital markets and a small demand for liquid assets in domestic currency, where furthermore the fiscal lag effect is strongly felt. Naturally, this happens if fiscal policies are not adjusted to "accommodate" service payments. But it is difficult to see any internal agreement being reached to distribute burdens as significant as those currently implied by Latin American debt. In these conditions, it can be expected that, when they take place, fiscal adjustments will be precarious, because there would be considerable resistance to accepting a system of public revenue and expenditure which would permanently free resources to meet these external payments. Furthermore, debt (with the consequent need to increase the trade balance) implies a relative price structure that can generate resistance. It is likely that inconsistencies in price and wage fixing would be more frequent in highly indebted economies. From this viewpoint, too, debt puts obstacles in the way of stabilization efforts.

Dornbusch's paper points to some of the more noteworthy aspects of the behavior of Latin American economies over the last few years. A very strong adjustment in the current account has taken place through a sharp contraction in imports and an increase in the volume of exports, partly offset by a price decline; all in all, the trade surplus is not able (exceptions aside) to cover the accrued interest. Adjustment has taken place at the expense of investment. Thus, not only has activity contracted (or its increase been significantly attenuated) but the sources of future growth have also been weakened.

During the period of gestation of the debt crisis and since it made its appearance, a series of messages has come from the industrial countries. At one point, it was the common view that capital flows provided an opportunity to improve allocation over time and that the accumulation of liabilities was not per se a matter for concern. When it became clear that the debt could not be serviced without disruption, financing suddenly contracted and an urgent demand arose for indebted economies to adjust. Frequent reference was made to the prospect of likely declines in world interest rates and the recovery of the industrial economies easing the debt problem and making the adjustment more bearable. In other words, we were invited to trust that forces exogenous from the point of view of those mainly concerned in the debt issue would intervene to soften the blow. In the event, the adjustment was long and costly, and the problem is still with us. No doubt domestic economic policies were frequently inadequate, but it also seems certain that external conditions did little to help indebted countries regain something of their dynamism. In a number of cases, the fall in the external interest rate was more than offset by worsening terms of trade; financing has not returned to normal and in general terms the debt issue continues to be linked to short-term renegotiations that postpone the search for any sustainable solution. Currently, stress is placed on the need to reconcile attention to debt with the need for growth. While it is important to go beyond mere adjustment by renewing emphasis on growth, the question arises of the circumstances in which such reconciliation would be feasible.

It seems obvious that growth requires more funds to be directed to investment and that they be used efficiently. There is considerable scope for improving economic policies. But it is difficult to consider this subject in isolation from debt: the instability the latter generates is a barrier to focusing on policies with a longer-term horizon, apart from its direct effect on the availability of resources. Likewise, as Dornbusch points out, it is far from certain that the capital currently invested abroad will ultimately be returned; perhaps one should consider this as a potential spin-off rather than as an alternative to relief on the payments involved. In the final analysis, the question is to define, however approximately, an economy's ability to make tranfers in such a way as to be compatible with a sufficient volume of investment and with some degree of distributive balance (without which it is difficult to envisage any lasting solution). Little progress has been made on a discussion of this subject. Dornbusch rightly points out that accounting changes from one form of debt to another do not solve the problem (especially when this change involves subsidies by the governments of the indebted countries), while, for example, to change part of the financial debt into direct investment would to a certain extent link payments to the level of income, that is, would convert an "unconditional" commitment to a conditional one.

Latin American debt has one special feature. The question of reparations in the 1920s involved governments directly and was the subject of diplomatic negotiation. For private debt, there is a mechanism for convening creditors to deal with situations in which the total amount of the debts exceeds the ability to pay. Here, neither alternative is available. Furthermore, no effort seems to have been made to evaluate the volume of resources that countries could permanently divert to service debt and whether it is thus necessary to reduce obligations, and to what extent, to reach a sustainable position. This is undoubtedly linked up with the trade policies of the creditor countries: it is obvious that with worse terms of trade and greater restrictions on market access, there will be fewer opportunities (and incentives) to meet external payments. On the other hand, it sometimes seems that the industrial countries are trying to maintain or increase the transfers they receive by way of interest and at the same time increase their exports to the indebted economies. As Dornbusch says, this position seems inconsistent.

Growth is ultimately the individual country's problem. But international circumstances, and particularly debt, impose severe restrictions. So far, the international financial system gives the impression of having concentrated its attention on avoiding major disruptions arising through inability to pay and, this being so, on seeking adjustments that would allow trade balances to be raised. This approach is not conducive to growth in the indebted countries, and it is not clear whether it can be permanently applied. Dornbusch's argument gives little cause for optimism about the immediate likelihood of current conditions changing. Given that there seems to be a longer-term problem, the question that remains is when and in what way it will ultimately be addressed.

Choice of Growth Strategy: Trade Regimes and Export Promotion

Julio Berlinski

The first section of the paper begins with a normative approach to the relationship between foreign trade and growth using the early statistical support provided by Simon Kuznets. Next, a more general discussion involves the relationship of trade regimes and growth. The issues presented are also intended to provide some insight into the political economy of protection in Latin America.

The second section of the paper is devoted to a discussion of the different instruments used in Latin America to control imports and promote exports and the role of foreign exchange regulations. The third section deals with the anti-export bias of the system of protection. The fourth section is concerned with the changes in import protection, especially their initial conditions, and reform proposals. Finally, the last section presents the principal conclusions of the paper: the implications of a trade regime for the choice of a growth strategy.

The Problem

In a pioneer work, Kuznets (1964) explored for a sample of 61 countries the relationship between foreign trade proportions, defined as imports plus exports divided by gross national product (GNP), and the size of nations and GNP per capita (GNP/N). The outcome showed those foreign trade proportions to be larger, the smaller the size of nations, measured either by their GNP or by population. The propor-

Table 1. Foreign Trade and Growth: Revisiting Kuznets' Hypothesis

Group	Observations	Intercept	GNP	Per Capita GNP	R^2	F	SSRE
Total	98	−0.93385	−0.24591 (6.875) *	0.34692 (6.989) *	0.3706	27.969 *	21.0599
I	28	−10.80487	−0.20325 (4.286) *	0.43010 (1.936) **	0.4521	10.316 *	3.2808
II	31	3.91733	−0.15990 (2.671) *	−0.48387 (2.339) **	0.4021	9.416 *	4.3542
III	20	−4.08468	−0.27156 (2.159) **	0.79037 (2.550) **	0.4474	6.881 *	6.6029
IV	19	2.29053	−0.26199 (3.561) *	0.00973 (0.032)	0.4609	6.840 *	2.5649

Source: Based on data from *World Development Report, 1985* (Washington: The World Bank, 1985).

NOTE: Group I (low-income economies) with GNP/N ranging from 120 to 400; group II (lower middle income) with GNP/N ranging from 440 to 1430; group III (upper middle income) with GNP/N ranging from 1640 to 6850; group IV (industrial market economies) with GNP/N ranging from 4780 to 16290. Estimates are ordinary least squares of a double logarithmic function where the dependent variable is the foreign trade coefficient (imports plus exports as proportions of GNP). Numbers in parentheses correspond to values of the *t* test. One asterisk indicates that the value is statistically significant at 1 percent and two asterisks at 5 percent.

tions can also be seen as a crude measure of the countries' dependence on foreign trade, which is likely to be greater if imports and/or exports are concentrated in a few key items. That heavy reliance of smaller countries on foreign trade is shown by the positive correlation of those proportions to GNP per capita once the size factor is taken into account.

A simple version of the Kuznets hypothesis is presented in Table 1 for 1983 data involving 98 countries. The aggregate estimates validate the hypothesis, the elasticity relating foreign trade coefficients and absolute GNP is of the expected sign (−0.25) and statistically significant;[1] on the other hand, the elasticity relating those proportions to GNP/N is positive (0.35) and also statistically significant. But when a more detailed breakdown of the data is made by classifying the

---

[1] The same sign will be found when population is used as the variable representing the size of nations.

98 countries into four groups, the smooth aggregate conclusions regarding the association between trade coefficients and per capita income do not hold in two cases: in the subset of industrial market economies (GNP/N between 4780 and 16290) the estimate is not different from zero, while in the lower middle-income countries (GNP/N between 440 and 1430) there is a change in sign. A more detailed discussion of the underlying sources of these discrepancies will be made in a future publication of mine to be entitled "Foreign Trade and Growth: Revisiting Kuznets' Hypothesis."

If those cross sections are considered the normal expansion path of any country through economic growth, then economic policy may be seen as an exogenous force which may induce divergences (retardation, acceleration) from normality. Some of these questions are explored in this paper by attempting to provide a general discussion of several issues arising from the trade regimes existing in Latin America, their relationship to export promotion, and what can be said about the sources of growth related to import substitution as well as to export activities. The paper will concentrate mainly on trade issues; no explicit consideration will be given to debt management problems or the relationship between current and capital accounts.

The trade regimes of the countries involved had as the basic instrument of import protection a national tariff. Their incentive signals were modified by the use of several instruments, among which were nontariff restrictions, tariff exemptions, nonneutral consumption taxes, taxes on traditional exports, and promotional schemes for nontraditional exports. Also, preference margins were negotiated in bilateral and multilateral agreements. This inventory should also include the exchange rate policy. The reason for having such a comprehensive approach is being reinforced by the recent experience regarding the use of exchange rates for stabilization purposes.

The need to consider the interaction of instruments seems to be essential in a discussion of the system of incentives, especially regarding tariff reform proposals. This is true because tariffs (explicit or implicit) have been shown to be a major component of total incentives provided to import substitution activities; also, foreign exchange regulations in some countries may have competed in the short run for such leadership. Last but not least, incentives to exports have to be consistent with protection provided to import substitution. This instrumental approach to growth strategy will allow us to look for some symmetry of incentives regarding export promotion, which, in turn, may help in attaining some of the objectives associated with increasing efficiency in resource allocation.

Devices of Trade Intervention

The different instruments used today in the trade regimes of Latin America are the result of decisions taken in the past by the countries involved—some are national initiatives, others bilateral or multilateral arrangements.

The historical sequence of the introduction of the different devices was, first, the tariff and traditional export taxation followed by fiscal incentives providing, among other things, tariff exemptions, and, second, the implementation of regional measures such as free trade areas or common markets. This was complemented by additional national legislation regarding quantitative restrictions, nonneutral consumption taxes, and the laws concerned with the promotion of nontraditional exports.

Import Protection

Since the early 1960s, import protection in Latin America has resulted from the interdependence of tariffs and/or quantitative restrictions with some regional devices. Many times the latter would affect the ranking of incentives underlying the structure of national legislation.

The Tariff. The national tariff has been the principal instrument used in Latin America to control imports. The pattern of rates can be summarized as follows: for produced goods the rates are higher for consumer goods than for intermediate or capital goods, while for complementary imports the rates are lower. Another aspect of the structure of protection is related to tariff exemptions provided by generous fiscal incentives. Given their size, the importance of these "tax expenditure" aspects should be stressed; the proportion of tariff-exempt imports was in 1979/80 the highest for Brazil (74 percent), followed by Argentina (44 percent), Mexico (61 percent), and Colombia (42 percent) (Berlinski, Camelo and Pazmino, 1984). The findings presented in Table 2 also show the large difference between the average tariff paid, which ranged from 7 to 14 percent, compared with corresponding ad valorem rates for imports outside the region (excluding imports from the Latin American Free Trade Association—now the Latin American Integration Association—countries) of 18 to 28 percent.

A word should be added about the beneficiaries of these tariff exemptions, especially regarding the effect on domestic prices of close foreign substitutes or the reduction in import costs. The former corre-

Table 2. Selected Latin American Countries:
Tariff-Exempt Imports, 1979–80

	Argentina	Brazil	Colombia	Mexico
		In millions of U.S. dollars		
C.i.f. value of imports	6,700	25,614	4,663	17,517
		In percent		
Tariff paid	10	7	14	7
LAFTA imports	14	3	5	4
LAFTA tariff	5	7	7	7
Proportion of imports on which tariffs are paid	42	23	53	35
Tariff rates	22	28	26	18
Proportion of tariff-exempt imports	44	74	42	61

Source: Berlinski, Camelo, and Pazmino (1984).
NOTE: Imports were used as weights for estimating tariff averages.

sponds to a case in which the size of imports is high, so that the imports may overflow to the open market and in so doing affect domestic prices downward; the latter corresponds to the more general case of dual markets, where cost savings on intermediate and capital goods increases the rate of return for the beneficiaries of tariff exemptions.

National tariffs were designed using as criteria the type of good involved and the domestic supply. Lower rates were applied to intermediate and capital goods, which basically are not produced in each country, while the highest rates were applied to consumer goods produced within domestic markets.

Nontariff Restrictions. National legislations introduced several instruments that affected the incentive content of the ad valorem tariff rates. This was done mainly by quantitative restrictions and import surcharges of different kinds, including the more common case of imposing consumption taxes, with lower rates on domestic supply than on competing imports. In addition, if for some products free trade within a subset of countries existed (owing to bilateral or multilateral agreements), those additional restrictions might have increased the level of protection provided to regional partners.

The existence of quantitative restrictions implies that the tariff may not be the relevant instrument of protection. In the absence of other instruments and if tariffs are not redundant, it is known that tariffs allow the domestic price of an imported good to increase above the border price level. But in several cases the implicit tariff might be different from the explicit one. The implicit tariff is reflected in the behavior of entrepreneurs; the explicit tariff reflects the nominal legal rates corrected (when required) for the existence of other price instruments (e.g., official prices of imports) or the ad valorem equivalent of other devices such as pre-import deposits. If quantitative restrictions become relevant, it will be found that the implicit tariff would be greater than the explicit one.

We have seen that the tariff was one among the instruments used for import protection. In many cases the effect of those nontariff restrictions set at the national level was of great importance. Therefore, they have to be seen together in order to have a correct understanding of the price signals concerning the profitability of investments. In addition, replacing quantitative restrictions with tariffs would provide a clear ceiling to domestic prices of import-competing goods; otherwise, implicit protection would fluctuate depending on shocks, most of them imposed by exogenous macrovariables.

Export Taxation (Protection)

Export taxation has been a traditional way of providing revenue to national governments, acting at the same time as an income tax substitute for groups generally hard to tax. Export taxes were also used to prevent windfall gains when export proceeds in domestic currency showed large fluctuations owing to increases in international prices or changes in the exchange rate. Also, setting nominal exchange rates in countries with a large dispersion in international competitiveness may require a complementary export tax. This is especially true when those products have some weight in the cost of living; that is, export taxes would act as a hidden subsidy on domestic consumption. In some countries, in addition to the taxation of traditional exports, quantitative restrictions have also been imposed. This seems to be related mainly to trying to keep foreign exchange proceeds under control.

One of the latest steps in the introduction of trade intervention measures was related to export promotion laws. These are generally intended to provide additional foreign exchange in trade regimes with high incentives for sales to the domestic market. While there are successful experiences, in several countries the laws were enacted too late and their coverage was too limited to have resulted in the removal of the discrimination against exports. We will come back to this in a later section.

The comparison of national regulations regarding export promotion devices shows that they consist mainly of the following:

(a) Drawbacks, the general idea of which is to provide neutrality to exporting firms, regarding the system of protection through tariff suspension (or rebate), mainly on inputs and capital goods. (b) Rebates on the f.o.b. value or value added, where nontraditional exports are defined by providing either a negative list of traditional exports or a positive list of what should be considered nontraditional. The rebates are in the form of cash refunds, or endorsable certificates that may have some maturity period before they can be used to pay taxes. (c) The provision of pre-export and post-export financing, in many cases with subsidized rates and long financing periods, which then represent an important component of the promotion package.

Export promotion schemes are very similar; basically they provide tariff exemptions on inputs and capital goods or rebates on nontraditional exports (and/or their increments) and provide pre- and post-export financing. But this might reflect only the intentions of policymakers. In some countries the incentive is (in absolute and relative terms) insufficient to overcome the costs imposed by the trade regime; in others, foreign exchange regulations may in the short run call into question the usefulness of an instrument like export protection, since it may have replaced, for example, the share of export proceeds sold in a free foreign exchange market. This means overlooking the volatility of nominal exchange rates compared with the need of having schemes that are able to remove the tax content of traded inputs. We shall come back to this subject when the sources of anti-export bias are discussed.

Multilateral Trade Arrangements

The institution of several multilateral agreements since the 1960s was intended to overcome trade limitations imposed by national boundaries. Among the agreements, we will mention as examples only the Central American Common Market (CACM) and the Latin American Free Trade Association (LAFTA). By negotiating a common external tariff and free trade between the countries involved, a strong incentive to existing activities related to the enlargement of domestic markets was implied in the CACM agreement. The analysis of benefits and costs of economic integration in Central America made by Cline (1978), in the tradition of an earlier similar work by Balassa (1975) concerning the European Common Market, showed little importance for the trade diversion measured, which I think underestimates the real magnitude. Recent negotiations of a new common external tariff (excluding Honduras) has brought back some of the earlier discussions, but apparently the benefits associated with the enlargement of domestic markets is still a strong reason for pursuing that kind of policy in small countries.

Regarding LAFTA, the original idea was based on two basic principles: reciprocity and the most-favored-nation clause, the first to protect the least developed countries (discriminatory), the second to extend to all members any tariff advantage granted. The gradual elimination of trade restrictions among the members during the transition period of twelve years did not take place; also, some of the instruments as designed did not prove to be practical. This agreement was later replaced by the Latin American Integration Association, with two basic instruments: regional preferences and negotiated bilateral agreements that might be granted to other members. Table 2 provides figures of the tariff rate paid, as well as the limited amount of trade, measured from the import side. The average tariff rate on imports from the region varied between 5 and 7 percent, and the size of trade was 3 percent for Brazil and 14 percent for Argentina. Here, one of the main problems has been the erosion of the preference margins negotiated in each case because of existing tariff exemptions on imports from outside the region, mainly on government purchases and several promotion schemes on particular economic activities.

Exchange Rate Regulations

The best way of looking at the interaction of trade policies and exchange rate regulations is to see them as a system of multiple exchange rates. At one end, the lowest nominal exchange rate would correspond to traditional exports where export taxes are imposed, and at the other end, final goods (mainly consumer goods) would correspond to imports substituted under high tariff barriers; somewhere in between would be nominal exchange rate for intermediate products and capital goods and also the rate on promotion of nontraditional exports.

Trade regimes in many Latin American countries are associated with overvalued exchange rates, which are made possible by the high international competitiveness of traditional exports, as well as with high tariff levels and/or quantitative restrictions on the import side. In addition, the existence of tariff redundancy, as well as of quantitative restrictions, may affect real exchange rates, owing to the fact that implicit protection of import-competing activities becomes endogenous and therefore subject to shocks, many of them imposed by macroeconomic policies.

Bias Against Exports

In this section the sources of bias will be discussed, as well as the changes introduced by some implemented reforms, together with new foreign exchange regulations. Two examples are given to relate these sources of bias to export performance.

Sources of Bias

Local producers have to buy inputs (from local or imported sources) that are protected at prices higher than the border level. In the absence of export rebates, the result would be negative effective rates of protection for exports. At the same time, given import restrictions, sales in the domestic market are made at prices higher than the international level, following generally the made-to-measure principle starting from input protection. Taking into account these effects, one can consider two sources of bias against exports (leaving aside adjustments of overvalued exchange rates): the absolute bias related to export taxation on the input side, and the relative bias owing to higher nominal rates of protection applied to domestic sales as compared to exports.

The most frequent case to be found in Latin America regarding the tradable sector can be broken down into three activities: agriculture, agro-industries (Industry I), and the remaining industries (Industry II). Absolute bias against exports measured by negative effective rates would be the highest in Industry II in the absence of export promotion, because of the tax imposed by input protection. The agro-industries internalize the international competitiveness of agriculture, receiving a high (many times the highest) positive effective protection for sales to the domestic markets; that is, in such a situation, even a uniform tariff on manufacturing will not produce uniformity in effective rates because Industry II is securing its tradable inputs at higher than border prices. In other words, while under the uniform nominal tariff hypothesis relative nominal bias against exports is the same for all industries, the effective bias is higher for Industry II.

In trying to provide estimates of absolute anti-export bias, Table 3 shows two examples of structures of protection that correspond mainly to the nonnatural resource-based industries of Argentina (1977) and Brazil (1981); they basically correspond to the so-called Industry II, since sectors excluded from the comparison are mainly primary production and processed foods. By computing the realized higher costs of inputs and an estimate of the corresponding protection

Table 3. Argentina and Brazil: Frequency Distribution of Absolute Anti-Export Bias

Rates	Argentina (1977)			Brazil (1981)		
	Total	Intermediate Goods	Capital Goods	Total	Intermediate Goods	Capital Goods
−49 to −25	7.5	9.1	8.3	0.0	0.0	0.0
−24 to 0	60.0	68.2	41.7	0.0	0.0	0.0
1 to 25	32.5	22.7	50.0	22.9	28.0	0.0
26 to 50	0.0	0.0	0.0	62.9	56.0	100.0
> = 51	0.0	0.0	0.0	14.3	16.0	0.0
Total (in percent)	100.0	100.0	100.0	100.0	100.0	100.0
Sectors	40	22	12	35	25	7
Mean	−6.2	−9.7	−2.2	37.0	37.3	35.9
Standard deviation	12.2	12.1	13.0	25.7	29.8	6.0
Dispersion	195.2	125.1	580.2	69.4	80.0	16.7

Source: Based on estimates of realized effective rates of protection on exports (Berlinski, 1977; and Tyler, 1983).

NOTE: Effective protection estimates are conventional partial equilibrium figures of realized protection using the Corden criteria for the treatment of nontraded inputs. No adjustment for overvaluation was introduced, since the figures involved for those years were very close (about 20 percent). To provide a similar basis for comparison of both sets of estimates, some Brazilian sectors were not included here; they correspond mainly to natural resource-based activities—primary production and processed foods. Estimates for Argentina do not include the subsidy content of pre- and post-export financing, owing partly to data shortcomings but mainly to frequent changes in procedures and rates.

to exports[2] the effective rates were obtained. The frequency distribution of the rates show that for Argentina only one third of the activities had positive rates, while 100 percent of Brazilian sectors had positive rates and about two thirds of them were in the range of 26 to 50 percent.

Within this general picture, Argentina's capital goods industry (with fewer observations) shows a better position but with a higher dispersion relative to intermediate goods. In Brazil, average rates are about the same for both types of goods, but with a substantially lower dispersion in capital goods (also with fewer sectors). The subsidy content of export financing for manufacturing was 8 percent in Brazil (see Tyler, 1983), which was not computed in the figures for Argentina, not because of lack of data but mainly because of the frequent

---

[2] As mentioned, both estimates are based on generalized price comparisons between domestic ex-factory prices and the c.i.f. price of imports competing (actually or potentially) with domestic production.

changes in procedures and rates. This does not seem to affect the basic message of stronger export promotion in Brazil but might reduce the bias measure in favor of Argentine capital goods.

As mentioned earlier, another source of anti-export bias is related to the lack of symmetry between nominal rewards for sales to the domestic market and to the export market. The relevant calculations for Argentina and Brazil are presented in Tables 4 and 5, where the bias measure was the ratio between protection coefficients (1 + rate), the numerator being the ratio of protection to domestic sales. The first set of columns corresponds to the nominal bias coefficient, which for Argentina (Table 4) shows the highest concentration of activities in the brackets of up to 1.5 (between 80 and 90 percent); this percentage is strongly reduced when we look at the relevant effective coefficients, which incorporate both bias measurements. The average bias for capital goods is lower, with a higher dispersion relative to the coefficients for intermediate goods.

For Brazil (Table 5), the concentration of activities in the same two brackets (up to 1.5) is also high (between 80 and 90 percent) for nominal as well as effective bias. But the composition within them is

Table 4. Argentina: Frequency Distribution of Relative Anti-Export Bias, 1977

Bias Coefficient	Nominal			Effective		
	Total	Intermediate Goods	Capital Goods	Total	Intermediate Goods	Capital Goods
< 1.0	17.5	9.1	16.7	17.5	9.1	16.7
1.0 to 1.5	70.0	81.8	66.7	35.0	36.4	50.0
1.6 to 2.0	12.5	9.1	16.7	27.5	36.4	16.7
2.1 to 2.5	0.0	0.0	0.0	7.5	4.5	8.3
2.6 to 3.0	0.0	0.0	0.0	7.5	9.1	8.3
3.1 to 3.5	0.0	0.0	0.0	2.5	4.5	0.0
> = 3.6	0.0	0.0	0.0	2.5	0.0	0.0
Total (in percent)	100.0	100.0	100.0	100.0	100.0	100.0
Sectors	40	22	12	40	22	12
Mean	1.3	1.3	1.2	1.7	1.7	1.4
Standard deviation	0.3	0.2	0.3	0.9	0.6	0.6
Dispersion	21.8	17.8	24.0	54.2	38.4	42.0

Source: See Table 3.

NOTE: The bias against exports is the ratio between protection coefficients (1 + rate) to domestic sales and exports, while nominal and effective refer to the corresponding protective rates.

Table 5. Brazil: Frequency Distribution of Relative Anti-Export Bias, 1981

Bias Coefficient	Nominal			Effective		
	Total	Intermediate Goods	Capital Goods	Total	Intermediate Goods	Capital Goods
< 1.0	45.7	48.0	57.1	48.6	52.0	57.1
1.0 to 1.5	42.9	44.0	28.6	34.3	32.0	28.6
1.6 to 2.0	11.4	8.0	14.3	14.3	16.0	0.0
2.1 to 2.5	0.0	0.0	0.0	2.9	0.0	14.3
2.6 to 3.0	0.0	0.0	0.0	0.0	0.0	0.0
3.1 to 3.5	0.0	0.0	0.0	0.0	0.0	0.0
> = 3.6	0.0	0.0	0.0	0.0	0.0	0.0
Total (in percent)	100.0	100.0	100.0	100.0	100.0	100.0
Sectors	35	25	7	35	25	7
Mean	1.0	1.0	1.1	1.1	1.0	1.2
Standard deviation	0.3	0.3	0.4	0.5	0.4	0.6
Dispersion	31.5	29.9	37.3	43.9	41.9	52.9

Source: See Table 3.

NOTE: The bias against exports is the ratio between protection coefficients (1 + rate) to domestic sales and exports, while nominal and effective refer to the corresponding protective rates.

different: about 50 percent of the sectors are in the <1.0 bracket, which means that nominal as well as effective incentives to exports are higher than those realized for sales to the domestic market. The average bias shows fewer differences between types of goods but also a higher dispersion for capital goods.

The comparison of anti-export biases between activities of Industry II type (nonnatural resource-based) for Argentina and Brazil shows that in Argentina there is stronger input discrimination (absolute bias) as well as an important differential reward to domestic sales (relative bias).

Changes in Anti-Export Bias

When the effect on growth of the import substitution industry slowed down, governments introduced several measures to promote nontraditional exports. As we have seen in an earlier section, the measures are generally designed to compensate the by-product effect of trade regimes on export profitability. Thus, drawbacks allow firms to secure inputs at international prices; rebates on f.o.b. values are also intended to compensate the high cost of inputs and in general they did not go beyond "tax" removal. Using our classification of bias, these devices are oriented toward the reduction of absolute bias.

Foreign exchange regulations and the setting of nominal exchange rates have also emphasized absolute bias, disregarding that in the medium run the relative bias measure is important in changing the profit equation of the firm. Otherwise, exports will be driven mainly by domestic recession, and the moment the recession is over the trade balance will be worse because of increased imports associated with the increase in domestic activity and decreased exports for the same reason. This would not be true if there was more symmetry between prices of products sold in the domestic market and those for the export market, and capacity may even be stretched to satisfy the demands of both markets.

A recent example of testing this positive correlation between incentives and the growth of exports can be seen in Balassa and others (1986) concerning Greece and the Republic of Korea. On the other hand, Teitel and Thoumi (1986), in trying to correlate the high rates of growth in manufacturing exports of Argentina and Brazil during the 1970s, did not find this conventional association. But the data on Brazilian incentives that they used correspond to legal nominal rates for 1977 (Tyler, 1983), compared with realized protection rates computed by the same author for 1980–81 and on which Tables 3 and 5 are partly based. This might change Teitel and Thoumi's conclusions, given the generalized high redundancy of tariffs found (Tyler, 1985). The result for Argentina is puzzling because the additional evidence provided in the earlier portion of this section is that the anti-export bias was still there. We were also aware that not including the interest subsidy content in those calculations might have influenced the results, especially for capital goods where the financing period is longer. The hypothesis developed by the authors is basically related to learning by doing, first selling to domestic markets and at a later stage becoming exporters. It is my impression that in testing the association of incentives and exports a high explanatory power would be found in the actual practice of marginal cost pricing for exports, in activities where competition among the few allowed them to charge fixed costs to domestic buyers.

Going back to the main discussion, absolute bias would have been reduced by export rebates, the provision of inputs at international prices, or by changes in the real exchange rate. While relative bias might have been reduced by the first measure if its magnitude went beyond "tax" removal, it would have remained about the same for any real devaluation given its protective effect on import-competing activities. Another way of reducing relative bias is through changes in import protection, which is discussed in the next section.

Changes in Import Protection

The purpose of this section is to point out some problems related to changes in import protection. Here, some elements regarding the structure of incentives and institutional constraints are introduced in order to stress the close relationship between initial conditions and policy reversals, especially procedures about the modus operandi of bankruptcies, the generous "tax expenditure" schemes, and the imperfect competition in domestic markets.

Initial Conditions

The initial conditions describe the points of reference for the evaluation of the reform proposals. This is important when the adjustments required imply a strong divergence from present conditions. Also, recent studies made of the Southern Cone liberalization programs show that credibility is crucial to success (Corbo and de Melo, 1985). The initial conditions should include not only the structure of protection categorized by anti-export bias (see preceding section) and high dispersion of protective rates but also the institutional framework and the functioning of markets for products and factors.

In Latin America it has become commonplace to discuss in limited circles some of the underlying problems of the present trade regimes: (a) the conflict between agriculture and industry, (b) the functioning of the bankruptcy laws, (c) the generous industrial promotion mechanisms, and (d) imperfections of markets. This seems to be what Keynes (quoted by Gardner, 1969, p. xi) has called inside opinion: "For there are, in the present time, two opinions; not, as in former ages, the true and the false, but the outside and the inside; the opinion of the public voiced by the politicians and the newspapers, and the opinions of the politicians, the journalists, and the civil servants, upstairs and backstairs and behind-stairs, expressed in limited circles."

It is an open question as to what extent this apparent dichotomy (outside-inside opinions) is real or simply represents the way pressure groups behave in order to defend their interests. In many cases I have found a rhetorical mix of vested-interest string-pulling and the existence of an old script followed by the bureaucracy, which is supposed to make decisions involving private rates of return.

Going back to the problems mentioned above, the conflict between agriculture and industry is best expressed by the process of setting the nominal exchange rates. This becomes difficult once relative domestic prices for some goods differ substantially from border prices. The distance between nominal exchange rates for agriculture (adjusted for export taxes) and those for industry-cum-protection is such that setting the exchange rate raises permanent tension between technical and political decisions.

Next, the bankruptcy laws seem to be functioning only for medium-sized and small firms—a strong restriction for any intended rationalization of the incentive system. The problem is more difficult when, in addition, projects are approved under the general belief that for several reasons protection is to be maintained for long periods of time. As usual, it is difficult to generalize, but my impression is that this protection network soon becomes a source of quasi-rents.

Another common feature is the implementation of a generous system of "tax expenditures," which supported private capital formation for long periods, extending private rates of return beyond conventional pay-off periods. In most cases, prices used in these evaluations were not even corrected to allow for the discrepancy between private and social opportunity costs, which describes the worst of the worlds.

Concerning the effects of market imperfections on products, firms were allowed a liberalized period of adjustment to the new situation. The asymmetry of rewards to domestic and export markets resulted in firms reducing exports based on reduced protection to domestic markets where the markets behaved as price leaders (Berlinski, 1982). Regarding the markets for factors of production, the effects of "tax expenditures," subsidized credit lines, and social security taxes in favoring more capital-intensive techniques are well known.

Corbo, de Melo, and Tybout (1985) provided a very comprehensive evaluation of the reasons for the failure of recent reforms in the Southern Cone. They mention (a) the policy inconsistencies associated with strong incentives to borrow from outside, the conflict between foreign exchange and trade policies affecting first the profitability of exports, and the lack of fiscal restraint, and at the micro level the failure to eliminate important distortions; (b) the adjustment lags related mainly to the thought that the rate of domestic inflation would rapidly converge to the rate of international inflation and the rate of devaluation; and (c) evasions of the intended reforms, related to the lack of long-term adjustment of the firms and their concentration in financial activities. Among the lessons drawn in the conclusions, we would have liked to see more about the adjustment costs associated not only with technical inconsistencies of the programs but also with other restrictions (bankruptcies, tax expenditures, imperfect markets) that may undermine the stability of any future policy package.

We have seen that recent changes in import protection were approached with inadequate attention to initial conditions when dismantling exercises started from highly distorted situations. For example, if the bankruptcy law could not be enforced for large firms, then credibility about sustaining those policies in the medium run would be the basic point of reference for entrepreneurs. Some of the entrepreneurs, while applauding the policy in public (outside opinion) but pointing out contradictions in limited circles, were postponing the decision to close down (if this would have been the case) by increasing their borrowing. The hope was that the snowball effect that follows this type of generalized attitude would lead to a policy reversal.

There is a need to look closely at outside and inside opinions when designing policy reforms, which will necessarily lead us to a compromise between the "best" policy generally represented by the economist's point of view and the one that might provide stable rules for the decision maker.

New Reform Proposals

Import substitution industrialization started in Latin America under high tariffs. The general pattern was to assign higher rates for consumer goods than for intermediate and capital goods, with a built-in escalation owing to the varying degrees of fabrication plus setting rates for complementary imports at a low fiscal floor.

It is well known that a tariff increases the price of imports, and in so doing may provide incentives to import-competing activities by increasing their factor rewards. But, if inputs are provided at prices higher than international levels, value added under protection increases less than the margin allowed by output protection. The measure that incorporates both effects is precisely the effective protection rate. The patterns of realized effective rates of protection for domestic sales used in Tables 4 and 5 will be presented here as examples: average rates in Argentina are higher for intermediate products than for capital goods and the opposite holds in Brazil. Their frequency distributions show a high concentration of activities (85 percent) on both ends (effective rates up to 25 percent and higher than 76 percent) for Argentina, while 69 percent of Brazilian sectors were located in the same bracket; that is, what makes the larger relative difference in anti-export bias between those countries is basically the export promotion system.

The rationalization of the structure of protection is related mainly to private rates of return of import-competing activities, fiscal revenues, and the effect on consumers. That is why the removal of special regimes for tariff exemptions is also involved, but, primarily, the rationalization should be concerned with the anti-export bias induced by tariff and nontariff measures. More specifically, this rationalization implies necessarily reducing the present dispersion of effective rates, which does not seem to be justified on normative grounds. This dispersion is related basically to differentials in protection of outputs and inputs, so that the adjustment should be oriented toward the reduction of high rates on consumer goods, increasing the so-called fiscal floor for imported inputs. This set of rules might also require changes in the exchange rate to maintain trade balances within desired limits.

How easy is the transition between an old and a new trade policy? That is a difficult question, not only on technical grounds but also looking at the political economy of the adjustment. The need to increase exports is a must in searching for sources of growth beyond cyclical fluctuations. This is leading us to look at the rationalization of incentives as a sequential process, where only a strong increase in exports will generate the credibility needed to introduce the required changes in import protection. In the meantime, the higher costs of traded (domestic and imported) and nontraded inputs (absolute bias) should be removed, and selective rebates to overcome the relative anti-export bias should be provided. Trade policies should be oriented toward the minimization of the domestic resource cost of earning or saving foreign exchange, giving priority to consolidating those activities with a comparative advantage based on actual exports. But, as pointed out by Cline (1984), as soon as export-led growth becomes increasingly popular, one should also be concerned with the possible aggregate implications regarding the protectionist responses.

Looking for similar points of view regarding the proposal of a phased increase in exports before putting more rationality into incentives to domestic sales, we have found Diaz-Alejandro (1975) deeply concerned about the transition between two trade regimes: how much of the old system has to be dismantled, as well as what is to be expected from the new trade policies? Another complementary view concerned with international regulations is that of Snape (1984) when analyzing

the rules of the General Agreement on Tariffs and Trade regarding
the code of subsidies. He suggests a change in Article 14 in order that
a developing country may grant export subsidies aimed at compensating the distorting effects of import barriers as a step in a program
of import liberalization.

Conclusions

Import substitution industrialization was promoted in Latin America under high tariff barriers. For existing industries, this meant an
increase in output and employment; for new industries, the protected
markets provided the captive domestic demand—an attractive point of
departure for many projects.

The structure of tariffs was designed to provide higher private
profitability for sales to the domestic market, mainly of final consumer
goods. At the same time this was eased by the availability of inputs at
near international prices owing to a generous system of tariff exemptions on intermediate and capital goods. Then tariff escalation was
built into the protective system. Also, there was a reinforcement of
trade intervention through quantitative restrictions, nonneutral consumption taxation, and other surcharges. In some cases where discriminatory arrangements were introduced, free trade within the
region (or a subset of it) enlarged the protected national markets.

Export promotion in Latin America requires some compensation
scheme in order to overcome the bias against the present protective
system. On the one hand, absolute bias should be removed in the short
run by export promotion devices; on the other hand, given the larger
reward received by sales to the domestic markets, selective rebates
should be granted, but in the medium term the profit equation of the
firm should be changed, which will lead to tariff reform; that is, here,
export expansion is presented as a prior step to an import liberalization process.

Compensation schemes have shown similarities among countries.
Some have tended to introduce drawbacks or export rebates; others,
given the scarcity of foreign exchange, have introduced free foreign
exchange markets where shares of export proceeds would be sold.
Here a distinction must be made between the domestic resource-based
industries and the remaining manufacturing activities. The former
are generally supplied with primary inputs at international prices,
while the latter are taxed by securing their inputs (domestic, imported) at higher than international prices.

In general terms, relative bias could be eliminated by designing a system that provides near symmetrical incentives for sales to the domestic market and to the export market. But, here, the higher the protection to import-competing products, the higher the fiscal cost to the treasury, so that this export promotion scheme would have to be funded by increasing taxes (or deficits). In other words, while the promotion basis for import substitution (except some tax expenditures associated with fiscal incentives) is taking place outside the treasury, export promotion requires an increase in expenditure or foregone fiscal revenues, which, if feasible, may induce retaliation. All of this leads to the need to introduce in the medium term a tariff reform.

The aim of tariff reform proposals is to change relative prices between importables and exportables in the economy. This can be done by simple rules, but, given the size of existing industries, what is needed are stable dismantling procedures and preannounced schedules. Here the main problem concerns the cost of adjustment of existing activities, which may not survive if profit rates are going down. This requires that policy measures be phased so as to provide at an early stage strong export promotion to allow for the rationalization of import protection (tariff and nontariff measures) in the medium term.

References

Balassa, Bela A., ed., *European Economic Integration* (Amsterdam: North-Holland, 1975).

———, and others, "Export Incentives and Export Growth in Developing Countries: An Econometric Investigation," Development Research Department, Discussion Paper No. 159, The World Bank (Washington, February 1986).

Berlinski, Julio, "La proteccion efectiva de actividades seleccionadas de la industria manufacturera Argentina" (Buenos Aires, 1977).

———, "Dismantling Foreign Trade Restrictions: Some Evidence and Issues on the Argentine Case," in *Trade, Stability, Technology and Equity in Latin America*, ed. by Moshe Syrquin and Simon Teitel (New York: Academic Press, 1982).

———, Julio Camelo H., and M. Pazmino, "Importaciones exentas de aranceles en algunos paises de la ALADI," *Integracion economica* (Buenos Aires), Institute for Latin American Integration (April 1984).

Cline, William R., "Benefits and Costs of Economic Integration in Central America," in *Economic Integration in Central America*, ed. by William R. Cline and Enrique Delgado (Washington: The Brookings Institution, 1978), pp. 59–121.

———, *Exports of Manufactures from Developing Countries: Performance and Prospects for Market Access* (Washington: The Brookings Institution, 1984).

Corbo, Vittorio, Jaime de Melo, and James Tybout, "What Went Wrong with the Recent Reforms in the Southern Cone," Development Research Department, Discussion Paper No. 128, The World Bank (Washington, July 1985).

Corbo, Vittorio, and Jaime de Melo, eds., "Scrambling for Survival: How Firms Adjusted to the Recent Reforms in Argentina, Chile, and Uruguay," World Bank Staff Working Papers, No. 764 (Washington, 1985).

Diaz-Alejandro, Carlos F., "Trade Policies and Economic Development," in *International Trade and Finance: Frontiers for Research*, ed. by Peter B. Kenen (Cambridge, England: Cambridge University Press, 1975).

——, *Colombia: Foreign Trade Regimes and Economic Development* (New York: National Bureau of Economic Research, 1976).

Gardner, Richard N., *Sterling-Dollar Diplomacy: The Origins and the Prospects of Our International Economic Order* (New York: McGraw-Hill, 1969).

Kuznets, Simon, "Quantitative Aspects of the Economic Growth of Nations: IX. Level and Structure of Foreign Trade: Comparisons for Recent Years," *Economic Development and Cultural Change* (Chicago), Vol. 13, Pt. II (October 1964).

Snape, Richard, "Subsidies of International Concern," Development Research Department, Discussion Paper No. 110, The World Bank (Washington, November 1984).

Teitel, Simon, and Francisco E. Thoumi, "From Import Substitution to Exports: The Manufacturing Exports Experience of Argentina and Brazil," *Economic Development and Cultural Change* (Chicago), Vol. 34 (April 1986).

Tyler, William G., "Anti-Export Bias in Commercial Policies and Export Performance: Some Evidence from the Recent Brazilian Experience," *Weltwirtschaftliches Archiv* (Kiel), Vol. 119 (1983), pp. 97–108.

——, "Effective Incentives for Domestic Market Sales and Exports: View of Anti-export Biases and Commercial Policy in Brazil, 1980–81," *Journal of Development Economics* (Amsterdam), Vol. 18 (August 1985), pp. 219–42.

Comments

Sterie T. Beza

Julio Berlinski's paper addresses a subject that has been traditional in the debate on economic policy in Latin America; one that has recently been the subject of renewed interest by specialists—that is, trade policy in the context of a growth strategy. But just as in previous decades the focal point was the role of an import substitution policy, in recent years emphasis has been placed on the need to expand exports.

Berlinski makes a contribution in this field from the perspective of economic policy execution in a world dominated by pressure groups, in which the problems of credibility are of primordial importance.

The starting point of his analysis is a statistical relationship, noted over twenty years ago by Simon Kuznets, between the relative size of a country's foreign trade on the one hand and the national product and per capita income on the other. Accepting this relationship, Berlinski appears to take it as given that, to promote the process of economic growth, it is desirable to increase the openness of the economy. This seems a reasonable proposition, although it is curious that in reproducing Kuznets' analysis for a recent period, Berlinski finds that the relationship is not valid for two of the four subgroups of countries analyzed. It would be interesting to know what the explanation of this phenomenon might be. He will possibly address it in a future paper.

Turning to the paper's central theme, the author emphasizes the fact that the high degree of tariff protection in many Latin American countries produces an anti-export bias that acts as an obstacle to any increase in foreign trade and, in the end, to any sustained growth in the economy. Doubtless the prices at which local producers buy their inputs are higher than international prices to the extent that imports are subject to taxes or other barriers, and in the absence of any off-setting measures, exporters are faced with negative rates of effective protection. This is what the author calls absolute anti-export bias. He also points to the existence of a relative bias when prices in the domestic market are higher than international prices as a consequence of tariff protection on exportable goods.

Once the problem has been identified, the question arises as to how to deal with it. Berlinski's proposal in this regard is, to my mind, the key point in the paper—but at the same time one of the most debatable. In principle, it would seem logical to think that the best solution would be to change the import system so as to make it more liberal. However, the author thinks that such a measure can be politically viable only if it is preceded by an expansion of the export sector. Such an expansion would be brought about by means of promotion mechanisms (such as tax refunds or subsidies) which would neutralize the anti-export bias of import restrictions. As a final objective the author favors the rationalization of incentive systems, in particular a tariff reform. However, he believes that this goal can only be reached in a sequential process, in which an increase in exports would enable the necessary credibility to be generated to successfully carry out such a tariff reform (and to eliminate other import barriers).

The author's postulates call for a number of comments. In the first place, one wonders what he has in mind when he says that the import liberalization effort will be credible only if it follows an expansion of the export sector. Is he thinking of the need for an expanding export sector to offset any possible short-term negative effect on the overall level of economic activity caused by the liberalization of imports? Or is he perhaps thinking of the creation of a new pressure group of exporters which could offset the protectionist pressures of the sectors that have developed under the protection of import restrictions? At any rate, it is important to note that the problems of credibility frequently arise from incompatibilities between different policies. From this he derives the importance of the different policy measures forming a harmonious whole.

There is a risk that the authorities may act as though the export promotion measures are without cost. One problem is the pressure that these measures bring to bear on public finances. This seems to be one of the factors that leads the author to recommend the eventual dismantling of the import-protection-cum-export-promotion scheme. But beyond this problem, unless there are sufficient unused resources that can be swiftly mobilized, the need arises to reduce consumption in order to leave room for the expansion of exports and to transfer the resources intended for the production of nontradable goods or of import substitution goods to the production of exportable goods. If export subsidies are high enough to make the export of import substitution goods profitable, there need be no change in the structure of production; that is, there would be no transfer of resources from inefficient industries to other more efficient ones. If, on the contrary, export subsidies lead to a transfer of resources to new export sectors, there could be positive results in terms of standards of living. However, there would still be adversely affected groups, who logically would tend to oppose the change. In both cases, to facilitate the expansion of exports, it would be necessary to reduce domestic consumption (at least temporarily), through fiscal policy measures, for example.

Another important consideration is that it would be extremely difficult in practice to establish a system of export refunds that could adequately neutralize the anti-export bias of protectionist measures, insofar as the effects of these measures vary from product to product. Obviously, a uniform system of refunds would not eliminate the distortions caused by those protection measures that produce differential effects. Furthermore a neutral tariff protection system offset by export subsidies would be very difficult to administer, even assuming that such a one could be designed. There would doubtless be strong incentives to evade the costs or to take advantage of the benefits of the system, with the result that in reality it would probably be difficult to avoid the proliferation of fraudulent practices and a negative fiscal effect.

It should also be emphasized that a sequential process of the kind favored by Berlinski would over time prolong the import restriction measures, which not only have an anti-export bias but also give rise to other distortions. There is no doubt that the great number of nominal and actual protection rates applied in many Latin American countries has a harmful effect on the allocation of resources, which to a large extent overflows into exports. In this area, it should be pointed out that the argument in favor of tariff protection based on the optimum tariff theory does not in general seem applicable to Latin American countries, owing to the nonexistence of monopsonies in the region. The justification for protectionist practices based on the existence of external economies may be valid, but it is generally accepted that the objectives sought may be achieved more efficiently by other means, for example, by means of direct subsidies to the production it is wished to promote.

Berlinski's paper includes a comparison of the protection schemes of Argentina and Brazil, and an estimate of the degree to which the anti-export bias has been offset by direct export promotion measures. This analysis seems to lead to the conclusion that there are no major differences between the two countries in the area of tariff protection policy, but that Brazil seems to have offset its anti-export bias to a much larger extent than Argentina. In this regard, it should be pointed out that, apart from the tariff protection on which Berlinski's analysis is based, both countries have used other protectionist measures, such as quotas or import prohibitions. Although the author recognizes the existence of such practices, for obvious reasons they are not reflected in his quantitative analysis. This, as well as the frequent use of tariff exemptions, may seriously affect the validity of the results of the analysis.

Apart from that, these results do not appear necessarily to support Berlinski's position in favor of a sequential process. On the one hand, although Brazil has doubtless had a more dynamic export sector than Argentina and greater economic growth in general over the last few years, there are no indications that it has made any progress in dismantling its import restrictions. As the author very rightly warns, the perpetuation of the system may give rise to problems both on the fiscal side and as a consequence of possible trade reprisals by other countries.

Another factor worth bearing in mind in evaluating programs aiming to liberalize imports, and which may have had implications in both Argentina and Brazil, is the existence of a broad sector of protected public enterprises. Unless the authorities are ready to act energetically to submit these enterprises to the same discipline as private enterprises, the import liberalization process may be obstructed. It is obvious that in those countries where the public enterprise sector carries a lot of weight, to exempt it from adjustment is costly in terms of both the direct impact of the exemption and the negative effect on the credibility of government policy.

Apart from the cases of Argentina and Brazil, Berlinski's paper does not give country experiences except in a very summary form; this despite the fact that some countries seem to have made some progress in rationalizing their import regimes and to have been able to develop somewhat dynamic nontraditional export sectors. These successes were certainly not achieved without difficulty, and the methods used included a combination of measures, including direct export promotion. However, it seems only fair to mention that the problem of import restrictions has been attacked more directly than the author suggests, and with a certain degree of success.

Many countries' experience also points to the importance of exchange policy. As a matter of fact, the experience of Argentina, Chile, and Uruguay over the past decade suggests that the difficulties they may have experienced in handling their economies, and specifically in their efforts to liberalize imports, were intimately linked with the overvaluation of their currencies. On the other hand, an active exchange policy less subject to ups and downs has probably been a key factor in the results Brazil has achieved. This is a point that the author does not ignore, but perhaps emphasizes less than he should. It must be stressed that, apart from encouraging the transfer of resources from the sector that competes with imports to the export sector, it is also necessary to ensure that there is a transfer of resources from the sector that produces nontradable goods to the sector that produces tradable goods.

By way of conclusion, I will take the liberty of turning back to some points that seem important to me.

First, although it cannot be denied that a sequential process could help reach the import liberalization objective, there are abundant reasons to doubt that this is the best way to do it. Berlinski's paper does not seem to adduce evidence that this method has been used with success thus far.

Second, any liberalization policy must undoubtedly lay emphasis on being credible. In doing this, it is essential that the various policies, including the exchange rate policy and the financial (above all, fiscal) policy, are mutually compatible. When the authorities announce their liberalization timetable in advance, which is clearly desirable in many cases, their credibility also will require them to strictly adhere to the established timetable.

Last, too much emphasis should not be placed on the relationship between trade and fiscal policies. It is important that the approach adopted of rationalizing trade policy is compatible with the objective of not negatively affecting public finance, and fiscal policy should try to facilitate the transfer of resources to the export sector. Furthermore, one cannot ignore the danger of the objective of rationalizing trade policy being thwarted by lack of action consistent with this objective in regard to public enterprises.

Germán Botero A.

Berlinski's paper summarizes existing trade policies in Latin America and concludes by suggesting that the way to return to free trade is first to promote exports and then to remove import tariffs. This commentary summarizes the distortions mentioned by the author using a model of the two sectors (one consumer good and one capital good) and two factors (capital and labor). The distortions are modeled as changes in the technique (capital/labor ratio) of production vis-à-vis the technique that would exist under free trade, and it is shown how the growth rate of consumption is maximized if distortions are eliminated. According to the author, the existence of distortions is explained by political pressures from groups of producers of the protected goods.

Let us assume an open economy that produces capital goods (importable good) and consumer goods (exportable good): its factors of production are capital that produces or imports and manpower. With free trade, the relative prices of the two products are equal to those on the world market, which means that there is a Pareto-optimal frontier on the economy's capacity for consumption. Preferences between present and future consumption determine the point on the consumption frontier at which the economy is located: ceteris paribus, an increase in the discount rate over time increases present consumption, reduces the accumulation of capital goods, reduces the capacity for producing goods in the following period, and consequently reduces future consumption.

An increase in domestic production of capital goods in the short term can be achieved by restricting trade through taxes on their importation. The production of consumer goods declines, and the whole frontier of consumption possibilities turns back to a lower Pareto level than the original frontier. Assuming normal goods, the reduction of income reduces demand: the country consumes less, accumulates less capital, and reduces the net present value of its consumption. Berlinski suggests that this loss of present and future consumption is caused by the (industrial) pressure groups that succeed in making governments keep up their protectionist policies.

The author recognizes that restrictions on trade must disappear if growth is to be promoted, but he emphasizes that the political viability of this aim depends on what compensation is given to the beneficiaries of the current customs tariff structure. He suggests that this might be achieved through an export promotion scheme, so that after exports increase the pressure groups can agree to a reduction of protection of the industrial sector.

Berlinski does not specifically spell out how to implement his proposal. It is obvious that the main restraint is where to find the resources to be used to increase the production of exportable goods. Ideally, as the long-term objective is to reduce distortions, they should not be obtained by means of indirect taxation. A choice must be made between direct taxes on the producers or taxes on the consumer's income. The former choice is surely not feasible, because of the political pressures mentioned by the author; the latter also runs up against political difficulties because taxes are usually already very high.

To sum up, the author describes existing distortions, points out the political difficulties of eliminating them, and formulates a strategy for reducing them slowly. However, his strategy calls for additional taxes, which may also encounter major political difficulties. The other alternative is to confront the pressure groups and gradually reduce trade restrictions.

Fiscal Policy, Growth, and Design of Stabilization Programs

Vito Tanzi

The objectives of Fund-supported stabilization programs include a balance of payments viable over the medium run, the promotion of growth under a stable economic environment, price stability, and the prevention of excessive growth in external debt. These objectives do not have the same weight, but each is important in stabilization programs. A narrow interpretation of the Fund's role would emphasize the balance of payments objective and de-emphasize the others.

This paper deals with the role of fiscal policy in stabilization programs, emphasizing the structural aspects of fiscal policies since, over the years, these aspects have attracted less attention than has demand management. The Baker initiative of October 1985 called attention to the importance of these structural aspects. The paper does not discuss other elements of program design, such as incentive measures implemented through the exchange rate, through import liberalization, through financial deregulation, or through pricing policy, even though these structural elements are obviously important. In countries where institutions necessary for the effective use of other policies are not adequately developed, fiscal policy may be the main avenue to economic development and stability, although, unfortunately, political pressures, external shocks, and administrative shortcomings have frequently weakened government control over this instrument. Tax evasion, inflation, and the proliferation of exonerations have reduced the government's ability to control tax revenues, while political pressures, fragmentation of the public sector, and inadequate monitoring

systems have undermined its ability to keep public expenditure in
check. Far from being the stabilizing factor in the economy that it
should be, fiscal policy has itself, in too many instances, become a
major destabilizing force contributing to disequilibrium in the external sector.[1]

In recent years the connection between fiscal developments and
external sector developments has been increasingly recognized. Some
have gone as far as to suggest a "fiscal approach to the balance of
payments" that considers fiscal disequilibrium as the main cause of
external imbalances.[2]

Although growth was always a primary objective of economic policy,
the sustained rates of growth experienced by most countries until the
mid-1970s (except for occasional and transitory periods of balance of
payments difficulties) made it possible for the Fund, in negotiating
stabilization programs, to concentrate on the objective of stabilization
in which it had more expertise and an accepted mandate. The increase
in oil prices during the 1970s and especially the more recent debt crisis
accompanied by the sharp fall in commodity prices brought about a
new environment in which external sector disequilibrium could not be
easily financed. This forced many countries to pursue (over longer
periods than had earlier been the case) stabilization policies aimed at
reducing external imbalances or the rate of inflation, policies that
some critics considered as inimical to growth.

In the face of external shocks, some countries (for example, the
Republic of Korea) succeeded in stabilizing their economies and in
advancing once again along the road of economic development.
Others were less successful. When the need to pursue stabilization
policies extended over several years, the short-run political costs of
these policies began to loom larger than the longer-run economic
benefits; political fatigue set in and some countries became restive
under the harness of traditional stabilization programs. The cries of
critics that stabilization policies were inhibiting growth became louder
and attracted a larger following. Critics advised policymakers to aban-

---

[1] In this paper the impact of fiscal developments on the balance of payments is emphasized. But, of course, the relationship is not unidirectional. In some cases fiscal disequilibrium may initially be created by developments in the balance of payments (say, a fall
in export prices). In those cases the important question is whether the government should
finance the shortcoming, or whether it should immediately or progressively lower domestic
spending to reflect the lower real income of the country. On this, see Tanzi (1986),
pp. 88–91; Tabellini (1985); and Chu (1987).

[2] For the connection between the fiscal deficit and the balance of payments, see Kelly
(1982), pp. 561–602. See also Tanzi and Blejer (1984), pp. 117–36.

don stabilization policies recommended by the Fund and to concentrate on growth, regardless of the consequences for the balance of payments and the rate of inflation. They espoused the position that inflation is a lesser evil than stagnation and that the external sector can be kept in equilibrium through quantitative restrictions and export subsidies, or by repudiating external debt obligations.

As already mentioned, stabilization and growth have always been legitimate policy objectives. Although in the past it was thought that at any given moment a country could focus on policies aimed specifically at one or the other of these objectives, the view that it is unwise to separate these objectives currently predominates. Stabilization programs must pay attention to growth to ensure that stability is not won at the price of stagnation.[3] Growth policy must pay attention to stability to ensure that the pursuit of growth is not aborted by excessive inflation or by pressures on the external sector, as has happened in several cases in recent years. Growth without stability may be technically impossible over the longer run; stability without growth may be politically impossible except in the short run. This paper attempts to reformulate the fiscal design of stabilization programs in order to emphasize the growth objective.

If stabilization were the only objective of economic policy, stabilization programs could rely mostly on traditional demand-management policies.[4] Stabilization *with* growth, however, requires that demand-management policies be complemented by policies aimed at increasing potential output. Misguided structural policies have reduced potential output by misallocating resources and by reducing the rate of growth of the factors of production. They have thus been the main cause of stagnation and a contributor to economic instability. The design of adjustment programs should integrate stabilization with growth, or demand-management policies with structural, supply-side policies.

Fiscal Policy and the Design of Fund Programs

Stabilization programs can, in theory, emphasize either specific or general fiscal policies. For example, the country and the Fund could

---

[3] This is particularly important in order to reduce over time the burden of the foreign debt of the countries.

[4] But, of course, changes in the exchange rate, which have often been part of traditional stabilization programs, have incentive effects in addition to their demand-management effect.

agree on a whole range of specific fiscal measures, such as changes in various taxes and tax rates and changes in specific public expenditures, subsidies, and public utility rates. These measures, however, would have to add up to the required adjustment in aggregate demand and supply. They must reduce the balance of payments disequilibrium and the rate of inflation to the desired level by reducing aggregate demand and by increasing aggregate supply. For identification I shall call this the microeconomic approach to stabilization programs, an approach that explicitly recognizes both the demand-management and the supply-management aspects of fiscal policy. It recognizes that fiscal policy changes usually affect not only aggregate demand but also aggregate supply.[5]

Alternatively, the country and the Fund could limit their agreement on a program to general, macroeconomic variables. In the extreme version of this alternative, the Fund and the country might not even discuss specific fiscal policies, but would limit not only their agreement but also their discussions to the size of the fiscal deficit and to the expansion of bank credit associated with that deficit. If specific policies are discussed, it would be to assess their immediate impact on the size of the fiscal deficit and on aggregate demand.

In this approach, supply-side aspects of fiscal policy (what I have called the supply-management aspects) would be largely ignored. I shall call this the macroeconomic approach to stabilization policy. This approach implies that once the size of the deficit has been determined, the balance of payments consequences of that deficit have also been determined regardless of the specific measures that the country will employ to achieve the stipulated level of fiscal deficit.[6] Whether the

---

[5] Over the years, what I have called the supply-management aspect of fiscal policy has received far less attention than the more traditional demand-management aspect. To put it differently, price (or micro) theory was rarely integrated with income (or macro) theory. Fiscal policy based on the Keynesian framework normally concentrated on the effects of changes in tax levels and public spending levels on aggregate demand. Supply management is a relative newcomer to economic policy, even though it had been clearly recognized by Joseph Schumpeter in his classic book, *The Theory of Economic Development*, first published some seventy years ago. Supply management emphasizes that the way the factors of production are used may be more important than their amounts. It emphasizes that growth requires not only that the factors of production keep growing at a desirable pace but also that they are allocated as efficiently as possible. If, for example, investment grows but is progressively channeled into less productive projects, the country's output may not grow.

[6] Most of the formal models that link the fiscal deficit to the balance of payments follow this approach. In these models, it is the size of the macrovariables (the saving rate, the investment rate, the fiscal deficit, etc.) that plays the leading role. These variables are rarely disaggregated, so that the possibilities connected with better resource allocation are not explored.

deficit is reduced by raising taxes or by cutting spending, and regard-less of the specific tax and spending measures used to achieve such a reduction, the balance of payments consequences are assumed to be the same.[7]

Although these alternative versions of the design of stabilization programs have probably never been pursued in their pure form, over the years the formulation of stabilization programs has been much closer to the macroeconomic than the microeconomic alternative,[8] in conformity with the common interpretation of the guidelines on con-ditionality.[9] Until recent years, stabilization programs established fis-cal ceilings on the basis of an implicit model that connected monetary expansion associated with the fiscal deficit to developments in the balance of payments. The countries themselves would then choose the specific ways in which the fiscal ceilings would be observed. Which tax rates should be changed, which new revenue measures should be adopted, and which expenditures should be reduced (or expanded) were left to the authorities to determine, although Fund missions did provide some advice based, where possible, on technical assistance reports. As Sir Joseph Gold put it " ... performance criteria ... must be confined to macroeconomic variables.... The concept of 'macro-economic' variables involves the idea of aggregation ... [and] includes the broadest possible aggregate in an economic category...." Gold goes on to state that " ... the Fund should not become involved in the detailed decisions by which general policies are put into oper-ation...." He concludes that "specific prices of commodities or ser-vices, specific taxes, or other detailed measures to increase revenues or to reduce expenditures would not be considered macroeconomic vari-ables" (Gold, 1979, pp. 32–33).

Specific measures (such as the elimination of subsidies) were on rare occasions made performance criteria in Fund programs, but the main reason for doing so was often deficit reduction and thus demand management.[10] Fiscal changes without direct and immediate bearing on the size of the fiscal deficit (say, revenue-neutral tax reforms) did not receive explicit attention in formal agreements, even though they might have a bearing on the efficiency of the economy. Changes that

---

[7] It must be understood that even this macroeconomic approach will have to depend on specific measures to raise revenue or reduce spending.

[8] The theoretical design of Fund programs as generally interpreted has been much closer to what I have called the macroeconomic approach.

[9] See, for example, Gold (1979), pp. 30–34.

[10] For subsidies, one additional reason was their direct effect on the current account of the balance of payments when the subsidy encouraged the consumption of an imported com-modity.

would increase the fiscal deficit in the short run but would have desirable supply-side effects on the economy over the medium run were not encouraged. The observance of the fiscal ceilings was the most essential fiscal element of a program.

If the country wanted advice on its tax structure, on the structure of its public spending, or on their respective administration, it could request technical assistance from the Fund. No conditionality was attached to the provision or the use of this advice, although Fund missions occasionally used technical assistance reports to provide advice to the countries, especially on how to raise revenues.[11] Technical assistance has been the major channel through which the Fund has directly influenced the structure of tax systems and their administration and, to a lesser extent, the structure of public spending.

With important qualifications, this macroeconomic approach to stabilization programs predominated until a few years ago. Starting with extended Fund facility programs, however, Fund missions began paying more attention to structural aspects in general and specific fiscal aspects in particular,[12] and today much more attention is paid to structural (supply-side) elements in stabilization programs. The transition from the macroeconomic to the microeconomic approach is, however, far from complete. The approach followed in negotiating stabilization programs begins with an estimation of the required reduction in a country's fiscal deficit, given its balance of payments position and the foreign financing presumed to be available, and proceeds, separately and often ex post, to a discussion of specific policies.[13] The connection that is likely to exist, especially over the medium run, between the "required" deficit reduction and the specific measures adopted to make that reduction possible is not accounted for in setting program ceilings. For example, the removal of growth-retarding taxes is not encouraged if alternative revenue sources are not immediately available, as such a removal will immediately increase the fiscal deficit and, given the underlying model used, will presumably lead to a deterioration in the country's external position. Thus, the approach still goes from the macroeconomic to the

---

[11] Technical assistance is provided by the Fund only at the request of a country's authorities.

[12] The extended Fund facility was established in September 1974 to provide financial assistance in support of medium-term programs for up to three years to overcome structural balance of payments maladjustments. The first request for this arrangement, by Kenya, was approved by the Fund in July 1975.

[13] In actual negotiations, the sequence may not appear as described but in essence it is.

microeconomic and much attention is focused on the size of the deficit and on its financing.

Nevertheless, recent Fund programs have increasingly recognized that the specific measures through which fiscal deficits are reduced may determine, especially over the medium and longer run, whether a stabilization program will have durable, beneficial effects on the balance of payments and on growth, or whether these effects will vanish as soon as the program is over. An adequate macroeconomic framework (consistent with a viable balance of payments and with price stability in the short run) is a necessary, but not a sufficient, condition for growth and for stability over the longer run. Stability requires in addition efficient structural policies.

Should the Fund and the authorities focus mainly on macro-economic fiscal variables, as has traditionally been the case? Or should they make specific fiscal policies of equal importance in a program? Putting it more starkly, should the Fund be prepared to walk away from an arrangement with a country in which resources have been badly misallocated, thus reducing its growth potential, if an acceptable core of structural policies is missing even though the traditional mac-roeconomic framework appears adequate? Should Fund missions start the analysis of a program by identifying such a structural core of required policies—that is, a set of specific supply-side measures—that must be implemented over the course of the program before the macroeconomic ceilings are set?[14] The answers to these questions are not as obvious as they might appear at first, as convincing arguments can be presented on both sides.

A first argument in favor of continuing with the traditional, macro-economic approach is that, at least in theory, this approach is objective. Whether or not performance criteria are satisfied is an issue subject, in most cases, to quantification and verification and thus beyond dis-pute.[15] As such, this approach reduces the uncertainty faced by au-thorities. They know that if the country satisfies the performance criteria it will obtain from the Fund the agreed financial support. And, once again, those performance criteria normally relate to macro-economic variables.

---

[14] This might require a change in the conditionality guidelines approved by the Executive Board. Of course, whenever there is no presumption that resources have been badly misal-located, Fund programs would continue to focus on a macroeconomic framework.

[15] "Performance criteria are always objective in order that a member will not be taken by surprise by a decision of the Fund to impede transactions under a stand-by arrangement. The member has maximum assurance, therefore, about the circumstances in which it can engage in transactions with the Fund."—Gold (1979), p. 32.

A second, and perhaps more important, argument is that performance criteria based on ceilings imply less political interference by the Fund in the internal affairs of countries than do criteria related to specific measures. Authorities are likely to object to having to agree to modify a tax in a given way or to modify the level or pattern of public spending.[16] Critics who find present Fund conditionality too rigid are likely to object even more to what might be seen as an extension of that conditionality. Examples of this reaction exist in connection with Fund recommendations to eliminate or reduce subsidies. Many observers feel that these are political decisions that should be left to the authorities and that the Fund should at best offer only an opinion on them.

A third argument in favor of the traditional approach is that discussions about fiscal ceilings, as well as the review of the outcome of these discussions at headquarters, require fewer and less specialized staff resources than do discussions of specific measures. For an institution concerned about its own budget, this is an important consideration. The design of a program can be based on a relatively straightforward view of the relationship between fiscal deficits and balance of payments. Once some assumptions are made, it is far easier to decide what the size of a fiscal ceiling should be than to decide the details of specific policy changes and how these changes influence program objectives.

A fourth argument, closely related to the preceding one, is that, at least in the fiscal area, it is far easier to write a letter of intent in which a country's formal commitments are couched in the form of general ceilings than to write documents that spell out formal commitments in terms of many specific policy changes. It is always difficult, for example, to specify the precise requirements of a tax reform.

There are, however, arguments that caution against exclusive or excessive emphasis on traditional performance criteria that emphasize fiscal ceilings. They favor paying close attention to the microeconomic aspects of fiscal policy, such as the structure of individual taxes, the structure of expenditure, the allocation of investment, the prices charged by public utilities, and public employment. To avoid any misunderstanding on this issue I should emphasize here that the questions raised below about fiscal ceilings should not be interpreted as supporting Fund critics of conditionality. They simply call attention to the arguments (a) that a good stabilization program must not rely exclusively on demand management and (b) that the ceilings used to

---

[16] A few programs have made the total level of public expenditure a performance clause. This can be considered a departure from the traditional narrow interpretation of conditionality guidelines. Generally, the formal agreements have focused on the difference between public expenditure and revenue (i.e., on the deficit).

serve demand management should not be set independently from the structural changes that the country is willing to make. The main justification for this change of emphasis is that, provided the supply response is not insignificant and occurs fairly rapidly, the more far-reaching the structural reform agreed to by the country, the greater will be that supply response (in terms of output, exports, capital repatriation, and the like). Such a supply response may imply that a less stringent demand-management policy may be necessary.

Problems have at times been encountered when ceilings have been imposed on macroeconomic variables. These problems are mentioned to indicate that a program that relies exclusively on performance criteria related to macroeconomic variables may not be capable of providing the hoped-for results. First, the longer ceilings on macro-economic variables are in use, the more ways countries learn to get around them. Ceilings are most useful when a country complies not just with the letter of an agreement but also with its spirit. Unfortunately, there have been instances in which countries have complied with the letter and defied the spirit of an agreement. They have engaged in operations aimed at circumventing the ceilings in order to draw resources from the Fund without making genuine adjustments. To deal with this problem, the Fund has been compelled, in some programs, to increase the number of performance clauses related to the fiscal deficit. This has created a perception of excessive conditionality.

Second, the usual formulation of a stabilization program may give the impression that the relationship between fiscal deficits and program objectives, and especially their relationship with the balance of payments, is clearcut and unambiguous. In other words, it may give the impression of a single-valued functional relationship—that is, so much fiscal deficit implies so much deficit in the current account of the balance of payments. Unfortunately, our knowledge about important economic relationships (such as that between changes in the money supply and changes in prices, and that between changes in prices, changes in nominal exchange rates, and their effects on the balance of payments) is too limited to inspire excessive confidence about the precise level of the fiscal deficit required to achieve a given change in the current account of the balance of payments or in other economic objectives. The truth is that a given fiscal deficit may be associated with a range of balance of payments outcomes.[17]

---

[17] Programs recognize this problem by including (a) reviews to ensure that additional measures are taken to stay on track and (b) a commitment to take additional measures as needed.

Third, the ceilings may, in some cases, divert attention away from
the basic objectives of economic policy. Meeting the ceilings may come
to be seen, within the program period, as an end in itself. During this
period, programs may be judged successful or not depending on
whether ceilings are being met rather than on whether the ultimate
objectives of the program (durable improvement in the balance of
payments, growth, price stability, and so forth) are being achieved.

Finally, and most important, excessive reliance on macroeconomic
ceilings may divert attention away from the quality as well as the
durability of the specific measures used by a country to comply with
its performance clauses. Let me give some examples, starting with the
question of the durability of the fiscal measure. The question to be
raised is: Will a fiscal measure have a permanent impact on the fiscal
deficit? Is, for example, a revenue increase or an expenditure cut of
such a nature as to affect the deficit for years to come, or is it of
a once-and-for-all type? This is an important question if the program's
objective is, as it should be, a permanent improvement in the
economy.

Sometimes tax payments by enterprises have been advanced at
the request of the government,[18] or public expenditures have been
postponed (through the building up of arrears or through the postponement of inevitable expenditures)[19] so that the country can meet
the fiscal ceilings and can, thus, make the next drawing. At other
times, temporary sources of revenue (once-and-for-all taxes, temporary surtaxes, tax amnesties, sales of public assets, and so forth) have
allowed the country to stay within the agreed ceiling without doing
anything to reduce its underlying or core fiscal deficit.[20] At times
governments have used up so much of their political capital in introducing these temporary measures that they no longer have the stam-
ina to make the permanent and growth-promoting policy changes
required to achieve durable adjustment with growth.

In addition to the question of the durability of the fiscal measures
(will their effects survive the program?), there is the important ques-

---

[18] A few years ago the government of a given country pressured a large foreign enterprise
to advance tax payments for the next three years so as to allow the country to comply with
the fiscal ceiling.

[19] This is common with real wages for public employees that are at times reduced to
unsustainable levels during the program but bounce back to a more normal level when the
program is over. Permanent adjustment would more likely result from a reduction of the
permanent public sector work force than from what is often a temporary reduction in real
wages. On the issue of arrears in the payments of goods and services by the government, see
Diamond and Schiller (1987).

[20] For a definition of the concept of core fiscal deficit, see Tanzi and Blejer (1984), p. 119.

tion of the quality (or, if one wishes, of the economic efficiency) of those measures. As far as short-term demand-management policy is concerned, whether a country reduces the fiscal deficit by raising revenue or by cutting expenditure is inconsequential.[21] It is also inconsequential whether it does it through the use of measures that have disincentive effects or through measures that do not have such effects. The stabilization program will fail if the ceiling is not observed; it will not fail if it is observed through growth-retarding measures.

The above discussion should not be interpreted as arguing that stabilization programs should no longer rely on demand management based on a macroeconomic framework that sets ceilings on relevant macroeconomic variables. In my view, the need for such a framework is too obvious to require justification. The discussion simply argues that this framework needs to be supplemented by measures aimed at ensuring that stabilization programs are, first, durable and, second, as growth-promoting as possible. Under present guidelines on conditionality, under which the Fund staff operates, the change advocated in this paper might not be possible. A decision by the Executive Board of the Fund states that "Performance criteria will normally be confined to (i) macroeconomic variables, and (ii) those necessary to implement specific provisions of the Articles or policies adopted under them. Performance criteria may relate to other variables only in exceptional cases..." (International Monetary Fund, 1986, pp. 27–28).

Stabilization Policy and Economic Growth

Growth-promoting stabilization policy requires that the reduction in the fiscal deficit be carried out through fiscal measures that are (a) durable in their effects and (b) efficient in their impact. In other words, the policies chosen must not self-destruct once the program is over and must achieve their deficit-reducing objective with the least possible inhibition of economic growth.

The efficiency of fiscal instruments is important for growth, as much recent work on this issue has demonstrated. Work effort, exports, productive investment, saving, capital flight, foreign investment, and so on, can be affected by the choice of specific fiscal instruments.[22] These choices may play a large role in determining the

---

[21] This is true regardless of the present level of taxation in the country.

[22] The Fiscal Affairs Department of the Fund has produced a series of papers on this issue in the past few years. Some of these papers are expected to be published in a forthcoming book. For specific studies of the relationship between export taxes and exports, see Vito Tanzi (1976), pp. 66–76; Okonkwo (1978); and Sanchez-Ugarte and Modi (forthcoming).

amount of foreign resources a country will have available during and after the program period. Thus, the relationship between changes in the size of fiscal deficits and changes in the ultimate objectives of economic policy, such as growth and stability, is inevitably influenced by the fiscal policy measures utilized. It can make a substantial difference to the growth prospects of a country if the fiscal deficit is reduced by eliminating a totally unproductive expenditure or by raising a tax that has strong disincentive effects, even though in terms of traditional stabilization policy (in terms of short-run fiscal deficit reduction) the result would appear to be the same. The more efficient the measures used to achieve a given deficit reduction, the greater will be the rate of growth, and, assuming an unchanged monetary policy, the lower will be the rate of inflation.

The implication of the above conclusion for stabilization programs is obvious: provided that a country is willing to implement a considerable number of structural measures early enough in a program so that the positive effects of these measures can be felt relatively soon, the Fund should be prepared to require less reduction in the overall fiscal deficit (i.e., to require less austerity) than it would if the structural package were less far reaching or if the country delayed its introduction. Thus, the Fund should explicitly recognize, at the time it enters into an agreement with a country, a trade-off between quantity and quality of fiscal adjustment, a trade-off that would also be influenced by the timing of the introduction of the structural measures. This trade-off should be recognized and, possibly, formalized in program design and negotiations.[23]

This is not the place to discuss in detail the quality of the fiscal measures that could form the structural core of a stabilization program, but a few examples may help convey the importance of this issue. Suppose that an agricultural commodity of wide consumption (say, wheat, corn, or rice) has been subject to an export tax in a country negotiating a Fund program. The elimination of this tax would reduce

---

[23] The potential output of a country is likely to grow if (a) the rate of investment grows while its average productivity and the average productivity of the other factors of production (labor, land, and so on) do not change; (b) if the average productivity of the factors of production increases owing to the removal of distortions, or to technological change, even though the supply of the production factors does not change. If the distortions have, as is often the case, reduced the country's ability to earn foreign exchange or have led to the misuse of the foreign exchange available, their removal will over time increase the flow of foreign exchange available to the country. In other words, the removal of the distortions would have the same effect as an increase in foreign lending to the country. It would thus reduce the need to constrain demand, as this need, in a typical Fund program, is often a function of the scarcity of foreign exchange.

tax revenue and thus raise the fiscal deficit. This, in turn, would have monetary and consequently balance of payments implications, which the macroeconomic framework of Fund programs would assess. But let us consider whether there are countervailing supply-side effects. The removal of the tax would raise the domestic price of the commodity and lead to a reduction in domestic consumption, thus making some additional supply available for exports.[24] In addition, the removal of the export tax would encourage producers to produce more of that product. When this additional production becomes available, exports will increase further. Since the availability of foreign exchange is always a key factor in a stabilization program, focusing only on the demand effect (through the increase of the fiscal deficit) that the elimination of the tax will have, and ignoring the supply effect (through the incentive to produce and export more), is likely to introduce a bias against the elimination of that tax. It may thus possibly lead to programs that require greater demand reduction than might have been necessary.[25]

Or suppose that some additional spending is carried out by the government to repair a road that facilitates the shipping of agricultural products out of the country. Here again the short-run negative effect on the balance of payments associated with the larger fiscal deficit is partly or fully neutralized by the positive effect associated with larger exports. These examples may be extreme but are far from rare. It would be easy to provide additional illustrations of the link between quantity and quality of fiscal adjustment. A perusal of stabilization programs indicates that, despite an increasing awareness of these issues, political difficulties, guidelines on conditionality, and timing concerns have prevented their formal inclusion in Fund programs.

In negotiating programs, the Fund has attempted, with increasing frequency, to ensure that cutbacks in government expenditure are focused on less productive activities. World Bank guidance is sought in this connection. Nevertheless, obvious political sensitivities have limited the degree of Fund involvement in decisions on expenditure policy. As a result, the expenditure policies pursued have in several

---

[24] It should be recalled that an export tax on a commodity X can be decomposed in a production tax on X and a consumption subsidy on X. Thus, the removal of the export tax removes the subsidy to domestic consumption and removes the tax on production. Domestic consumption falls while production and, presumably, exports rise.

[25] Of course, if the authorities propose to reduce the fiscal deficit through an increase in export taxes, then the negative supply-side effects of this policy would require even greater demand management than when these effects are ignored.

instances not been as supportive of the growth objective as they could have been.[26]

An examination of actual cutbacks in capital expenditure in various countries indicates that they have at times been borne by some of the more productive projects. To reduce the budget deficit, cutbacks have sometimes affected productive, externally financed projects despite the fact that loans for part of the total cost of the projects were highly concessionary. At other times, cutbacks have focused on productive, domestically financed, small-scale projects, while externally financed, highly visible, but less productive projects backed by important donors have been protected. Even where a core investment program has been agreed between the country and the World Bank, higher implementation rates for lower-priority projects have often occurred.

A common feature of such policies has been the disproportionate cutback in expenditure on materials, supplies, and maintenance relative to other types of expenditure. As a result, roads, bridges, public buildings, irrigation projects, airports, and other public sector infrastructure have deteriorated by more than would have been necessary, notwithstanding the inevitability of certain adjustments necessitated by the debt crisis.[27] Inadequate maintenance eventually requires expensive projects for reconstruction of deteriorated plants and equipment.[28] In agricultural regions, impassable roads have drastically limited the impact of market-oriented policies aimed at encouraging increased agricultural production. Shortages of materials and supplies have also dramatically limited the productivity of public sector employees, whether in education, medical care, agricultural extension, or tax administration. Across-the-board cutbacks in expenditure have been common. Such an approach fails to address the enormous waste of expenditure in many politically sensitive but unproductive sectors, including defense spending. Significant cutbacks in public sector employment remain the exception. As a result, efforts to cut the public

---

[26] At this point it may be useful to state the obvious: government decisions are often influenced more by political considerations than by considerations of economic efficiency.

[27] These expenditures are generally classified as "current" rather than "capital" expenditure. Therefore, the common view that stabilization programs must protect "investment" may not necessarily lead to the best policy. In some cases, the most productive expenditures are "current" ones.

[28] There is now a growing concern among some experts that the present reductions in fiscal deficits associated with these lower expenditures for maintenance of roads and other infrastructure will necessitate much higher expenditures (and thus higher deficits) in future years, as the lack of maintenance will require expensive rebuilding. This is again an example of the shifting of the fiscal deficit from the present to the future.

sector wage bill have typically resulted in a deterioration in real wages, often greatest among the higher-paid civil servants. The factors encouraging corruption, low productivity, and multiple jobs of civil servants have therefore been intensified.

Tax increases have in some instances included measures that can be expected to have detrimental effects on growth. This has at times occurred in countries that already have very high tax ratios. For example, on many occasions the rates of export duty have been raised (or an export duty has been imposed) following devaluation, on grounds that the exporters would enjoy some sort of "windfall" profit. However, devaluations often simply offset past cost increases. Import surcharges have been levied, or the rates of import duties have been raised, for balance of payments and revenue reasons. As these surcharges have been imposed on products already highly taxed, they have, by increasing the differences between taxed and untaxed imports, increased distortions and reduced growth prospects.[29] Surcharges on the income taxes of individuals and corporations have often been used. Sometimes countries have raised payroll taxes or taxes on interest incomes with undesirable repercussion on employment, saving, and capital flight. In a few cases countries have levied taxes on expatriate employment, or have raised the rates of mining taxes, or have levied taxes on foreign exchange transactions, thus discouraging foreign participation in economic development.

The main point of this discussion is worth repeating. The impact of changes in fiscal deficits on economic objectives depends to a considerable extent on the quality of the specific measures employed. A change in the quality of those measures will change the relationship between the fiscal deficit and the balance of payments, especially over the medium and longer run. The required reduction in the fiscal deficit (the required austerity) needed to achieve a given effect on the basic objectives of economic policy will be more severe as less efficient measures are chosen. For this reason, stabilization programs should systematically deal with microeconomic issues of public finance in addition to other structural policies. Programs must include needed structural changes and must integrate them with the macroeconomic framework.

Several problems arise in connection with the implementation of the approach suggested in this paper. They relate to (a) our knowledge of

---

[29] Imports subjected to import duties are often less than 50 percent of total imports, so that substantial rate increases on the taxed imports are needed to generate significant tax revenue. Of course, as the rates go up so does smuggling.

incentive effects, (b) timing considerations, and (c) political implications.

As to the first point, one could argue that not enough is known about the incentive effect of particular policies to place precise quantitative values on them. This is apparent, but irrelevant. Stabilization programs often rely on exchange rate devaluation even though precise estimates of these responses are not available. They also rely on changes in real interest rates even though, again, the size of the response of financial (and real) saving to changes in real rates cannot be known with precision. The important point is to have a sense of the direction of the effects and some "feel" for their size. If one waits for precise and objective quantifications of these effects, no formal agreement on a stabilization program would ever be included.

As to the timing issue, one could agree that the choice of better policies would in time bring about a more efficient economy and higher rates of growth. But what about the present? Wouldn't, for example, the elimination or the reduction of an efficient tax or an increase in a highly productive government expenditure raise the deficit in the short run, thus necessitating more external or inflationary financing? A simple answer to that question is that important structural changes often bring with them immediate changes in expectations that can influence individuals and corporations to make further changes reinforcing their initial effects.[30] For example, changes that create an environment more favorable to the private sector may encourage individuals to repatriate capital, encourage foreign enterprises to invest in that country, and facilitate foreign borrowing. More foreign money is likely to be made available to countries pursuing structural reforms.[31] Still part of the answer is the fact that, as shown in the example of the export tax, some real effects will often occur early. If structural changes are made early in a program, or even before its formal approval by the Fund, their supply-side effects would probably also occur within the program's duration, so that the initial negative effect on the size of the fiscal deficit could be balanced by a positive effect in the latter phase of the program. Reluctance to allow some initial expansion in the deficit through, say, the removal of inefficient taxes may contribute to the postponement of essential structural adjustment.[32] Finally, this timing question is not limited to

---

[30] This is particularly true when the attitude of the government indicates that these changes are not likely to be reversed soon.

[31] It should be recalled that the Baker initiative is postulated on this assumption.

[32] Many structural changes can be made to be revenue neutral by removing some taxes (adding some expenditure) while at the same time adding some other tax (reducing some other expenditure).

these policies. For example, the existence of J-curve effects indicates that the same problem exists with exchange rate devaluation. Also, so-called ratchet effects may postpone the time when the impact of demand-management policies is felt on effective demand.

The proposed departure is not without political implications. The conditionality guidelines may have to be amended to make it possible for the Fund to include formally in a stabilization program understandings about tax or expenditure reforms in the countries that approach the Fund for programs and where there are significant structural distortions.[33] In some ways this would be a change more of form than of substance, because the Fund has already in recent programs been involved in structural aspects and has tried to persuade some countries to implement particular policy changes. The countries' authorities may object to the proposed change, especially if they perceive it as additional conditionality without their receiving anything in return. Nevertheless, if they became aware that, at the time a program is negotiated, there might be some trade-off between the size of the required macroeconomic adjustment on the one hand (the required austerity) and structural changes on the other, their possible objection to the proposed change might in some cases be less than one would assume a priori.

Concluding Remarks

The above discussion indicates that, if at all possible, a more inductive approach to determining the particulars of the fiscal policy required in stabilization programs would be desirable. In this approach, in addition to identifying the range of adjustment needed at the macroeconomic level, the Fund, in cooperation with the country's experts, would make an inventory of the various changes in both the level and structure of taxes and of public expenditure that would be required to promote the country's growth objective.[34] It would have to take into account the importance that the country's authorities attach to such objectives as equity and the provision of basic needs. The task would then be to determine whether the proposed changes add up to a macroeconomic adjustment package that is consistent with the balance of payments objective. The structural adjustment would be made up of a basic structural core of fiscal measures representing a sine qua

---

[33] That is, some of the documents that reflect the formal understandings between the Fund and the country must spell out the details of the agreement between the two parties as to the tax modifications, changes in public expenditures, and so forth.

[34] Obviously, other structural aspects would also be considered.

non for a program. If this structural core did not add up to the macroeconomic adjustment assumed to be needed, the Fund and the local experts would look for progressively less efficient ways to add to revenues or to reduce expenditures. Should the country's economic difficulties be assumed to originate exclusively from excess demand (that is, if no major structural problems are identified), the negotiations would proceed along more traditional lines.

The country's authorities would be aware that there is a trade-off between the size of the needed demand constraint and the extent of the structural changes. They would know that the more daring and timely they are in introducing structural changes, the more flexibility they would have in demand-management. In essence, the program would be made up of three elements, possibly all of major importance: (a) the traditional macroeconomic framework with ceilings and targets; (b) the structural core; and (c) the investment core, which presumably would indicate, on the basis of World Bank recommendations, the minimum investment, as well as the allocation of that investment, consistent with both growth and balance of payments objectives.

One should not underestimate the difficulties, both technical and political, that a formal pursuit of this alternative would present; and one should recognize that this alternative would be considerably more labor intensive for both the Fund and the countries' experts and policymakers. It is an alternative that requires further thinking before it can be fully implemented.[35] Initial experimentation in well-chosen and willing countries would be indispensable to a full assessment of its general feasibility and to an outline of the procedural steps to be followed.

In this year when the Nobel Prize in economics has been given to James Buchanan for his contributions to public choice theory, it may be appropriate to conclude this paper with a few highly personal thoughts on the political implications of the suggestions it contains.

While aggregate demand may grow independently of structural policies, so that a traditional stabilization program would be sufficient in itself to bring about the needed reduction in that demand and thus the needed adjustment to the economy, it is more often the case that excess demand exists not (or not only) because demand has grown more than it should have, but because supply (including that of foreign exchange) has been constrained by misguided structural policies.

---

[35] The full and formal introduction of structural changes in the theoretical design of Fund programs should be considered one of the main challenges to our future research effort.

For example, financial savings may have been reduced by constraints on nominal interest rates or by excessive taxation of interest income; this reduction may have constricted the supply of domestic financial savings available to finance the deficit and private investment in noninflationary ways, and, because of capital flight, it may have reduced the availability of foreign exchange.[36] Agricultural output may have been reduced by low producer prices that necessitate the import of food. Agricultural exports may have been limited by excessive export taxes, by overvalued exchange rates, and by low prices paid to producers. Food supplies may have been limited by deteriorating transportation systems because of misallocation of public expenditures. In all these examples it is the supply that has been reduced, thus creating imbalances that, in time, manifest themselves as excessive demand. In these cases, demand-management policies alone would reduce the symptoms of these imbalances but would not eliminate the causes. Thus, stabilization programs might succeed stabilization programs without bringing about a durable adjustment unless the basic causes of imbalances are addressed.

One major difficulty in dealing with these basic issues is that the policies that I have called "misguided" may be misguided only in an economic and not in a political sense. Public choice theorists would emphasize the fact that these policies may be quite rational, at least in the short run, if assessed from a purely political viewpoint.[37] They would argue that structural problems exist not necessarily because policymakers made technical mistakes in their policymaking, perhaps because of poor economic understanding. Rather, public choice theorists would argue that through these policies policymakers have tried to promote their own political objectives. Furthermore, the time horizon of policymakers is generally so short that they do not take into full account the long-run implications of their policies on the economy. These policies create "rents" for groups whose support the government needs in order to stay in power, even though they may in time reduce the level of income for the majority of citizens.[38]

---

[36] For an analysis of the ways in which deficits get financed in developing countries and on the limits to those sources of financing, see Tanzi (1986), pp. 139–52.

[37] All the literature on rent-seeking that represents an important chapter of public choice would support this view. See especially Buchanan, Tollison, and Tullock (1980); and Tollison (1982), pp. 575–602.

[38] For example, if agricultural prices are kept low in order to subsidize the real wages of urban dwellers, the government may acquire the support of the latter, but the cost may be a low rate of growth and increasing economic difficulties over the longer run. See, for example, some of the studies in Harberger (1984).

If this public choice interpretation of economic policy is at least partly valid, and I do not know to what extent it is, it implies that policies aimed at structural reforms will often be resisted more than macroeconomic stabilization policies. They would be resisted because they would remove these rents from precisely those whose support the government needs and would thus reduce the leverage that the policymakers have for staying in power. In part, structural reforms would reduce the *raison d'être* for the government in power. As a consequence, it would seem to follow from these theories that major structural reforms have the best chance of being carried out when there is a major political change—that is, when a government that has long been in power is replaced by a totally different one—so that the political interests of the new policymakers are not tied to existing structural policies. This public-choice-inspired hypothesis should be amenable to testing. It seems to have some plausibility, but only a careful analysis of actual situations can assess its validity as a useful tool to explain changes that occur in economic policy.

References

Buchanan, James M., Robert D. Tollison, and Gordon Tullock, eds., *Toward a Theory of the Rent-Seeking Society*, Texas A&M University, Economic Series, No. 4 (College Station: Texas A&M Press, 1980).

Chu, Ke-Young, "External Shocks and the Process of Fiscal Adjustment in a Small Open Developing Economy," IMF Working Paper, No. 87/11 (Washington: International Monetary Fund, March 2, 1987).

Diamond, Jack, and Christian Schiller, "Government Arrears in Fiscal Adjustment Programs," IMF Working Paper, No. 87/3 (Washington: International Monetary Fund, February 10, 1987).

Gold, Joseph, *Conditionality*, IMF Pamphlet Series, No. 31 (Washington: International Monetary Fund, 1979).

Harberger, Arnold C., ed., *World Economic Growth* (San Francisco, California: Institute for Contemporary Studies, 1984).

International Monetary Fund, *Selected Decisions of the International Monetary Fund and Selected Documents*, Twelfth Issue (Washington, April 30, 1986).

Kelly, Margaret R., "Fiscal Adjustment and Fund-Supported Programs, 1971–80," *Staff Papers*, International Monetary Fund (Washington), Vol. 29 (December 1982), pp. 561–602.

Okonkwo, Ubadigbo, "Export Taxes on Primary Products in Developing Countries: The Taxation of Cocoa Exports in West Africa" (unpublished; Washington: International Monetary Fund, November 29, 1978).

Sanchez-Ugarte, Fernando, and Jitendra R. Modi, "Are Export Duties Optimal in Developing Countries?: Some Supply-Side Considerations," in *Supply-Side Tax Pol-*

icy: Its Relevance to Developing Countries (Washington: International Monetary Fund, forthcoming).

Tabellini, Guido, "Fiscal Policy Response to the External Shocks of 1979 in Selected Developing Countries: Theory and Facts" (unpublished; Washington: International Monetary Fund, December 26, 1985).

Tanzi, Vito, "Export Taxation in Developing Countries: Taxation of Coffee in Haiti," *Social and Economic Studies* (Kingston), Vol. 25 (March 1976), pp. 66–76.

———, "Is There a Limit to the Size of Fiscal Deficits in Developing Countries?" in *Public Finance and Public Debt*, ed. by Bernard P. Herber (Detroit, Michigan: Wayne State University Press, 1985).

———, "Fiscal Policy Responses to Exogenous Shocks in Developing Countries," *American Economic Review, Papers and Proceedings* (Nashville, Tennessee), Vol. 76 (May 1986), pp. 88–91.

———, and Mario I. Blejer, "Fiscal Deficits and Balance of Payments Disequilibrium in IMF Adjustment Programs," in *Adjustment, Conditionality, and International Financing*, ed. by Joaquin Muns (Washington: International Monetary Fund, 1984), pp. 117–36.

Tollison, Robert D., "Rent Seeking: A Survey," *Kyklos* (Berne), Vol. 35 (Fasc. 4, 1982), pp. 575–602.

Comments

Luis Jorge Garay S.

The purpose of Vito Tanzi's paper, "Fiscal Policy and Stabilization Programs," is to show some methodological and operational problems that are inherent in the traditional adjustment programs of the International Monetary Fund, even within their own theoretical framework.

The paper has the merit of spelling out certain basic problems in the analytical framework, with particular attention to the fiscal area, although the naming and conceptual interpretation of the two alternative approaches contrasted with each other are unfortunate. To call the approach that is put forward as a framework of reference the "macroeconomic approach" is inappropriate, because strictly speaking the subject of study in a macroeconomic approach is the analysis of the behavioral interrelationships between those factors that play a decisive role in the evolution of a specific economic phenomenon. In point of fact, the operational approach adopted by the Fund is based on a partial study of disequilibrium situations at given moments in time, but not on a study of the behavioral relationships of the various components of factors that determine the disequilibrium itself, of the dynamics of the process leading to the disequilibrium, or of the transition to the path to equilibrium. The approach advocated by Tanzi also suffers to a large extent from this kind of fundamental shortcoming.

In this context, a "macro approach" to tackling the problem of fiscal deficit has to focus on the dynamics of the process that generates the deficit; dynamics that include not just various facets of the economy but also various instances over time and between sectors within the public sector.

The difference between a macro approach and a mere "aggregate approach" is radical and can, in general, lead to substantially different economic policy considerations. It is therefore appropriate for me to try to clarify the scope of the essential contrasts between them, making brief reference to certain basic shortcomings of the aggregate approach that could be avoided, or at least reduced, in the context of a strictly macroeconomic approach.

In the first place, a purely aggregate approach does not guarantee the ability to identify a serious partial or even quasi-generalized disequilibrium situation. Indeed, in practice it is feasible and in no way surprising to observe an "apparent" fiscal equilibrium at the aggregate level for the public sector as a whole, despite the fact that behind it there lies a significant range of partial disequilibria, which, although they may even offset one another (in terms of monetary value) between the various official entities, are nonetheless the clear expression of a typical disequilibrium situation. To use the terminology of recent economic theory on the subject to illustrate this, rather than being a symptom of a state of equilibrium, a situation of this kind is in reality merely one of a number of temporary situations that are generated in a disequilibrium process. To place special emphasis on the aggregate of public sector deficit, without having sufficient understanding of the process by which the fiscal disequilibrium is generated, of the instances of actions, or of the timing of the factors acting upon it, quite frequently leads to fiscal aggregate adjustment programs with a short-term horizon, involving the adoption of policies and corrective measures that are certainly effective in swiftly controlling the deficit level, but which may actually generate conditions that foster disequilibrium in the medium term. This runs counter to the whole purpose of the adjustment program, which is to facilitate the transition to equilibrium.

Second, the fact that most adjustment programs are short-term rather than medium-term tends to encourage the authorities to apply discretionary measures that have a visible impact soon after their introduction, which may not be the most appropriate way of achieving all their objectives, of encouraging continuity in a recovery program of the kind referred to in the adjustment programs, or of guaranteeing the consolidation of some of the vital conditions for economic growth with stability in the medium term.

There is not necessarily a one-to-one relationship between a program's targets and the specific policy measures that will guarantee attainment of those targets. In practice, to the extent that some leeway is given in the choice of measures, the possibility increases of medium-term criteria coming into play in seeking to comply with the spirit of the adjustment, and of policy priorities additional to those established in the program being taken into consideration. Such leeway, obviously, can be correspondingly broader, ceteris paribus, the more flexible the program is toward changes in the environment (as is explained below), the longer the period prescribed for reaching the proposed targets, the less the relative intensity of the adjustment in terms of the magnitude of the initial disequilibrium, and the smaller the range and depth of the disequilibrium process that one is trying to correct.

Consequently, only when the costs and benefits over time and the trade-offs between targets have been weighed in a medium-term context and of the various modalities of adjustment will it be possible to define a "desirable" program in which the flexibility, durability, intensity, extent, and "quality" of the adjustment can be duly reconciled.

Third, the time horizon, the level of aggregation, and the selection of reference parameters used to frame the traditionally tailored adjustment programs have contributed to the imposition of qualificatory standards on the attainment of the set targets, which in principle do not adequately take into account the number of significant changes that take place in the environment (both domestic and international) in which the performance of the economic aggregates for the design and specifications of the program was simulated.

Despite this, it must be recognized that from the outset two exception clauses were established regarding compliance with adjustment programs arranged with the Fund: (i) the so-called waiver clause, under which compliance with a target or targets is waived provided the deviation in compliance is slight and reversible in the short run and that it is not detrimental to compliance with the program as a whole, and (ii) the modifiability clause applicable in cases of substantial alterations in the environment—large, irreversible, and quasi-generalized—which make it necessary to change the program in order to ensure that all those alternative measures that would be suitable in the new circumstances are adopted, as well as to ensure that the spirit and the quality of the adjustment "desired" at the outset are complied with. This latter modality has been applied only on very few occasions in very special situations, for which reason, at least until now, it has not been possible to attain a reasonable degree of flexibility in the traditional criteria for certifying compliance with a program.

Fortunately, about last October the way began to be opened in the desired direction by another form of exception, intermediate between the other two, included in the financial agreement signed by Mexico and the Fund, which provides for the introduction of adjustments in a target or targets functionally related to the degree of alteration (or change) in one or several of the economic variables that decisively affect the behavior of the aggregates of the economy, but on condition that not only the spirit of the core of policies and measures stipulated therein but also their orientation, intensity, and arrangement over time remained intact. One outstanding example of this kind of cause is the unforeseen, drastic, and lasting change (in terms of the program horizon) in the world price of a product whose exports generate a large proportion of the foreign exchange of the program country.

Fourth, because the traditional adjustment programs are based on one and the same analytical framework, regardless of the nature, depth, and scope of the disequilibrium process, the consequent therapy for rehabilitation, based on a diagnosis derived from the framework referred to, has of necessity taken a standard form. However, to avoid entering into a discussion which would not be appropriate in this commentary, suffice it to say by way of illustration that there is a near consensus on the desirability, or at least the expediency, of adopting shock tactics for those economies subject to acute, lasting, and quasi-generalized disequilibrium. Obviously, such therapy contrasts fundamentally with the one prescribed by the orthodox approach to adjustment.

In these circumstances, it seems clear that the more severe the maladjustment the more the modalities, intensity, and duration of the recovery process will need to take into account the inherent conditions of the dynamics of disequilibrium. It should be remembered in this respect that regardless of the analytical framework adopted no theory has yet been developed (even for simplified systems) to study the "optimum" level of maladjustment or disequilibrium, let alone one on a "desirable" framework for transition to equilibrium. The absence of such a theory makes the application of a single set of universal "hard-

and-fast" rules regarding the "desirable" depth and timing of the adjustment even more vulnerable.

Having mentioned some of the theoretical and conceptual defects and lacunae in the aggregate approach, and the difficulties—some of them insuperable in practice—of the strict macro approach, we should also mention a number of basic institutional and operational precepts in the traditional programs which further exacerbate some of the problems just mentioned. Three of them, to refer only to those most relevant in the area of public finance, relate to the procedural and operational area of expenditure policy and to the infrastructure available for its effective execution.

In the economic analysis of public finance, according to effective operations at the cash level, the traditional approach is posited on the following basic tenets: unity of the cash area in the public Treasury, an automatic and efficient system of transfers within the State, and perfect fungibility of money in the process of public expenditure. While such premises are intimately interrelated, their relevance varies according to the stage in the process of expenditure in question. Thus, for example, the fungibility of money is fundamental in promoting adequate temporal and financial synchronization between the budget operation and the execution of the expenditure. The efficiency of the transfer system is important in promoting timely and decisive mobilization of resources between public entities (in the form of "pure" transfers or "soft" loans, among other mechanisms) as a prerequisite for the productive and (socially) profitable use of the financial surpluses that some of these generate. As is evident, the unity of the cash area ensures careful coordination between the moment the financial resource enters the cash process (for example, as a budget counterpart resource), the moment at which it generates the expenditures commitment, and the moment at which the expenditure is paid out in the cash process.

However, given that in practice such tenets are difficult to satisfy, compliance with the targets of a fiscal adjustment program whose design does not take due account of the scope and implications of failure to observe its conditions can lead to such problems as (i) accentuating the existing distortions in budget execution by not taking due account of the pressure of overhanging commitments from previous exercises (for example, by departing from a proposal to "reorganize" the accounts payable of the Treasury), (ii) obstructing proper synchrony between budget management and expenditure execution, which not only hinders the efficient and timely allocation of resources but may also even encourage such anomalies as "overfinancing" the

overall fiscal deficit (with the consequent building up of the cash
position, most of the time drawn from costly credit resources), and (iii)
obstructing a "balanced" relationship between the priorities of fiscal,
monetary, exchange (e.g., accumulation of international reserves) and
debt policy targets, even to the extent of placing disproportionate
emphasis on some of these policies at times when action on the others
would be appropriate. (It comes as no surprise to see fiscal policy
being made relatively subordinate to short-term money management.)

Thus, for reasons of an operational and institutional nature, a reduction in the level of disequilibrium, or even its stabilization at a
"desirable" level (in this case, of the overall fiscal deficit for effective
cash-based operations) does not necessarily imply that there has been
a corresponding real adjustment (of public finances), or that the
transition has been made to the path of medium-term equilibrium. On
the contrary, more likely than not the adjustment will be merely
"apparent, sporadic, and partial," failing to counteract the factors
determining the disequilibrium. Here, indeed, we find another of the
problems that can be best dealt with by a strictly macroeconomic
approach (or at any rate with better data with which to judge than in
the case of a purely aggregate approach).

Before concluding, I would like to review some of the ideas with
which Tanzi winds up his paper, with particular reference to the
development of an approach to the design and specification of
"macroeconomic structural adjustment" programs. Although sticking
as closely as possible to the traditional framework as their scheme of
reference, these programs would include a structural core of measures (with special importance in the fiscal area) and an investment
allocation core in line with the targets of economic growth and
"viability" of the balance of payments in the medium term.

As the above-mentioned approach contemplates adjustment in the
medium-term and long-term horizons and as this in turn gives it a
structural rather than a current or short-term character, there immediately arises the institutional concern as to what should be the proper
international institution to promote the implementation of this kind of
adjustment program. According to the division of roles under the
Bretton Woods Agreement, the task would most properly be carried
out by the competent authorities of the World Bank rather than
those of the International Monetary Fund. Although it is, so to say,
artificial to set forth with complete assurance a universal rule for
demarcating the boundaries between short-term and medium-term
policies, because a medium-term policy would in any case by its nature
include a body of short-term measures, what is undeniable is that the

further one moves into the framework of a macroeconomic adjustment with a medium-term horizon, with structural implications and with action required at the level of investment allocations, the more suitable the World Bank rather than the Fund will be to take charge of putting into practice programs such as those referred to.

Despite the above, there remains not just an element of contradiction, but also a lack of definition such as to the order of priority of objectives, policies, and conditionality consistent with these two kinds of adjustment programs, when we are at a transitional stage between these alternative approaches. This has been a frequent occurrence in the recent past, with program, sectoral, and structural adjustment credits granted by the World Bank simultaneously with the traditional stand-by programs agreed with the International Monetary Fund.

Consequently, in order to avoid the harmful coexistence of cross-conditionalities with mutually contradictory criteria, as has happened in some countries, it would be necessary to thoroughly revise the functions of the World Bank and the Fund with regard to the incorporation into the world monetary system of an approach to adjustment different from the one currently in use, such as a macroeconomic structural adjustment would constitute.

Ricardo Hausmann

The paper presented by Vito Tanzi falls under the heading of the new thinking on adjustment with growth that has been gaining ground since 1985, in that it analyzes the way in which the International Monetary Fund has defined adjustment programs and proposes an alternative view which, he suggests, could make for a better connection between stabilization and growth.

The Fund's stabilization programs have been based on the Polak model, which links domestic credit expansion with the level of international reserves, using the accounting identity developed through the monetary approach to the balance of payments. This identity stipulates that international reserves are the difference between the demand for money, considered as endogenous, and the expansion of domestic credit. This identity is formally defined as follows:

$$RIN = M2 - CDF - CDP,$$

where RIN is the level of net international reserves and CDF and CDP are domestic credit to the fiscal sector and domestic credit to the private sector, respectively.

The programs operate by defining desired levels of international reserves, growth, and inflation and thereby calculate the private sector's demand for money and credit. The accounting identity is used to calculate the public deficit that would be consistent with the abovementioned targets. Consequently, according to this approach there is a fairly direct link between the fiscal deficit and the performance of the balance of payments.

Tanzi attacks this view by suggesting that the performance of the balance of payments is not unconnected with the particular way in which the reduction of the fiscal deficit is addressed. He illustrates this argument by referring to the adverse effects of taxes on exports and of cutting back on infrastructure maintenance. The first example increases domestic demand and reduces the supply of exportable goods, with the result that the contraction in domestic demand via a reduction in the fiscal deficit must be greater than it would be in an alternative program not using this instrument. The second example emphasizes the impact on the supply of exports and supports the same argument. Other examples relate to the durability of the proposed fiscal changes. The temporary and unsustainable reduction in the public administration wage bill, the postponement of necessary projects, and a reduction of priority investments are examples of less-than-optimum fiscal adjustments using a medium-term logic.

Tanzi consequently proposes a new way of addressing stabilization plans so that fiscal reforms can be lasting and support the needed adjustment in the balance of payments, given their effects not only on aggregate demand but also on the supply side.

The microeconomic approach he proposes would begin with an analysis of the specific revenue and expenditure reforms and then ascertain whether they provide the requisite adjustment at the macroeconomic level. Tanzi also discusses the advantages and disadvantages of this system, highlighting the political interference that this new system would imply, the lack of a clear Fund mandate in these areas, and the inadequacy of the Fund's budget to cope with this kind of program.

The need to change the way in which the Fund formulates its adjustment programs reflects a shortcoming of the Polak model. Tanzi recognized this but limits his criticisms to the failure to consider the microeconomic impact of fiscal policy on supply. This would seem to be the right time to mention other limitations of the Polak approach that should be taken into account when redefining the adjustment programs.

The Polak approach assumes that tax policies affect demand in the same way irrespective of the form they take. However, it is obvious that not every tax increase produces a similar reduction in domestic expenditure. For example, an increase in domestic taxes to offset a reduction in fiscal revenue from exports resulting from a deterioration in the terms of trade is proportionally more contractive. Likewise, a progressive income or wealth tax reduces real domestic expenditure to a lesser extent than an increase in indirect taxes on mass consumer goods.

Another assumption generally used is the stability of demand for money. This assumes a stable demand for external financial assets by resident agents. However, capital flight is frequently a countercyclical phenomenon, as economic recession reduces the return to fixed assets and increases uncertainty, thereby encouraging the outflow of capital. A reduction in economic activity causes a fall in international reserves, which makes an interest rate hike necessary, as well as further contraction of demand, leading to the need for an overadjustment to cope with the capital flight.

It is important to stress that despite the fact that the Fund's Articles of Agreement do not question capital controls, it has neither developed nor proposed any policies to limit the flight of foreign exchange by administrative means and, at the same time, it has not criticized those governments of industrial countries that have converted their financial markets into tax havens for funds coming from other countries. The impact of a recessionary adjustment on capital flight and the demand for money deserves more extensive consideration than the Polak model has suggested.

In Polak's approach it is impossible to analyze the medium-term consequences of short-term adjustments. In particular, declining public and private investment brought on by contractionary policies in the fiscal and monetary areas delay the adjustment of the productive infrastructure and make lower growth rates in medium-term demand a necessity. The compensation over time cannot be analyzed. In this regard, adjustment programs tend to be less than perfect in that they are based on the implicit hypothesis of credit rationing. Consequently, it generates a short-term adjustment greater than that which would result from optimization over time. This results in a lower growth rate in the country and greater balance of payments difficulties, which in turn lead to a request for additional medium-term resources from the Fund and the World Bank.

The deterioration of the fiscal accounts of Argentina, Mexico, and Venezuela partly reflects the consequences of the earlier vicious circle of external public indebtedness and private capital flight. Real deval-

uation produces a redistribution of wealth taking the form of capital
gains for external asset holders and fiscal deficits reflecting the loss of
capital in the public sector.[1] Polak's answer would be to translate this
loss into a contraction of domestic absorption via fiscal restraint without reflecting the specific characteristics of this situation. This points
to the possibility of more carefully defining the causes of fiscal deficits
in order to design policies more relevant to each situation. In particular, a tax on external asset holdings and the income they generate,
combined with an international system for fiscal cooperation, would
help to reduce the contractionary impact of fiscal correction.

The Polak model does not distinguish between the different effects
on the balance of payments of cuts in expenditure on tradable goods
and of cuts in expenditure on nontradable goods. The former
strengthens the balance of payments whereas the latter only produces
a contraction in domestic activity, especially when there are idle resources. The composition of public expenditure between demand for
tradables and nontradable goods is, consequently, together with exchange policy, an important instrument for making changes in the
structure of expenditure (expenditure switching), thus avoiding the
inefficient cuts in economic activity that are characteristic of more
aggregated approaches, such as Polak's (expenditure cutting).

The thrust of these arguments is that the range of restrictions involved in the current approach used by the Fund to design the fiscal
packages within its stabilization programs should be expanded. The
revision proposed by Tanzi could be a propitious occasion to tackle
these other issues, and expand the range of effects to include those not
previously taken into account. In particular, Tanzi would like to limit
criticism to the contradictions between deficit reduction and the economic distortions generated with regard to the microeconomic model
of general equilibrium. It would, however, be advisable to delve further into the other macroeconomic aspects that appear to have received insufficient attention under the traditional approach.

Tanzi's paper seeks a greater degree of integration between stabilization and growth. For this, either explicitly or implicitly, a growth
theory is needed to serve as a framework for operative decisions.
Nothing explicit about this is stated in the paper. However, from the
examples proposed, an implicit theory that seems to support the proposition can be deduced.

[1] On this question, see Miguel Rodríguez, "Consequences of Capital Flight for Latin
American Debtor Countries," in Capital Flight and the Third World Debt, ed. by John
Williamson and Donald R. Lessard (Washington: Institute for International Economics, forth-
coming).

This theory appears to affirm the following: some fiscal policies tend to generate distortions in relative prices, producing an inefficient allocation of resources and consequently a lower growth rate. A fiscal reform to reduce distortions will consequently permit increased growth in the medium term.

There is no doubt that this argument contains an element of truth. There are fiscal practices which act as bottlenecks to development. However, this does not necessarily mean that the allocation of resources generated by more extensive use of market mechanisms is an adequate guide for the allocation of budget resources. The dynamic comparative advantages and externalities require analysis and attention that are difficult to reduce to the argument in favor of the elimination of distortions. In the case of externalities such as public goods, the market fails by definition. The allocation of resources in this area calls for a body of criteria that are not easy to systematize and include in a generic view of the necessary changes.

The experience of successful developing countries highlights the importance of dynamic comparative advantages. This assumes government planning and direction, a feature common to the Republic of Korea, the Taiwan Province of China, and Brazil, to generate an allocation of resources that the market would not recognize as efficient in the short run. In oil exporting countries, the "Dutch disease" makes an explicit policy necessary to avoid having market signals work against industrial and agricultural activity. The decline in the terms of trade for primary commodities and energy has reduced the relevance of static comparative advantages as a resource allocation mechanism consistent with a successful development strategy. The coordinated allocation of public resources through expenditure in education, technology, financial subsidies, and trade policies and through government purchases seems to be a frequent practice in the successful countries mentioned above, but is a violation of the general equilibrium model.

A specific discussion of the fiscal reforms that the Fund would propose in the new adjustment programs could not leave out these subjects and consequently calls for some explanation of the theory and strategy of growth going beyond the mere reduction of distortions.

Given the stage that consideration of the relationship between stabilization and growth appears to have reached, it would seem a little premature to increase substantially the conditionality of Fund loans. In the first place, the tax question is still a very sensitive issue from the political point of view, as it involves questions of constitutionality. The separation of powers that is a feature of democratic republics has given the Legislature power over the budget. This means that the Executive Branch is not able to commit itself regarding aspects of conditionality such as those assumed in Tanzi's proposal. Programs would require the conditional approval of the Executive Branch and a lengthy Legislative debate before they could be accepted. This is incompatible with the time frame and urgency generally associated with Fund programs.

The problem is exacerbated by the cartelization of the international financial market through bank advisory committees, which also require prior agreement with the Fund. The democratic principle that emerged from the American Revolution that there should be "no taxation without representation" would in practice mean that the major stockholders in the Fund are overrepresented with regard to the very interests that democracy should in theory reconcile.

Furthermore, there is the question of the risk, which is unevenly distributed between countries and the Fund. As Tanzi rightly points out, our knowledge of the behavior of the various real economies is limited, despite which policy decisions still have to be taken. Put in other terms, there is a problem of our ignorance of economic dynamics when it comes to preparing policy measures. This ignorance carries with it the risk that the economy may not react in the way theory would have it. This risk, which could be called the "ignorance risk," falls wholly on the countries. Consequently, it is to be hoped that the countries will show a stronger aversion to the ignorance risk than has the Fund. The fiscal reforms resulting from Tanzi's microeconomic approach would reflect this asymmetry, which would make the discussions difficult. Matters are made worse by the fact that the ignorance risk increases exponentially as one attempts to move toward more specific reforms.

Consequently, if experimentation with the new approach is not coupled with a risk redistribution scheme, only the countries whose state is most critical, that is, those that have suffered the greatest erosion of their sovereignty, would be ready to participate.

One way of redistributing risk would be to tie in contingent Fund financing if the measures do not produce the expected results. For example, an export tax reduction that did not generate the expected improvements in the balance of payments would lead to an additional loan from the Fund. In this way, the countries' reluctance to absorb the loss of fiscal revenue would be reduced because the Fund would partly cover the ignorance risk. This would not be an easy scheme to implement in many cases, but it does demonstrate the desire for change that would exist in countries if the risk were more fairly distributed.

Last, it might be advisable to change the way in which the Fund has been operating. At present, the Fund's financing is secondary to the conditionality imposed by the agreement, as the emphasis lies in its being a requirement of the international banking community. It would perhaps be interesting for Tanzi's ideas to be implemented, at least initially, in countries that are not renegotiating their external debts and not suffering from an acute stabilization problem. From this viewpoint, the agreement with the Fund would be seen more as financing for a structural change than as a circumstantial stabilization measure. It would imply a redefinition of the roles of the Fund and the World Bank, as the traditional division of labor between these two institutions runs counter both to Tanzi's proposal and to the approach to implementation that is suggested here.

Adjustment, Indebtedness, and Economic Growth: Recent Experience

Guillermo Ortiz

More than four years have passed since the outbreak of the debt crisis. During this time, considerable experience has been gained with regard both to the ability of the world economy and the international financial system to respond and to the nature and effectiveness of the adjustment programs implemented by the indebted countries. An initial phase, in which there was a dramatic improvement in the external imbalances of the indebted countries, was followed by a short period during which it was thought that the strategy adopted in 1982 might effectively restore the economic growth and creditworthiness of these countries and ensure the resumption of voluntary credit flows from the international banking community. However, it soon became evident that the position of the indebted countries was still deteriorating, and in late 1985 the U.S. Secretary of the Treasury made an important statement on the debt problem in which he acknowledged that only economic growth could overcome these difficulties.

Since then, it has become fashionable to talk about "growth-oriented adjustment programs." The factor supposedly distinguishing these from the more traditional programs—that is, the growth-stimulating component—is their emphasis on the implementation of policies promoting "structural change." The logic of this approach is that measures to curb demand have in most cases failed to revive the indebted countries' economies, and on the other hand have been extremely costly in terms of production and consumption. As a result, priority must now be given to stimulating aggregate supply.

154

Much has been said and written about the best policies for improving the allocation of resources (essential components of the structural change strategies), about policies on exchange rates, interest rates, and flexible and appropriate prices and tariffs (avoiding overvaluation and paying higher rates), about trade liberalization, and about the privatization of public enterprises, the reduction of fiscal deficits (and, in general, of public sector participation in economic activity), and so forth.[1] But what has yet to be defined is how and under what conditions the growth is to occur—before, after, or at the same time as stabilization. Nor has the problem of financing been resolved, or that of the institutional framework in which this growth is to take place, or whether it is feasible given the existing amounts of and burden posed by debt.

This work does not presume to help resolve these issues, but is rather a collection of observations on some relevant aspects of recent experience that could be useful in formulating a "new strategy," which pinpoints some conceptual and operational problems that have been encountered at different levels. The paper is organized as follows. Section two provides a brief review of how the debt strategy has developed, with emphasis on the problem of financing (section three). The adjustment process is then examined in general in section four, with attention to how the existence of high indebtedness levels has caused problems and raised obstacles specific to the adjustment process. Finally, the last section raises a number of questions on the possible significance of a new stage of adjustment with growth.

Implementation and Results of Debt Strategy

In evaluating the status of and outlook for the debt problem, the Managing Director of the Fund took note of some of the major achievements made through early 1986. *First,* there had been a sharp turnaround in the external imbalances of the developing countries, the magnitude of which "few could have imagined." The current account deficit of the indebted countries had dropped from the equivalent of 30 percent of their exports in 1982 to 3 percent in 1985; *second,* the developing countries had taken firm adjustment measures, reflected primarily in large cuts in their fiscal deficits and a notable improvement in the competitiveness of their exports; *third,* debt servicing had continued, and principal had been restructured in an orderly fashion (de Larosière, 1986).

---

[1] See, for example, Balassa (1986).

Along with these achievements, it should be added that the pragmatic and cooperative approach adopted at the onset of the crisis—
and which the Fund played a central role in formulating—not only
successfully prevented a destabilization of the international financial
system but also helped to establish mechanisms enabling the indebted
countries to cope with the initial stages of adjustment. A cornerstone
of this strategy was the adoption of a "case-by-case" approach;
although there were aspects common to all the countries affected, the
circumstances of each in terms of debt level and structure and of
payment capacity were sufficiently dissimilar to merit individual treatment. Another essential aspect of this strategy was the negotiation of
"concerted" financing packages, involving a mix of resources from
official and multilateral institutions and from commercial banks. The
latter were frequently obtained under considerable pressure from the
governments of industrial countries and from multilateral institutions.

Thanks to the balance of payments progress mentioned above and
the fact that some of the heavily indebted countries, helped by a
favorable external environment, appeared to be recovering from the
sharp recession of 1983, the debt problem appeared to be on the road
to recovery toward the end of 1984.[2] Indeed, as shown in Table 1, the
Latin American and Caribbean countries as a whole achieved a slight
increase in per capita gross domestic product (GDP), while the indicators that measure these countries' payment capacity (debt/export
and debt/GDP ratios) developed favorably. However, the factors on
which this optimism was based were of short duration. The slowdown
in the pace of world economic activity, the continuing decline in commodity prices, and the decrease in the growth of international trade
in 1985 and in 1986 to date have meant considerably less bright prospects.

Four years after introduction of the adjustment strategy, we must
ask ourselves what have been the costs of adjustment and the distribution, what is the present situation of the indebted countries in terms
of their capacity to continue servicing their external debt and to
return to a path of sustained economic growth after four years of
adjustment, and whether the restoration of normal debtor-creditor
relationships is yet in sight. Although the adjustment process is far

---

[2] This viewpoint was widespread in the private financial and governmental circles of the
creditor countries and in international organizations. It is reflected, for example, in the
positive tone of the conclusions drawn in September 1984 by the Interim Committee on the
outlook for the world economy and the debt problem. Cline's noted study appeared at about
the same time (1984); it, too, took an optimistic view and supported implementation of the
strategy in the form in which it had evolved.

Table 1. Latin America and the Caribbean: Selected Economic Indicators, 1982–86

	1982	1983	1984	1985	1986[1]
	Annual growth in percent				
GDP	−1.0	−3.1	3.2	3.7	2.7
GDP per capita	−3.3	−5.3	0.8	1.5	0.5
Volume of exports	−2.5	8.5	8.6	−1.7	0.6
Volume of imports	−1.8	−3.2	−1.2	−0.7	1.3
Terms of trade	−5.4	−3.0	3.5	−2.6	−17.5
	Billions of U.S. dollars				
Current account balance	−41.9	−10.7	−3.1	−4.6	−17.1
Net resource flow[2]	−5.5	−19.2	−24.8	−33.4	−31.4
	Ratios				
Debt/GDP	43.5	48.5	46.9	46.1	46.9
Debt/Exports	273.1	290.4	275.2	296.2	331.7
Interest/Exports	32.0	30.6	29.6	28.9	27.7

Source: International Monetary Fund, *World Economic Outlook: A Survey by the Staff of the International Monetary Fund* (Washington, October 1986).

[1] Estimates.

[2] Difference between debt service payments and new borrowing.

from complete and the problems associated with excessive indebtedness will probably continue into the foreseeable future, there have already been many studies that try to evaluate both the results and the feasibility of continuing with the strategy followed so far.[3] As regards the first question, the magnitude and distribution of the costs of adjustment, suffice it to say that the 1980s are being referred to as the "lost decade" in most countries with debt problems—particularly in Latin America—in view of the highly likely prospect that per capita incomes in 1990 will be less than in 1980.[4] Up to 1985, per capita GDP in Latin America and the Caribbean had fallen by more than 6 percent (Table 1), and wages and per capita consumption declined even more sharply.[5]

---

[3] An interesting study by Sachs (1986) summarizes the academic debate on the debt problem and also contributes new ideas. The study under Taylor's direction (1986) is an effort to compare the recent adjustment experience of the indebted countries and to evaluate the policies recommended by the Fund.

[4] Excluding Brazil and Cuba, the ECLAC estimates that per capita output in Latin America fell by 8.8 percent between 1981 and 1985 (United Nations, 1986).

[5] See ECLAC's 1986 Annual Report, according to which the urban minimum wage had declined in real terms, since 1980, by 13 percent in Brazil, 24 percent in Chile, 40 percent in Ecuador, 28 percent in Mexico, and 47 percent in Peru.

Two aspects of recent experience are of particular relevance to this document. First, the fiscal adjustment implemented by the countries with debt problems has resulted in severe contraction of public investment. According to the UN Economic Commission for Latin America and the Caribbean—ECLAC—(1986), gross capital formation for the Latin American countries declined in real terms by about 23 percent on average. Except for Colombia, all countries in the region experienced a sharp contraction, in excess of 30 percent in the case of the Southern Cone countries. The drop in investment is due to the type of fiscal adjustment the indebted countries have been forced to implement, and certainly raises serious doubts as to the possibility of returning to a satisfactory rate of growth in the future. It would be no exaggeration to say that, in some countries, the severe contraction of investment in basic infrastructure has already seriously impaired their potential for economic growth.

The second noteworthy aspect is the great vulnerability of the indebted countries to adverse changes in the international environment. One development widely discussed in 1984 was the indebted countries' seeming emergence from the stage of import compression and their prospects of entering a new phase of economic growth stimulated by increased exports, leading to an easing of the debt burden. These predictions were based on more favorable performance of the world economy and trade than had been anticipated (Table 2). However, a drop in the rate of growth of the world economy was enough to significantly alter the growth prospects and payment capacity of the indebted countries.[6] This point may be illustrated with some figures. In April 1985, the Fund projected in its *World Economic Outlook* that the combined debt/export ratio of the countries experiencing debt problems would be approximately 246 percent in 1986 and 186 percent in 1987. In the financial year ended April 1986, these figures were revised to 275 percent for 1986 and 261 percent for 1987. The latest projections (October 1986) contain yet another revision for 1986 and 1987: to 292 percent and 285 percent, respectively. The projected debt/export ratio has been increased by 46 percentage points in the course of 18 months.

---

[6] Although there has been a considerable slowdown in economic activity in the industrial countries since 1984, particularly in light of the favorable effects that it was assumed would follow from the drop in oil prices, these countries still cannot be said to have entered the recessionary stage of the economic cycle.

Table 2. Growth of World Economy and World Trade: Projections and Results

Rates of growth in percent

Year	Values Observed	Values Projected in *World Economic Outlook*					
		August 1983	October 1984	April 1985	October 1985	April 1986	October 1986
GDP of industrial countries							
1983	2.6	1.9					
1984	4.7	3.3	4.9				
1985	2.7		3.4	3.0	2.8		
1986					3.1	3.0	2.8
World trade							
1983	2.9	0.5					
1984	8.6	4.5	8.5				
1985	3.1		5.5	5.4	3.5		
1986					4.3	3.7	3.5

Source: International Monetary Fund, *World Economic Outlook: A Survey by the Staff of the International Monetary Fund* (Washington, various editions).

The impact of the slowdown in world economic activity on the indebted countries' growth prospects and creditworthiness was compounded by the development of the terms of trade. Apart from the "normal" effect on revenues implied by a deterioration in the terms of trade, for the indebted countries it entails an additional burden, in that the real interest rate that effectively applies to them is the rate found by deflating the nominal interest rate by export unit values. Accordingly, despite the drop in the nominal interest rate, most Latin American and Caribbean countries have experienced a considerable increase in the real rate; the terms of trade for this group of countries have declined by more than 20 percent since 1982 (see Table 1). Concerning Mexico, for example, recent estimates indicate that the transfer of resources abroad attributable to shifts in the terms of trade, even after taking into account the favorable impact of the lower nominal interest rate, has amounted to approximately US$30 billion since 1982 (Table 3).

Clearly, the negative correlation between internal adjustment and external environment has meant far higher costs in terms of products and wages, and has introduced considerable uncertainty as to whether some countries will be able to continue servicing their debt.

Table 3. Mexico: Implicit Transfer of Resources Resulting from Movements in the Terms of Trade

In billions of U.S. dollars

	1982	1983	1984	1985	January–June 1986
Exports of goods and services					
At current prices	26.1	27.2	30.1	27.7	10.6
At 1980 prices	29.2	33.7	35.0	34.2	16.5
Implicit transfer	3.1	6.5	4.9	6.5	5.9
Imports of goods and services					
At current prices	20.3	12.8	16.2	18.8	8.6
At 1980 prices	18.0	11.1	13.7	15.8	7.3
Implicit transfer	2.3	1.7	2.5	3.0	1.3
Interest payments					
Current payments	12.2	10.1	11.7	9.9	4.4
At 1980 rates	11.6	12.3	12.5	12.5	6.4
Effect of interest rates	0.6	−2.2	−0.8	−2.6	−2.0
Total net transfer	6.0	5.0	6.6	6.9	5.2

Source: Bank of Mexico. Based on new series on unit values of imports and exports.

Financial Aspects

Regarding the third question raised in the previous section, the prospects for restoring normal debtor-creditor relationships now seem considerably diminished in comparison to what was projected in 1984 when the first multiyear rescheduling agreements were reached. This is hardly surprising in view of the deterioration of the economic situation and creditworthiness of a large number of indebted countries and the policy being pursued by the international banking community of proportionately reducing their exposure in the developing countries and of voluntarily extending new loans to only a select group of countries with no debt-servicing problems, principally in Asia. Total new credit to the developing countries from the international banks has declined from US$82 billion in 1981 to US$34.7 billion in 1983, US$16 billion in 1984, and only US$9 billion in 1985. The total portfolio involving this group of countries increased by only 1.6 percent in 1985. The regional distribution pattern (Table 4) illustrates this process clearly. Asian countries received 25 percent of total loans in 1983, but 56 percent in 1985. In the latter year, the increase in the portfolio

Table 4. Bank Lending to Developing Countries, 1983–85

In billions of U.S. dollars

	1983	1984	1985
Total	34.7	16.4	8.9
Increase as a percentage of portfolio	7.0	2.9	1.6
Africa	4.8	0.2	1.0
Asia	8.8	8.2	5.0
Europe	2.8	2.2	3.2
Middle East	3.5	− 0.4	− 2.1
Latin America and the Caribbean	14.8	6.2	1.9

Source: International Monetary Fund (Washington, various publications).

corresponding to the countries of Latin America and the Caribbean was less than 1 percent. From another perspective, new bank lending accounted for about 10 percent of the interest paid by the countries of the region.

It has become increasingly difficult to work out concerted financing packages with the commercial banks. Disbursements of such financing to all developing countries during 1985 amounted to only US$5 billion, half the amount granted the year before. New financing commitments assumed by banks during 1985 and the first half of 1986 amounted to only US$2.5 billion against US$16.5 billion in 1984. Even when the amounts in the financing package recently arranged for Mexico are included, total estimated flows for 1987 are substantially lower than for this year. One explanation for the increasing difficulties experienced in arranging new financing packages is that the banks are now a far less cohesive group than when the debt problem arose in 1982. Because the banks have different regional interests, have pursued different capitalization and funding practices, and must deal with banking regulations specific to each country, the problem of spreading risks and possible losses has become far more complex. Advisory committees appear to be playing a less effective role, in that the banks comprising the committees represent increasingly diversified groups.

An ostensibly positive aspect of decreased cohesiveness of the banking community is that it would allow for a wider range of financing arrangements, such as the automatic capitalization of interest. However, one problem met with in trying to broaden the range of financing is that the banks not only encounter difficulties in reaching agreements with their own customers on the terms and conditions of new financing, but increasingly have problems reaching agreement among themselves as well. This phenomenon—which is typical of the decision-making process in cartel-type organizations—has to some extent been fostered by the approach adopted by the governments of creditor countries and by multilateral organizations. Allegedly in order to preserve the stability of the international financial system and be able to respond "systematically," a system of "rewards and penalties" has been set up whereby the indebted countries must individually negotiate with groups of creditors, thus institutionalizing the banking cartel.

The system of rewards and penalties, however, has become increasingly lopsided. Clearly the "reward" to be received by the indebted countries that have pursued intensive adjustment programs would be the restoration of economic growth and normal relationships with creditors, factors which in turn should lead to recovery of their debt-servicing capacity. However, the anticipated growth did not materialize, and the chance of restoring "normal" relationships with creditors—a return to spontaneous or voluntary leading—is still very remote for most of the indebted countries. Indeed, some of the contradictions inherent in the strategy pursued have become more obvious, particularly following negotiation of the financing package recently concluded with Mexico:

• On the one hand, banks that have already withdrawn from voluntary financing are more and more reluctant to participate in concerted financing schemes. When they do so, they use various means to minimize their participation as much as possible. The economic subcommittees seek to reduce the financing requirements derived from balance of payments projections agreed with the multilateral organizations. Similarly, the banks try to obtain guarantees from the latter for at least part of the financing to be committed. On the other hand, they warn against initiatives on the part of the debtors and against interest capitalization schemes, arguing that these imply a departure from normal commercial practices.

• On the whole, the banks are inflexible in granting general concessions, such as the elimination of surcharges, partial debt cancellations, or the granting of interest rates below the prevailing market rates. Such proposals are felt to be premature, among other reasons, because the establishment of criteria on which to base the granting of concessions and the scale of such concessions pose considerable problems. Similarly, the banks argue that once such practices have been introduced, it would be difficult to prevent their extension to cases where they are not fully justified. The banks maintain, however, that each case is considered separately and on its own merits.

• Perhaps the most obvious paradox is that, although creditor governments, banks, and multilateral institutions have defended the implementation of a case-by-case strategy from the outset, the fear of setting a precedent seems to be a decisive factor in the course of negotiations. This was more than evident throughout the recent negotiations with the commercial banks on the Mexican financial package.

The banks' reluctance to provide an increased flow of financing to the indebted countries and their inflexibility in granting concessions raise serious doubts as to the viability of the current strategy. First of all, it is clear that no genuine system has actually been adopted for considering each case individually, adjusting the amount and terms of the financing to individual requirements. In fact, the strategy has been one of uniform treatment, in which a series of ritual steps or stages must be adhered to by the indebted countries (beginning with a Fund-supported adjustment program and followed by agreements with the World Bank, etc.) if they wish to obtain from the banks any arrangement on a rescheduling of debt principal or—perhaps—a reduction in surcharges. Similarly, through the official creditor members of the Paris Club, the indebted countries can aspire to negotiate restructurings—possibly under more favorable terms than those obtained from the banks, provided they have agreed upon a Fund-supported program—but risk losing additional import credits guaranteed by official agencies.[7]

Adjustment Process

The other aspect of the debt strategy is the adjustment process being pursued by indebted countries on the basis of programs supported by Fund resources. Historically, the developing countries have adopted this type of program in situations characterized by "unsustainable disequilibria" (of a temporary nature) in their balances of payments. Although the Fund staff has frequently stressed that it is advisable for members to approach the Fund before imbalances become more severe, adjustment programs are frequently introduced when the situation has reached at least a certain degree of seriousness. This was surely the case before the debt crisis became manifest, and has unquestionably been the norm since 1982, even though the notion of temporariness has obviously changed.

---

[7] Brazil is facing many problems in its relations with the Paris Club because it has not negotiated a program with the Fund.

In general, the term *unsustainable disequilibria* is understood to mean current account deficits that cannot be financed by a voluntary contraction of external credit or the use of international assets. Given the sharp cutbacks in external financing in recent years and the virtual disappearance of the voluntary financing referred to earlier, the margins of what could previously be considered a sustainable disequilibrium have contracted considerably. Traditionally, distinctions have been drawn for program design purposes on the basis of whether the causes of imbalances were domestic or external. The origins of the debt problem have been widely discussed and documented, and while discussion continues as to whether the principal factors responsible for the crisis were inadequate financial policies or events outside the control of governments, it is clear that both came into play.

Although, in designing programs, an effort has been made to adapt them to the nature of the disequilibria, to the availability of resources, and to the macroeconomic objectives sought, the general lines of these programs have changed only slightly over the years. Given that the fundamental objective of the programs is to restore a balance of payments position that is viable in the medium term, the type of measures normally included consists of a mix of policies aimed at reducing domestic "absorption" and redirecting the spending required by various sectors (Guitián, 1981). Although the programs applied to indebted countries in recent years have placed more emphasis than in the past on measures designed to improve resource allocation and promote "structural change," it is clear that demand-management policies have remained the backbone of these programs.

It is widely known that the theoretical underpinning of the programs supported by the Fund is based on the works by Polak (1957) and Robichek (1967, e.g.). Even at the risk of oversimplification, it is worth reviewing briefly the analytical basis of program design, which may be summarized in two equations:[8]

(1) Δ International Reserves = Revenue – Absorption
    (= Consumption + Investment) + Δ External Financing;

(2) Δ International Reserves = Δ Demand for Money –
    Δ Domestic Credit from the Banking System to the Public and Private Sectors.

The first equation results from combining the identity of the national product with the definition of the balance of payments, while

---

[8] Various documents provide detailed descriptions of the formulation of Fund programs. See, for example, Dell (1982), Buira (1983), and International Monetary Fund (1981 and 1984).

the second is obtained from the balance sheet of the banking system and from the equilibrium condition of the money market. The first equation shows that for a given level of external financing, and considering the difficulty of increasing the product in the short term, improving the balance of payments (reflected in an increase in international reserves) requires a reduction in domestic absorption. This may be achieved by reducing government spending, raising taxes, or both measures combined. In turn, to achieve domestic and external equilibrium simultaneously, it is normally necessary to apply measures to redirect spending, this because, if we assume an initial position of disequilibrium, reducing domestic demand alone provides no guarantee of equilibrium in both sectors in the absence of perfect price flexibility. Among such measures, for theoretical and other reasons it is normally advisable to opt for exchange rate adjustments. The second equation, on the other hand, provides us with the working tool for correcting the external imbalance (provided that the demand for money is a stable and predictable function), namely the reduction of domestic credit. In fact, this equation represents the rudiments of financial programming and usually serves as the basis for establishing the criteria or quantitative targets for financing of the public deficit.

In practice, exercises in financial programming normally start from a predetermined amount of external financing, making certain assumptions about the trends of the fundamental macroeconomic variables (nominal GDP, inflation, exchange rate and interest rate developments, exports, etc.) and about the functional behavior of certain others (the demand for money and other financial assets, and imports), and use these to derive the size of the public sector deficit that is consistent with a particular target for rebuilding international reserves and financing the private sector. This is an iterative exercise that should converge on reasonably consistent macroeconomic scenarios; these in turn are used as the basis for negotiating the program. In fact, if the demand for money is a relatively stable function throughout the length of the program (or if the velocity of circulation is more or less constant), controlling the monetary aggregates through the use of targets for credit expansion, the public deficit and international reserves may make it possible to roughly approximate the projected development of nominal GDP, except that the extent to which the contraction has an impact on inflation and the growth of real GDP is indeterminate and the latter normally constitutes the adjustment variable. It is specifically because of this that Fund programs are frequently criticized for having a pronounced contractionary bias that works against economic growth.

The debate on whether Fund programs are or are not contractionary in nature dates back at least to the celebrated structuralist/
monetarist controversy of the 1950s, a debate revitalized of late in
light of the results obtained so far in the application of adjustment
programs—especially in Latin America—since 1982 (Taylor, 1986).
While this topic is of the utmost importance, and without seeking to
join this debate, it should be noted that a substantial proportion of the
discussion on the possible recessionary effects of adjustment programs supported by the Fund appears not to have been focused on the
most relevant aspects of the current problem. On the one hand, the
policies designed to reduce aggregate demand do, by definition, have
some contractionary effect, at least in the short term. In addition,
depreciating the exchange rate frequently has an initial impact that is
recessionary.[9] On the other hand, the positive effects on economic
activity of eliminating distortions or of changing relative prices are
normally not immediately of sufficient magnitude to offset the recessionary impact of measures to contain aggregate demand. As a
consequence, it is extremely difficult to conceptualize a program
aimed at correcting macroeconomic disequilibria that grow out of
excess demand which does not have a negative impact on economic
activity in the short term. However, this does not necessarily justify the
conclusion that the program in question is biased against economic
growth. It may be argued, and indeed has been argued by persons
defending the design and implementation of the programs, that a
return to a viable balance of payments position is a necessary precon-
dition for renewed economic growth. It might also be asked whether
there is any alternative to the application of adjustment measures in
that, in the absence of a program, there will be an adjustment to a
balance of payments crisis anyway, but in a disorderly manner and at
a social cost that would ultimately be far greater (Khan and Knight,
1985).

It could almost be argued that some degree of initial deterioration
in economic activity (and, of course, a reduction in consumption) is an
unavoidable cost of restoring domestic and external equilibrium. In
turn, such a deterioration will be a function of the financing available,
the magnitude of the disequilibria that were to be corrected, the rigidities and distortions brought about by them or by institutional factors
and, to a significant degree, by the initial holdings of assets and liabilities of the transactors in the economy. However, this does not

---

[9] Edwards (1985) provides a recent empirical analysis of this point.

invalidate observations to the effect that some programs make no effort to minimize the social cost of adjustment, or that their design entails some bias toward overshooting balance of payments targets and underestimating the effective degree of adjustment (e.g., Dell, 1982). Another type of concern that has frequently been voiced is the operational workings of the programs. In particular, the logic of establishing performance criteria with respect to given variables presumes that these variables can be controlled by the authorities and that their behavior has a direct impact on the macroeconomic targets and objectives. In some cases, however, the variables supposedly under the control of the authorities in fact are quite endogenous.[10]

One relevant point is that orthodox or traditional types of programs, while they may have a contractionary bias, may be extremely effective in helping to restore external equilibrium, providing a sound basis for future growth, when they are applied in countries where the disequilibria are moderate. In the worst of cases, the additional social cost of overshooting external targets at the cost of a greater downturn in economic activity would not be politically intolerable so long as this is an effort to correct imbalances that are not disproportionate. However, in cases involving the type of disequilibria affecting the highly indebted countries, the problems associated with designing and implementing adjustment programs take on a new dimension.

While the Fund has accumulated vast experience with adjustment programs, their implementation in countries where the public and private sectors are heavily indebted, both domestically and abroad, is relatively recent. It should be recalled that the last episodes of generalized external debt moratoria in Latin America occurred in the 1920s and 1930s, well before Bretton Woods. A high level of indebtedness has significant consequences in the process of adjusting to external disequilibria that are not always recognized and incorporated into the design of programs. One important point is that, in addition to the "flow" imbalance represented by the current account deficit, the disequilibrium represented by high indebtedness entails problems more directly related to a "wealth" imbalance. Correction of the external deficit (or economic stabilization) does not resolve the problem of long-term dynamics complicated by the existence of high debt levels. In this regard, if countries have borrowed "excessively"—judging from a current cross section of relative prices and the perception of

---

[10] As indicated in the next section, for example, the public sector deficit is extremely sensitive to the behavior of the exchange rate and inflation rate (see Córdoba, 1986).

creditors—the adjustment may be conceived as a process of "debt elimination" or amortization.[11] This process applies, of course, both to the external and the domestic debt, although the economic implications of actual amortization of the two types of debt, of course, have quite distinct effects. Their most obvious difference is that amortization of the external debt entails a net transfer of resources from abroad, while payment of the domestic debt has redistributive effects only domestically.

The experience of Latin America in recent years illustrates this process clearly. Indeed, an assessment to the effect that the current strategy is viable in terms of the extent to which the above objectives are achievable is effectively a contention that the transfer of resources involved may occur at the same time as the indebted countries recover some measure of economic stability and begin to grow. It should thus come as no surprise that the efforts made to judge the viability of this strategy quantitatively as regards long-term dynamics consist in simulation models designed to identify which conditions must be fulfilled for a transfer of resources and economic growth to occur simultaneously.[12]

Impact of Indebtedness on Adjustment Program

We now turn to specific illustrations of the manner in which the existence of a high level of domestic and external indebtedness complicates adjustment processes and affects the impact of the measures normally included in stabilization programs. The examples set forth below do not, of course, constitute an exhaustive list.

Exchange Depreciation

The quite sizable adjustments in the real exchange rate carried out by various Latin American countries in recent years have had significant contractionary and inflationary effects simultaneously.

In accordance with traditional approaches, depreciation of the exchange rate should be reflected in an increase in the production of

---

[11] One process resembling the "real amortization" of the external debt, in terms of the transfer of reserves it entails, is the increase in its balance resulting from the impact on the balance of payments of changes in the terms of trade and interest rates. As noted earlier, in Mexico, the increase in the nominal balance of the debt attributable to adverse terms of trade has amounted to almost US$30 billion since 1982.

[12] The widely known study by Cline (1984) and the works of Selowsky and van der Tak (1986) and Ortiz and Serra (1986) are examples of this type of exercise.

marketable goods stimulated by increased external demand for exports and domestic demand for import substitutes. However, various authors have noted that in practice—especially in the developing countries—many devaluations have been followed by some type of economic recession. Worse still, it is not always clear to what extent the lower level of economic activity can be attributed to the exchange rate change. Díaz-Alejandro (1965) observed that the redistributive effects associated with exchange rate depreciation could have a negative impact on economic activity to the extent that they result in a transfer of income toward sectors with a lower propensity to spend.[13] In addition, other authors have indicated that there are supply-side mechanisms whereby a devaluation may have a recessionary impact (Van Wijnbergen, 1986; and Gylfason and Risager, 1983). Furthermore, when the public and private sectors are indebted in foreign exchange, the possible negative effects of a reduction in the exchange rate may be amplified considerably. Tanzi and Blejer (1986) note that one initial and obvious outgrowth of the existence of public debt is that it must be serviced, and there is therefore an increase in the associated payments (either in the form of higher interest rates or through the effect of an exchange rate reduction on debt service expressed in terms of domestic currency) which increases the public deficit. It is clear that measures taken to reduce the deficit will have some impact on economic activity, with the added difficulty, as the authors observe, that on many occasions the type of adjustment that occurs is inefficient and tends in the long run to affect the potential for economic growth. For example, as noted earlier, it has been seen that the drastic fiscal correction brought about in Latin America in the past four years has had an impact in particular on cutbacks in public investment. On occasion there has also been recourse to tax measures that introduce distortions and run counter to the medium-term and long-term objectives of deregulating trade and promoting exports, such as the increases in tariffs or export taxes.

Regarding private debt, exchange rate depreciation may have a significant recessionary impact by affecting the investment decisions of enterprises. A devaluation has the immediate effect of revaluing upward those assets of an enterprise that are denominated in foreign exchange, while the revaluation of its other assets (to the extent they include marketable goods) may not be immediate or in the same proportion. This negative "risk effect" may directly affect the cost and

---

[13] Krugman and Taylor (1978) have formalized these and other possible contractionary effects of a devaluation on aggregate demand.

amount of financing available to the enterprise, giving rise to liquidity problems that obligate the firm to rebuild its working capital before undertaking new investment projects. Likewise, the uncertainties about future exchange rates that may be induced by a devaluation may prompt enterprises to restructure their obligations by paying off their credits in foreign exchange ahead of schedule. These effects were significant in the 1976 devaluation of the Mexican peso and explain the substantial decline in private investment that was noted in the following year (Córdoba and Ortiz, 1980). More recently, the potentially devastating impact on economic activity represented by the exchange losses incurred by enterprises following the 1982 devaluations prompted Mexico's financial authorities to establish mechanisms to spread such losses over time. A further effect of exchange rate devaluation on the financial position of enterprises is that they endeavor to make up for foreign exchange losses and restore their liquidity position by increasing prices beyond the level justified by just the impact of the exchange rate on imported inputs. To the extent that effective protection allows for such a shifting of prices to the consumer, it will increase price inertia and make it extremely difficult and costly to reduce inflationary pressures.

Inflation and Fiscal Deficit

A high level of external indebtedness is not the only factor complicating the stabilization process. The existence of a significant amount of domestic debt may also pose important problems for the implementation of adjustment programs, especially in countries with a high rate of inflation. If the domestic debt is in the form of bonds whose yield is adjusted in order to compensate the holders of such bonds for the erosion of capital caused by inflation, an increase in inflation will have a disproportionately large impact on the interest bill paid by the government. If we assume, therefore, that the nominal value of the gross domestic product increases pari passu with the rate of inflation, as the latter increases the financial requirements of the public sector will increase in relation to GDP, creating the impression that public finances are deteriorating even though this is not necessarily the case.[14] These effects significantly complicate the management of public finances within the adjustment process by giving equivocal domes-

---

[14] It should be borne in mind that the types of fiscal measures (such as price and rate increases for goods produced by the public sector) and exchange rate measures normally included in programs frequently have a significant inflationary impact at the outset.

tic and external signals as to the fiscal effort being made by the authorities.

While the inflation may be fully predictable, for economic policy purposes the implications of the distortions it causes in measurement of the fiscal imbalance are less important. In this case, for a given financial structure of the public sector, it is possible to make a target for the real debtor position of the government compatible with a particular level of financing requirements. However, given that inflation is not a sure thing, it may happen that, even when the nominal targets for the public deficit are not met, the real adjustment in public finances that is sought under the program is in fact taking place. In an inflationary environment, an increase in the financing requirements of the public sector does not necessarily lead to increased pressures on aggregate demand or the balance of payments, in that these increased requirements may simply reflect accelerated amortization of debt principal which should not be expected to have an impact on aggregate demand. For this reason, a more appropriate yardstick for the fiscal position of the government is the operating deficit, a concept which encompasses only the real portion of the interest paid on the public debt. A further argument in favor of incorporating this measurement of the fiscal deficit in adjustment programs is that it is more directly controllable by the authorities.

Indebtedness and Capital Flight

Capital flight is a topic that has received considerable attention of late. It has frequently been said that a country unable to keep its residents' savings from being sent abroad has little hope of attracting capital flows from abroad. In particular, in negotiations with creditor countries, the international banking community has used such arguments in asserting that capital flight occurs because countries are applying incorrect policies.[15]

Unquestionably, capital flight originally arose from a perception on the part of savers that the policies implemented lacked coherence. A classic example of this is the outcome of an exchange rate policy that results in undervaluation of the exchange rate (such as the "tablita" in Argentina or the "managed floating" of the Mexican peso in

---

[15] It is to some degree ironic that the banking community has been so insistent on this topic, in that more than a few banks have directly promoted capital flight through their branches in the capitals of Latin America. Intense debate has also arisen with respect to the amount of such flight; the various estimates available show quite a wide range of results (see Zedillo, 1986).

1980–81), with the resulting pressure on the exchange market being financed by borrowing abroad. Under current circumstances, however, indebted countries may experience both capital flight and exchange rate instability, even though they are pursuing coherent macroeconomic policies (on exchange rates, interest rates, etc.).

The debt problem involves more than just the external debt. When it also includes the domestic debt, and the financial position of the public sector is precarious and vulnerable, the sudden emergence of an additional fiscal imbalance (caused, for example, by a disruption on the supply side or a deterioration in the terms of trade affecting tax revenues) may cause concern on the part of savers, who may fear that the government will be compelled to impose some kind of tax on the holding of financial assets, either in the form of higher inflation or via some other confiscatory mechanism. In these circumstances, the natural reaction of the public will be to try to unload this type of asset. Paradoxically, if the public perceives that the government is firmly resolved to fulfill its external commitments, it may have even greater doubts about the government's capacity to continue servicing the domestic debt. The notion that overall indebtedness has reached limits that exhaust the capacity to borrow additional amounts abroad, and that there is thus a problem with the basic solvency of the public sector, may go a long way toward explaining capital flight under present circumstances.[16]

Adjustment and Growth?

A fundamental issue to be resolved in the design of "growth-oriented" adjustment programs is the temporary nature of the measures they include. It has been said that the orthodox or traditional measures for curbing demand that are applied in the heavily indebted countries under Fund-supported stabilization programs, while succeeding in producing sharp turnarounds in external positions, have not been successful in either reducing inflation or restoring the conditions needed for growth. The hypothesis is that the debt problem raises problems of "access" whose dynamics work at cross-purposes with efforts to stabilize the economy in a dimension of "flows." The dynamics of inflation and its inertial forces—which are reflected in

---

[16] Ize and Ortiz (1986) developed a model that reflects these concepts and includes the endogenous determination of the maximum amounts of domestic and external indebtedness that may be incurred by the government.

both the amount of debt and the impact of stabilization policies— have meant that the trade-off between output and short-term inflation has proven more costly than past experience with stabilization (in countries without debt problems) would have indicated. For these and other reasons, the anti-inflationary programs implemented in Argentina, Brazil, and Israel have been focused on directly controlling the pricing process.

By definition, structural adjustment processes require a relatively long-term outlook in order to obtain results. To ensure their continuity, adequate financing must be available and they must not be jeopardized by exogenous shocks. In turn, this financing will require an updated institutional framework. However, the banks appear reluctant to participate. The Fund, which has played a preponderant role, is an institution whose resources are revolving in nature and are intended to support programs for correcting temporary balance of payments imbalances, not problems of a more structural type. The final question is whether the financing will have to come from additional indebtedness or whether the amounts and burden of debt must be reduced as a prerequisite to the resumption of growth (Dornbusch, 1986).

References

Balassa, Bela A., *Toward Renewed Economic Growth in Latin America* (Washington: Institute for International Economics, 1986).

Buira, Ariel, "IMF Financial Programs and Conditionality," *Journal of Development Economics* (Amsterdam), Vol. 12 (February/April 1983), pp. 111–36.

Cline, William R., *International Debt: Systemic Risk and Policy Response* (Washington: Institute for International Economics, 1984).

Córdoba, José, "El Programa Mexicano de Reordenación Económica, 1983–1984" (mimeographed; Ministry of Budget and Programming, Mexico City).

———, and Guillermo Ortiz, "Aspectos deflacionarios de la devaluación del peso mexicano de 1976," *Demografía y Economía* (Mexico), Vol. 14 (No. 3, 1980), pp. 291–324.

de Larosière, J., "How Is the Fund Helping the Indebted Countries," Address by the Managing Director of the International Monetary Fund before the Los Angeles World Affairs Council, Los Angeles, California, March 19, 1986 (Washington: International Monetary Fund, 1986).

Dell, Sidney, "Stabilization: The Political Economy of Overkill," *World Development* (Oxford), Vol. 10 (August 1982), pp. 597–612.

Diaz-Alejandro, Carlos F., *Exchange-Rate Devaluation in a Semi-Industrialized Country: The Experience of Argentina, 1955–1961* (Cambridge, Massachasetts: MIT Press, 1965).

Dornbusch, Rudiger, "The Bradley Plan: A Way Out of the Latin Debt Mess," *Washington Post*, August 27, 1986, p. A19.

Edwards, Sebastian, "Are Devaluations Contractionary?" National Bureau of Economic Research, Working Paper No. 1676 (New York, August 1985).

Guitián, Manuel, *Fund Conditionality: Evolution of Principles and Practices*, IMF Pamphlet Series, No. 38 (Washington: International Monetary Fund, 1981).

Gylfason, Thorvaldur, and Ole Risager, "Does Devaluation Improve the Current Account?" *European Economic Review* (Amsterdam), Vol. 25 (August 1983), pp. 37–64.

International Monetary Fund, *World Economic Outlook: A Survey Prepared by the Staff of the International Monetary Fund* (Washington, various issues).

——, IMF Institute, *Financial Policy Workshops: The Case of Kenya* (Washington: International Monetary Fund, 1981).

——, *Analyse et programmation financières: Application à la Côte d' Ivoire* (Washington: International Monetary Fund, 1984).

——, *Programación financiera aplicada: El caso de Colombia* (Washington: International Monetary Fund, 1984).

Ize, Alain, and Guillermo Ortiz, "Fiscal Rigidities, Public Debt, and Capital Flight" (unpublished; Washington: International Monetary Fund, August 22, 1986).

Khan, Mohsin S., and Malcolm D. Knight, *Fund-Supported Adjustment Programs and Economic Growth*, International Monetary Fund, Occasional Paper No. 41 (Washington, 1985).

Krugman, Paul, and Lance Taylor, "Contractionary Effects of Devaluation," *Journal of International Economics* (Amsterdam), Vol. 8 (August 1978), pp. 445–56.

Ortiz, Guillermo, and Jaime Serra Puche, "A Note on the Burden of the Mexican Foreign Debt," *Journal of Development Economics* (Amsterdam), Vol. 21 (April 1986), pp. 111–29.

Polak, J. J., "Monetary Analysis of Income Formation and Payments Problems," *Staff Papers*, International Monetary Fund (Washington) Vol. 6 (November 1957) pp. 1–50.

Robichek, E. Walter, "Financial Programing Exercises of the International Monetary Fund in Latin America," Address to a Seminar of Brazilian Professors of Economics, Rio de Janeiro, Brazil, September 20, 1967 (mimeographed; Washington: International Monetary Fund).

Sachs, Jeffrey, "The Debt Overhang of Developing Countries," Conference on Debt, Stabilization, and Development, World Institute of Development Economics Research, held in Helsinki, Finland, August 1986 (forthcoming).

Selowsky, Marcelo, and Herman G. van der Tak, "The Debt Problem and Growth," *World Development* (Oxford), Vol. 14 (September 1986) pp. 1107–24.

Tanzi, Vito, and Mario I. Blejer, "Public Debt and Fiscal Policy in Developing Countries," paper prepared for International Economic Association Conference on the Economics of Public Debt, held at Stanford University, June 24–26, 1986.

Taylor, Lance, "Economic Stabilization–Recent Experience in the Third World," Conference on Debt, Stabilization, and Development, World Institute of Development Economics Research, held in Helsinki, Finland, August 1986 (forthcoming).

United Nations (1986), Economic Commission for Latin America and the Caribbean, *The Economic Crisis: Policies for Adjustment, Stabilization and Growth* (Santiago, Chile: CEPAL, 1986).

Van Wijnbergen, Sweder, "Exchange Rate Management and Stabilization Policies in Developing Countries," in *Economic Adjustment and Exchange Rates in Developing Countries*, ed. by Sebastian Edwards and Liaquat Ahmed (Chicago: University of Chicago Press, 1986).

Zedillo, Ernesto, "Capital Flight: Some Observations on the Mexican Case" (Washington: Institute for International Economics, October 1986).

Comments

Jorge Marcano

I basically agree with the author's assessment and description of the existing external debt situation. I will make an alternative submission, illustrating the viewpoint of creditors and of most of the international organizations and their belief that the strategy is working and has been strengthened. It is not a view to which I would subscribe, but it is the prevailing view on the other side of the negotiating table vis-à-vis the debtor countries.

I will therefore describe the strategy and its recent development.

First of all I should like to run through some known facts about the strategy, such as the diagnosis, the objectives, and the tactics for achieving them. To put the diagnosis in simple terms, the problem of external debt is a liquidity problem.

At one time or another there have been interest rate rises that have aggravated the existing situation, problems with repayment dates being concentrated within a short period as a result of the way in which external indebtedness has been tackled, and the very important phenomenon known as contagion.

The aim is a return to normality, which is seen as the re-establishment of the flow of funds from the commercial banks to the debtor countries. The tactics are based on two fundamental rules, namely, case-by-case treatment and a combined effort versus unilateralism. Here, the advisory committee of commercial banks plays a fundamental role. So long as ideas are kept within the confines of those rules, there is no problem. If someone breaks the rules, the full weight of the sanctions of the commercial banks and public institutions descends on his head. The reason for the case-by-case approach is that, in the early days, the international financial system could not have withstood a generalized bankruptcy of the debtor countries, but with the passage

of time the commercial banks would find themselves better placed to
absorb losses (and if one looks at the banks' balance sheets since 1982,
that is precisely what they have been doing), and it would also be
possible to confine the problem to a much smaller number of countries, isolating the most problematical cases, to which radical measures
could be applied. These circumstances explain the approach adopted
by the banks since 1982.

The statistics show that matters improved substantially in the great
majority of debtor countries during 1984–85, to the point where their
situation was becoming manageable. And then what happens? A drastic deterioration in their terms of trade, particularly in those countries
affected by the steep decline in oil prices, such as Mexico and to a
lesser extent Venezuela and Ecuador. These countries were seen as
shining examples of the success of the strategy, and were being
groomed by the international economic community for a return to the
"voluntary" financial market, in other words, access to normal commercial bank credit.

What is the flaw in this strategy? Are the creditor banks possibly too
cautious? And where do the designers and overseers of this strategy
direct their efforts?—toward dealing with the aftereffects, which
means renegotiating the agreement in the cases of Mexico and
Venezuela and some special measures in the case of Ecuador. This
means offering new alternatives, and we start to hear talk about
stand-by loans, as in the case of Mexico, and about growth, albeit more
rhetorical than real. The Baker proposal shows how politically convenient it can be to change tack, but even before that, of course, people
had already been thinking about growth. The hardest part is putting
pressure on the banks to participate in a scheme where they will have
to put in more money.

The picture as I have described it makes it fairly unlikely that the
banks will make any concessions on accepting losses of any kind. The
preferred strategy is to move toward a normalization of financial
flows. When general proposals such as those of Senator Bradley of the
United States Congress are put forward, the reply will be that it is
undesirable to set precedents. For this reason, I do not think that
solutions of the kind which offer generic concessions are likely to
win the day. The problem may in fact transcend the question of the
indebted countries of Latin America. The Bradley proposal on reducing interest rates could generate calls within the United States for
similar solutions to the problems of credit for energy costs, mortgages,
and so forth, in that country. Once the senators have done their sums,
I wonder if they will still look so favorably on this kind of proposal.

This, then, is the view which is now tending to prevail, and it will have to be considered in the debate on external debt.

Leonidas Ortega

I think that Guillermo Ortiz's paper, with which I agree, is extraordinary, particularly in the clarity of its ideas. The only thing I might question is that the title given to the subject, by connecting adjustment policy problems with those derived from indebtedness and growth, could be understood as meaning that each process is conditioned by the other and that they are interdependent. Indebtedness and growth certainly are, while adjustment is necessary only when practices occur that are not appropriate for the proper management of economic policy. To bind these three ideas together could lead us to distort the true nature of the problem, and we might consequently create situations that are not appropriate for the political, social, and economic stability of our countries.

I would very particularly stress that in Guillermo Ortiz's paper, as in those of the other exponents, although expressed in different terms, there is one common denominator: their analyses conclude by emphasizing that the external indebtedness problem took shape and its consequences started being felt many years ago, and since that time, both creditors and debtors have accumulated considerable experience in handling negotiations and in designing and enforcing the economic policies that such circumstances require. It is striking that in this commentary, as in others of its kind on this subject, the intellectual effort of the distinguished minds at work continues to focus on analyzing the contributing factors, the magnitudes and the effects, and the future that we might expect in our societies as a result of external debt under the present rules of the game. On the other hand, very little of this intellectual effort is directed to the creative work of seeking pragmatic solutions.

It is stated again and again that there are many solutions to the problem of external debt; it is emphasized that the success of any one of them will be just as much characterized by and dependent on the political determination in the minds of those who will have to choose and then impose it as it will on the resolution required to enforce it. Although the point made is genuine and of quite valid significance, I think that it is not very pragmatic simply to state it, without completing it with the corresponding contribution of a solution.

Naturally, thinking more as a lawyer than as an economist, I would say that what is missing is the determination by somebody to work on a viable solution from the political, legal, financial, and social viewpoints, both in the creditor and in the debtor countries, so that the incentive or coercive forces of the state for this very reason push for its rapid implementation.

By way of support for some concrete thinking along these lines, I am wondering this afternoon why the International Monetary Fund cannot make one of its basic purposes to demand that creditor and debtor countries adopt political and economic measures that would offer a final solution to the debt problem?

For this course not to be adopted by an institution such as the Fund, whose purpose, among others, is to seek equilibrium in the economies of its member countries, is to reject the use of its basic function and to turn all its other efforts into acts of only temporary worth that are mere palliatives for the serious problems of the world that it oversees; and what is more serious, to make the economies of our countries pay a price that will erode their social bases, which will never recover, thus endangering the international economic system, and the sociopolitical structures of the world and particularly those of the Latin American region.

One of the recommendations or measures the International Monetary Fund might adopt along the lines of what I am thinking could be to redefine the objectives of the World Bank, the Inter-American Development Bank, or of any other similar institution or, perhaps, to create a new financial institution that could be given, as its specific purpose, the restructuring of the indebtedness of our countries in terms of cost and maturity. They would be adapted to the internal realities of each individual country so that our people would not be subjected to adjustment pressures caused by external indebtedness or sacrifice the requirements of growth, on which any ambitions for political, economic, and social development are predicated.

Such an institution would be given resources to carry out its commitments by means of capitalization, or rather, by the contributions that international banking institutions would make to its capital—from the accounts receivable or obligations vis-à-vis the developing countries, or those of Latin America. In due course, these could be reinforced by contributions in kind of uncommitted exportable surplus products provided by the debtor countries to pay any shareholdings they may wish to subscribe to, as a means of obtaining greater influence in the new organization.

The new contributions in kind would be a major source of resources to be channeled to Latin America, as well as a means of linking the commercial future of Latin America with the destiny of its debt, as the new institution would, because of the interest there would be in converting the contribution in kind into cash, be its best ally in opening new markets for their products.

In exchange for its contribution from the accounts receivable of the developing countries, or those of Latin America, international banks would become owners of shares in the institution. These shares could be bought and sold on the capital market or be used by them to support the issue of any kind of securities they might wish to issue. Failing this, they might be used as an instrument to guarantee extraordinary credits that might be obtained from the central banks of their respective countries.

This difficult situation can be faced only with a positive attitude, with a free rein being given to the imagination, and with iron determination.

I think that only by creating a financial institution to tackle the serious problem of debt can we overcome the great conceptual abyss that stands between the debtors' and the creditors' intentions; the first are rooted in the political responsibility and vision of those who govern, and the second only in the responsible opinions of the administrators who work toward strictly financial and economic goals.

The prescription that my thoughts lead to after Guillermo Ortiz's presentation by no means claims to be anything other than an exercise intended to stimulate in you the overriding need to redirect this kind of effort toward other channels and toward the obvious possibility of obtaining pragmatic results from such intellectual and physical efforts as this, which are very frequently made in this Continent.

Trends and Prospects for Savings in Brazil

Carlos A. Longo

Brazil, like most Latin American countries, is characterized by the scarcity of voluntary resources for long-term investment. Perhaps it is a cultural problem or simply the result of the poor distribution of income. The fact is that rarely have increases in investment depended significantly on the mobilization of voluntary savings via the financial or capital market. After a brief encounter with nationalistic populism, the second Government of Vargas ended in 1954 with the stabilization crisis presided over by Ministers Gudin and Bulhões. Once this very brief crisis was over, the development-oriented Government of Juscelino Kubitscheck opted for the expansion of investment in infra-structure, the construction of Brasilia and, through the use of tariff barriers, started off the process of import substitution financed through the issuance of currency rather than through voluntary savings.

The result of this orgy of development was that while gross domestic product (GDP) grew, inflation started to do the same. When the new Government of Jânio Quadros took over in 1960, savings and liquid investments had dried up in the face of the uncertainty as to price developments and government intentions. The Government of President Goulart which took over in 1961, after Quadros resigned, in no way changed the uncertainties of the situation. Far from being concerned about investments, this Government, with leanings toward the labor movement and socialistic sympathies, spurred on inflation by granting wage readjustments much larger than the budget had allowed for.

The inevitable fall of Goulart led the Castelo Branco Government to adopt a policy that was simultaneously orthodox, as it cut down excess demand, and progressive, because it completely reformed the institutions. The bank reform, the capital market reform and the tax reform all date back to this time.

Saving has been systematically declining in Brazil since the beginning of the decade and the conventional instruments for financing the public deficit are practically exhausted. The current rise in growth could suddenly be cut off if thorough institutional reforms are not undertaken. This paper begins by taking a retrospective look at the evolution of the instruments of financial intermediation in Brazil. Next we will look at the decline in saving in recent years, on the basis of national accounts data. In section four, we will present a brief overview of the main investment increases. Section five highlights the problems faced by the Government in financing the deficit, and last we will present possible scenarios and prospects for attracting savings in Brazil.

Composition of Financial Assets

Brazil's financial institutions underwent profound changes in the mid-1970s, having hitherto essentially been banking institutions. The 1959–64 acceleration of inflation and the Usury Law (maximum annual interest rate 12 percent) accentuated the tendency to short-term lending and promoted financial disintermediation. Loans for crop financing and long-term loans were granted selectively at highly subsidized rates by the offical banks (Banco do Brasil, BNDES, savings banks). The stock markets dealt almost exclusively in exchange operations and, on a limited scale, government securities.

Law No. 4595/64, which organized the monetary system, established the Central Bank and the National Monetary Council. Law No. 4728/65 imposed discipline on the capital market by regulating the operations of the brokerage companies, establishing investment banks and distribution companies. The monetary correction mechanism was instituted by law No. 4356/64 with the establishment of ORTNs. Law No. 4380/64 established the National Housing Bank, which became the leading institution of the Housing Financing System (SFH), composed of real estate loan companies, savings and loan companies, and the federal and state savings banks. The introduction of the monetary correction mechanism helped rehabilitate the public debt as a noninflationary instrument for financing budget deficits. Savings deposits with monetary correction that would finance SFH loans grew rapidly from 1970 onward. Last, the investment banks were authorized to attract resources via fixed-term deposits with monetary correction.

The creation of various compulsory saving mechanisms also dates from this time. In 1967, enterprises began withholding 8 percent of wages to be invested in the Guarantee Fund for Time of Service (FGTS), essentially an unemployment and retirement insurance fund, whose resources were allocated to the BNH. In 1971, enterprises were required to withhold 0.75 percent of their turnover for the Social Integration Program (PIS), which guarantees the employee a remuneration of 3 percent a year over the monetary correction, the BNDES being responsible for the use of these resources.

The 1964–65 reform favored the accumulation of financial assets, whose balance as a percentage of GDP rose between 1965 and 1975 from 23.9 percent to 32.8 percent, the level to which it has only recently returned. Even this percentage is not significant if it is compared internationally; in some European countries with the same per capita income the rate is as high as 100 percent. The increase took place despite the decline of monetary assets from 20.6 percent to 13.1 percent of GDP, thanks mainly to the growth in indexed assets—passbook savings accounts, fixed-term deposits, and federal public debt—which led to nonmonetary assets rising from 3.2 percent to 19.7 percent during this period. The gradual and persistent decline of the stock of money after the reform is attributed to not only the growing complexity of the market but also to inflation, which rose from 20 percent a year during the 1967–75 period to 40 percent in 1976–79, then to 100 percent during the 1980–82 period, and finally to 200 percent in 1983–86 (see Table 1).

With the change in the currency unit in February 1986 (the cruzado plan) there was a sudden rise in monetary assets, as inflation fell from almost 14 percent a month to about 1.5 percent. Indexation was suspended, being kept only for passbook savings accounts. Currently, most fixed-term deposits and government securities are negotiated at nominal rates with maturities no longer than 60 days.

Saving in Decline

The evolution of the financial assets in the hands of enterprises and individuals is a slender indication of aggregate savings. Compulsory saving, new stock subscriptions, and investment funds and the savings of enterprises (retained earnings), government saving (current account surplus), and external saving (current account balance) must also be considered. On the basis of the national accounts, it is possible to obtain a gross capital formation series broken down by source and

Table 1. Principal Financial Assets

As a percentage of GDP

	1950	1955	1960	1965	1970	1975	1980	1985	1986
Bank notes	7.7	6.1	5.1	3.9	2.7	2.2	1.7	0.6	1.3
Call deposits	14.4	14.2	16.3	16.7	11.5	10.9	6.7	2.3	7.9
Savings deposits	—	—	—	—	0.8	4.0	5.8	8.8	8.2
Term deposits without monetary correction	4.4	2.1	1.0	0.6	—	—	—	—	5.0
Term deposits with monetary correction	—	—	—	—	1.8	4.0	3.8	6.0	—
Bills of exchange	—	—	0.2	1.6	3.1	4.0	1.6	1.9	1.1
Housing financing notes	—	—	—	—	0.8	0.6	0.1	—	—
State and local government public debt	—	—	—	—	0.4	1.0	0.9	1.2	1.6
Federal public debt without monetary correction[1]	3.1	1.1	0.3	0.1	0.2	1.6	1.1	1.0	—
Federal public debt with monetary correction[1]	—	—	—	1.0	3.7	4.2	2.5	7.6	10.2
Monetary assets	22.1	20.3	21.5	20.6	14.2	13.1	8.5	3.3	9.2
Nonmonetary assets	7.5	3.2	1.5	3.2	11.0	19.7	15.9	26.7	26.4
Financial assets	29.6	23.5	23.0	23.9	25.2	32.8	24.4	30.0	35.6

NOTE: Balances at June 30, from 1970; until 1965 as reproduced in A. Lemgruber, *Un Análisis Cuantitativo del Sistema Financiero* (Rio de Janeiro: IBMEC, 1978).
[1] Held by the public.

uses, which clearly shows the colossal fall in savings recorded since 1980.

Gross capital formation reached unprecedented levels close to 30 percent of GDP in the mid-1970s thanks to the very positive contribution of government saving (direct administration), state enterprises, and foreign savings. This composition did not fundamentally change until 1979, when, faced with the second oil shock and high international interest rates, the Government refused to make a compensatory readjustment.

When the international financial market was paralyzed in 1982, gross capital formation fell to 16.9 percent and is currently holding at this level, with some difficulty, exclusively through the contribution of private sector saving. Government savings and foreign savings disappeared a long time ago. The effect of this state of affairs on investment is obvious. The Government, either directly or through state enterprises, reduced its investments, and even the private sector did the same, to levels about half of those recorded halfway through the previous decade (see Tables 2 and 3).

Table 2. Sources of Gross Capital Formation

In billions of current cruzeiros

	1986	1985	1984	1983	1982	1981	1980
Gross capital formation			63,463	20,413	10,797	5,441	2,965
S_P				17,306	7,700	4,063	1,885
S_E	—	—	—	—	—	—	228
S_G	—	—	—	902	170	269	169
S_X	—	−84	658	4,009	2,965	1,108	682

	1979	1978	1977	1976	1975	1974	1973
Gross capital formation	1,409	919	625	434	299	197	124
S_P	807	587	396	264	184	109	76
S_E	161	147	92	46	46	26	16
S_G	140	85	97	70	38	32	30
S_X	287	126	56	63	54	48	10

Percentage of GDP

	1986	1985	1984	1983	1982	1981	1980
Gross capital formation	—	—	16.4	16.9	21.2	21.3	22.5
S_P	—	—	16.5	14.3	15.1	15.8	14.3
S_E			—	—	—	—	1.7
S_G	—	—	—	−0.7	0.3	1.0	1.2
S_X	—	—	−0.1	3.3	5.8	4.3	5.1

	1979	1978	1977	1976	1975	1974	1973
Gross capital formation	22.3	24.4	25.1	26.7	29.6	27.8	25.6
S_P	12.8	15.6	15.9	16.2	18.2	15.4	15.7
S_E	2.5	3.9	3.7	2.8	4.5	3.6	3.3
S_G	2.2	3.7	3.9	4.3	3.7	4.5	6.2
S_X	4.5	3.3	2.2	3.8	5.3	6.7	2.0

Source: National Accounts: SEST and Central Bank—the sum of the lines differs from gross capital formation because of changes in the current cruzeiro. Until 1980, national account figures are as reproduced in L. Lago and others, *El Combate de la Inflación en el Brasil* (Rio de Janeiro: Paz e Terra, 1984).

NOTE: S_P = private sector savings; S_E = state enterprise savings; S_G = government savings; S_X = external savings.

Investment Peaks

Three investment peaks followed by stabilization crises have taken place in Brazil since the Second World War. The expansionary Government of Getúlio Vargas was followed by a short contraction in 1954–55, under Ministers Gudin and Bulhões. At the end of the decade, there was a colossal expansion in investment during the Kubitscheck Government financed in the final analysis through the moneti-

Table 3. Uses of Gross Capital Formation

In billions of current cruzeiros

	1986	1985	1984	1983	1982	1981	1980
Gross capital formation			63,463	20,413	10,797	5,441	2,965
I_P				18,270	9,610	4,804	1,660
I_E	117,027	44,507	21,646	6,370	3,383	1,980	917
I_G	—	—	—	2,143	1,187	637	286

	1979	1978	1977	1976	1975	1974	1973
Gross capital formation	1,404	919	625	434	299	197	124
I_P	517	515	384	262	211	139	95
I_E	744	290	154	106	46	29	10
I_G	147	113	82	65	41	28	18

Percentage of GDP

	1986	1985	1984	1983	1982	1981	1980
Gross capital formation	—	—	16.4	16.9	21.2	21.3	22.5
I_P	—	—	—	9.8	12.3	11.0	12.6
I_E	3.3	3.2	5.5	5.3	6.6	7.7	6.9
I_G	—	—	—	1.8	2.3	2.4	2.1

	1979	1978	1977	1976	1975	1974	1973
Gross capital formation	22.3	24.4	25.1	26.7	29.6	27.8	25.6
I_P	8.2	13.6	15.7	16.1	20.9	19.6	19.7
I_E	11.7	7.7	6.1	6.5	4.5	4.1	2.0
I_G	2.3	3.0	3.3	4.0	4.1	3.9	3.7

Source: National Accounts: SEST and Central Bank—the sum of the lines differs from gross capital formation because of changes in the current cruzeiro. Until 1980, capital account figures are as reproduced in L. Lago and others, *El Combate de la Inflación en el Brasil* (Rio de Janeiro: Paz e Terra, 1984).

NOTE: I_P = private sector investments; I_E = state enterprise investments; I_G = government investments.

zation of the public deficit, as the financial and capital markets were just getting under way. After a brief contractionary and expansionary period under Jânio and Goulart, respectively, there came the fiscal and monetary contraction that went hand in hand with the strategic plan of action of Castelo Branco's Government, conducted by the Campos and Bulhões duo. The present banking, financial, and tax structure and the increase in investment that took place in the following years are due to the basic reforms introduced during this period.

The modernization of the institutions simultaneously produced more voluntary saving, an increase in autonomous investments, and fiscal surpluses in the current account. It is true that after 1969 the

Costa e Silva Government opted for a gradualistic policy in the struggle against inflation, which meant the generalization of the indexation process through which the ORTN turned into a second unit of account in Brazil. While on the one hand indexation initially made it easy to go along with inflation and forestalled capital flight, on the other hand it consolidated currency issue as a way of financing the public deficit.

The possibilities for reducing the monetization of deficits were abandoned after the first oil shock. Faced with the wide availability of external financing, the Government tried to raise the level of public investment (II PND). It stimulated attraction of external loans directly by state enterprises or indirectly via the financial system. The result was that Brazil absorbed the external shock with these loans, reduced the growth rate to a certain extent, doubled the rate of inflation, increased public and private investment, financed the current account deficit, and even accumulated reserves.

Since 1979, Brazil has been undergoing a stabilization crisis the consequences of which are still unforeseeable. Faced with two unfavorable external shocks (oil prices and interest rates), inflation running at over 50 percent, and dwindling reserves, the recently elected Figueiredo Government opted for an expansionary fiscal and wage policy (subsidies for agriculture, substitution of imported energy, and six-monthly wage readjustments above the level of inflation), and a contractionary monetary policy (domestic credit controls), with the object of continuing to attract external resources and substituting imports without reducing the level of activity.

A combination of ill-chosen initiatives—a maxidevaluation followed by prefixed exchange rates and monetary correction at unrealistically low levels—accelerated inflation and further damaged the balance of payments. When prefixings were suspended, a fiscal contraction followed, and then reversed itself during the period leading to the 1982 elections. When the external debt refinancing process was suddenly broken off, Brazil moved into the severest recession in its history. In 1983, a new maxidevaluation and wage restraint raised the exchange/wage ratio to close to 70 percent.

As a result of these measures, inflation climbed to a new level (200 percent annual), and Brazil generated a trade surplus that since 1984 has allowed it to keep the current account balance in equilibrium, with full payment of external debt interest, without new money. Driven by export growth, and more recently by an expansionary fiscal and monetary policy, Brazil began to grow again, but inflation did the same.

This growth probably lacks internal sustainability, as since the beginning of the decade investment in Brazil has been inadequate and the instruments of financial intermediation, capital, and public-deficit financing are essentially the same as they were twenty years ago.

Deficit Financing

For a given level of inflation and use of capacity, there are three main definitions of deficit: deficit in the meaning usually employed, that is, the public sector borrowing requirement, which is measured by the difference between the total use of current and capital resources of the government and its ordinary revenues. This concept is particularly useful as an indicator of the government's tax burden on the financial market. The nonfinancial deficit, also called primary deficit, is simply the public sector borrowing requirement less public debt interest payments. This is frequently used as an indicator of the government's pressure on aggregate demand. Last, we have the deficit that is of particular interest in examining the government's contribution to aggregate savings, that is, the current deficit. This deficit is measured by subtracting capital expenditure from the public sector borrowing requirement.

We can conclude from a superficial examination of the figures that the deficit recently stabilized at between 6 percent and 8 percent of GDP and that the nonfinancial deficit and the current deficit are close to zero. There are no reliable estimates, but there is no indication that the public sector borrowing requirement has been very different in the past. At the same time, data suggest that until 1980 the nonfinancial deficit was positive, since public debt had not reached its present proportions: the financial charges component was less of a burden on government expenditure than it now is. Consequently, at that time, the fiscal pressure on the level of activity was meaningful, and particularly so on investments. However, as we saw earlier, the current deficit was negative during the previous decade, which suggests that the Government was financing a good part of its investments from its own resources (generated by current revenues). Thus at that time, the Government's contribution to aggregate savings was not to be disdained.

The public deficit measured indirectly as the difference between (federal, state, and local government) public sector debt balances from one year to the next, plus currency issue, plus seigniorage excluding inflation on debt service, amounted to 6.8 percent of GDP in 1982 (a

5.5 percent basic increase and 9 percent increase in debt), 6.5 percent in 1983 (1.7 percent basic increase and 4.8 percent debt increase), 6.2 percent in 1984 (2.7 percent basic increase and 3.5 percent debt increase) and 8.7 percent in 1985 (2.7 percent basic increase and 6 percent debt increase). Public debt rose from 27.2 percent of GDP in 1981 to 50 percent in 1985, and currently, 55 percent of the debt is external (mainly federal state enterprises), 25 percent consists of federal government bonded debt, 10 percent is federal state enterprise debt with the domestic financial system, and 10 percent the debt of states and municipalities. As indicated, the deficit is largely financed by the inflation tax, despite which the debt/GDP ratio continues to rise. There are also circumstantial economic reasons for the existence of a higher-than-desired debt. The fact is that the economy has been operating beyond the level of full employment since mid-1986. Furthermore, with the change in the monetary unit and the consequent remonetization of the economy, the Government will have to replace currency issue with net placements of securities in new credit operations.

Monetization of deficit has always been a widely used procedure in Brazil. The creation of the Central Bank in 1964 did not prevent the Banco do Brasil from continuing to operate as a monetary authority through the so-called *conta de movimento,* to which until quite recently the negative sum of the asset and liability operations of the subsidized credits was debited. Also, with the growth of the public enterprise sector, the federal budget gradually declined, because these entities today control resources three times larger in absolute terms. Last, with the transfer in 1982 of the federal public debt to the Central Bank (Complementary Law 12/72), the atrophy of the fiscal budget was complete.

This situation started changing slowly in 1979 when the Secretariat for Control of State Enterprises (SEST) was created, along with the Planning Secretariat of the Presidency of the Republic. SEST now consolidates the balance sheets of 179 enterprises in the federal state production sector (SPE), although fewer than half a dozen (PETROBRAS, ELETROBRAS, TELEBRAS, VALE, RFFSA) are of major importance. SEST also consolidates the budget of the social welfare system (SINPAS). Until last year the budget for the official banks—Banco do Brasil, BNDES, Savings and Loan Bank, BNH, and so on—was included in the SEST global expenditure program. However, it was not made public in 1986.

From 1985 the federal budget included a provision for fiscal expenditures that had previously come under the monetary authorities—subsidies to agriculture, exports, and financial charges on bonded debt. Recently the rediscount facility (*conta de movimento*) of the Banco do Brasil was frozen and the Banco do Brasil was formally separated from the Central Bank: its deposits no longer form part of the money supply and are now subject to a legal reserve requirement. The subsidies administered by the Banco do Brasil will be financed by the recently created Secretariat of the Treasury under the Ministry of Finance. Despite these praiseworthy innovations, one cannot ignore the fact that the "credit budget" and the public debt are still essentially administered by the Central Bank. It should also be remembered that the federal budget is sent to Congress on the last day of August, while that of the state enterprises is submitted on the last day of the year. Consequently, over and above a shortfall in the coverage of these budgets, there is an obvious gap between the dates on which they are presented.

Despite everything, the Sarney Government is not overawed by the size of the deficit. It complies with the changes already made in the budget process and suggests that the recently created compulsory "loan" (in fact a subscription) on the purchase of fuels and the sale of vehicles, together with a new tax on travel abroad, will suffice to finance the deficit henceforth. The cruzado plan, which confined itself to knocking three zeros off the old currency, and to converting wages and contributions by half, financial contributions by their maximum value, and fixed contracts in nominal terms by their discounted value according to the official conversion table, would be sufficient to eliminate inflation, and even indexation.

The indexation process is not without complications. As we have seen, it played an indispensable role in restoring the credibility of public credits after 1964 and in making long-term loans and the housing financing system possible. Once generalized throughout the economy, indexation with high inflation rates means the automatic monetization of part of the public deficit. The government cannot drastically reduce indexation while inflation remains in three figures; public financing cuts would generate colossal adjustments in the distribution of income and would not prevent inflation stabilizing, even at high levels. But, with the change in the monetary unit and low inflation, let us say 20 percent annual, the financing cuts could make indexation redundant. The Government has not yet made any attempt along these lines and, on the contrary, is trying to make the freeze redundant by means of messianic appeals for increased output.

Mobilization of Savings

The economic policy of the Sarney Government has not been clear and firm enough to reverse the decline in savings and stimulate investment to increase capacity. The President, supported by a fragile coalition of parties, has been unable to adopt the unpopular measures that seem inevitable if the economy is to be rehabilitated on a sustainable basis. The stabilization crisis, which began toward the end of 1980, may continue despite the dizzy growth of the last two years. A stop-and-go policy has prevented structural reforms from taking place since 1979. This Government took over in March 1985 with an economy already on the road to full recovery, real wages increasing faster than productivity, and external restrictions (oil prices, dollar and interest rates) moving in a favorable direction.

Despite the rhetoric, the Government postponed the debate on the more pressing reforms and embarked on a markedly expansionary policy from August on. The monetary reform did not change this situation and, on the contrary, stimulated demand through real wage increases and price freezes, many of these set at below the average variable cost. Small and medium-scale enterprise owners, whose products are not easy to control, are occupying the position of the traditional firms. The production of consumer durables grew through July by 30 percent over the same period in the previous year, but intermediate goods did not exceed 8 percent. Stocks are low, and in order not to lose the market, many firms are raising wages even higher with a view to holding on to their workforce. Here there are problems both of maladjusted relative prices, and of excess demand, characterized by the increasing prevalence of speculation, shortages, deterioration of quality, or the "disguising" of products to get around the freeze. Meanwhile, the official indexes do not reveal this inflation.

Once the process of remonetizing the economy was exhausted, and with reluctant acceptance of the diagnosis of a feverish condition, the Government in July issued a range of fiscal measures to keep under its administration approximately 2 percent of GDP during the following 12 months. The compulsory "loan" will be used in the National Development Fund (FND), together with any yield there may be from a limited number of selected public enterprise shares and new uses of the pension funds of state enterprise officials. The implementation of these measures was marked by inertia and confusion. For a start, a compulsory subscription, which may or may not have residual value, was called a loan. Furthermore, as it is a "loan," the official inflation indexes do not take into account the price increases of fuels and vehicles, thus creating a monthly 2 percent to 3 percent lag of these indexes against the others, with negative repercussions on the financial market and on the Government's own credibility. These problems would not have arisen if the Government had openly confessed that demand was overstimulated and that conventional measures (tax increases, placement of securities, and reduction of expenditure) would have to be adopted to finance and/or reduce the deficit.

In the past, periods of high investment were possible thanks mainly to forced saving (currency issue), and external saving (loans), apart from domestic saving protected by indexation of the financial market and the balance sheets of enterprises. Capital flight did not become a serious problem, as it did, for example, in Mexico and Argentina, because in Brazil, exchange and monetary policies, in general terms, kept real interest rates positive. Currently, these requirements are seriously compromised. The monetary reform is not allowing the deficit to be financed through currency issue at the same rate as hitherto, at least for the time being. External savings, in the form of new loans, essentially depend on the general condition of the economy and on an ambitious renegotiation program which in turn depends on the success of the cruzado plan. To erase the memory of inflation, the Government prohibited indexation of the balance sheets of enterprises and of almost all securities on the financial market; as it is known that the projected inflation rate is not less than (let us say) 20 percent annual, the distortions that these measures introduce in saving, investments, and the placement of resources are evident.

The most significant changes announced or actually undertaken by this Government (freezing the *conta de movimento*, budget unification, creation of the Secretariat of the Treasury, setting up the FND, creation of Central Bank bills, etc.), are partial and consequently insufficient, in view of the magnitude of the problems that have to be faced. They are not part of a plan to cover all the Government's financing and resource use needs. In this sense, they do not break with the inertia of recent years in fiscal and monetary affairs, and the Government is having to adopt stopgap measures that revolve around the general problems but do not solve the fundamental issues of reducing the public deficit and of stimulating savings and investment.

Currently, most state enterprise prices are totally out of phase (50 percent below 1980 prices), and they cannot invest as much with their own resources as they would wish. They even transfer a large proportion of their financial costs to the Banco do Brasil and to the BNDES. These banks guarantee the financial charges of the state enterprises but transfer the account to the Central Bank which is relieved when the Treasury declares a compulsory "loan" and compensates it—albeit partially—for these expenditures. The contradictions of the Housing Financing System are also well known—a decade of inequality between price indexes, wage changes, and monetary correction of savings pass-books and the symmetry of the system for making services and the debit balance current—gave rise to uncovered liabilities in the system of about US$20 billion, which will become due in the next few years. The continuing lack of transparency in the public sector accounts is thus notorious.

Some not inconsiderable disadvantages of this state of affairs are the discrepancies and uncertainties about the ideal compensation policies. These distortions originate not only in the diversity of viewpoints regarding the behavior of the economy and the probable incidence of specific measures, but also particularly, in the case of Brazil, in the lack of reliable information. For example, only recently, the Government admitted that, far from disappearing, the public deficit, excluding inflation, is running at about 5 percent of GDP. Even so, doubts remain about this estimate itself.

One crucial element in calculating the deficit is the choice of trans-actions to be included in the calculation. If this universe is limited to the federal government, the following budgets can be distinguished: the fiscal budget per se, employment funds (FGTS, PIS/PASEP, FND), the funds for direct distribution (SINPAS, FINSOCIAL, PIN/PROTERRA), those of public service enterprises (ELETROBRAS, TELEBRAS, RFFSA, etc.), those of public enterprises (PETROBRAS, VALE, SIDERBRAS, etc.), those of the official banks (BB, CEF, BNH, BNDES) and any funds and programs still administered by the Central Bank. The fiscal budget and the budget of the SEST seem gen-erally to be in balance, as the former does not include all of the expenditures which are a central government responsibility—essen-tially the financing requirements of official banks, whose expenditure program takes up almost 10 percent of GDP. The SEST covers part of its deficit with a capital increase supplied by means of fiscal resources.

With an overall view of the fiscal accounts, it is possible to avoid taking casuistic measures and plan for institutional reforms. For ex-ample, to reduce the deficit it would be inadvisable to raise (let us say) income tax, even though it represents over half of the federal revenue. Given the considerable segmentation of the Brazilian public sector, a linear cut of 10 percent in its total expenditures would be equivalent, from a financial point of view, to a 100 percent increase in income tax. Furthermore, in Brazil, income tax is essentially an indirect tax; 40 percent of collections come from enterprises (IRPJ), 20 percent from interest and dividend remittances abroad and 20 percent from financial market yields, taxed exclusively at source. Consequently, in order not to further penalize middle-class wage earners and consumers, a tax reform that would broaden the concept of income and include all sources of income in the individual return, would be a prerequisite to raising the income tax.

The Government possesses an ever-dwindling range of instruments to reduce the deficit and stimulate investments, other than the publication of yet more packages of measures or sheer direct intervention. Recently, with the intention of extending the deadline for financial operations concentrated in the under-60-days range, the National Monetary Council decided to tax heavily short-term operations by individuals and nonfinancial enterprises. There is a growing expectation that between the November elections and the end of the year, the Government will promote a new package of fiscal measures. This climate is clearly not compatible with renewed investment. The prerequisites for establishing confidence in the financial and capital markets include the revision of the short-term fiscal and monetary policy, the launching and consolidation of institutional reforms and the renegotiation of the current external debt on a permanent basis.

The new set of fiscal measures should include an explicit statement of, and a once-and-for-all answer to, the question of financing and reducing the public deficit. With regard to outflows, the Government should not shy away from announcing cuts in expenditures and increases in taxes and tariffs. Obviously this calls for unpopular measures, such as the managed unfreezing of prices and the revision of the wage "trigger" (automatic readjustment of wages whenever inflation reaches 20 percent). The strict monetary policy recently readopted should be continued in order to keep real interest rates at levels no lower than 10 percent or 12 percent a year. Furthermore, the monetary authorities would reduce uncertainties if they could agree to set their monetary expansion targets, even though this may be difficult because of the current confusion about the budget. The return of indexation for placements and contracts of more than one year is indispensable to reactivate long-term investment. It will no longer be possible to put off fixing an exchange devaluation policy.

Until the various budgets are standardized, simplified, and submitted simultaneously to Congress, budgetary programming will not be taken seriously. A tax reform to broaden the bases of the main taxes (the income and value-added taxes), would allow the present excessive number of parafiscal taxes and contributions to be reduced (single taxes, FINSOCIAL, PIS/PASEP, PIN/PROTERRA, Wage-Education, etc.). An effective separation of the Banco do Brasil and the Central Bank will take place only when a federal credit budget is instituted (consolidation of the financial programming of official banks) with prior provision of noninflationary resources. The administration of bonded and financial public debt, which is currently a federal responsibility, should be transferred from the Central Bank to the Secretariat of the Treasury, and the systems (SFH) and enterprises that are verging on bankruptcy should be capitalized, privatized, or simply dissolved. A realistic tariff policy would help reduce subsidies and raise the investment capacity of the state productive sector.

With an annual inflation rate of 20 percent, an extension of the floating rate mechanism for credit operations of more than one year, which is what the Government seems to want, does not seem possible. Consequently, there should be several instruments together to attract financing. Pre-fixed interest on very short-term operations (LBC), should form part of the Central Bank's portfolio in managing the liquidity of the system. Floating interest rates for maturities of up to 360 days and the monetary correction of interest would be the basic rule for operations with maturities of more than one year. Currently, the tax bite is one of the main cost elements of loans; taxing at source could be lower and compulsorily considered as an early return. The expansion or contraction of each of these market segments will naturally depend on business trends, the level of inflation, and the actual conduct of fiscal and monetary policy.

Financial intermediation outside banks (bonds without specific guarantee, "commercial paper") or even the involvement of banks in business intermediation (mergers, expansion, and associations) and in advising enterprises, have not been sufficiently developed in Brazil. Nevertheless, if there is a new rise in investment, these nontraditional sectors and the capital market should have an historical opportunity to increase their share of the market. The easy phase of large investments in import subsitution seems to be over—Brazil imports barely 3 percent of GDP, excluding oil. The transition to mature industrialization will call for the large-scale absorption of imported technology, a process that depends on competitive and decentralized investment methods.

The consolidation and renegotiation of the external debt must be preceded by the restructuring of the liabilities of the highly indebted enterprises. Part of this debt, which in some enterprises takes up 90 percent of their liquid assets, would be capitalized with the Treasury, which will take over the burden of financial charges to creditors. (In fact it has already done so in many cases.) It would then be necessary to restructure on a longer term (let us say 25 years) the maturities of the principal of a large proportion of this debt. The interest would be paid in full, but on the understanding that at least half would be reinvested in Brazil. The exchange devaluation policy would explicitly strive to maintain the par value, which has not happened, while not neglecting the evolution of the balance of payments. Renegotiation of the debt, fiscal adjustment, and institutional reforms would be prerequisites for attracting risk capital on a large scale, financed through domestic and foreign savings.

Comments

Aldo A. Arnaudo

The decline in investment and voluntary (private) saving ratios is the main concern of the paper. The 1980s have seen a substantial drop in investment expenditure per domestic unit of production as compared to the previous decade. A similar development can be observed in Argentina. The two countries' experience seems to indicate that this decline is connected with external debt service payments rather than with the suspension of foreign capital inflows, a phenomenon that would also explain the sharper drop in the figures for Argentina.

Investment is financed by private savings, by the savings of state enterprises (depending on the tariffs for public services), government savings (depending on taxation), and foreign savings, practically nonexistent at present. If the private savings ratio were raised it would be possible to increase investment and the main restriction on "most Latin American countries,... the scarcity of voluntary resources for long-term investment" (p. 180) would disappear. An orthodox Keynesian position would conclude that this is impossible, but social behavior as regards savings is quite complex and has been shown to be affected by the institutional framework.

Longo outlines the mechanisms used in his country to stimulate private savings, setting forth the instruments and their results. It is not my intention here to discuss these experiences, but rather to make a comparative analysis between Argentina and Brazil and to consider some vital aspects to guide future action.

Gross Capital Formation and Sources of Financing

Percentage of GDP, averages

	Argentina		Brazil[1]	
	1976–80	1981–84	1976–80	1981–84
Gross capital formation	22.4[2]	15.8[3]	24.2	18.9
S_P	11.8[4]	14.1[4]	15.0	15.4
S_E	3.9[5]	−2.5[6]	2.9	—
S_G		−4.1[6]	3.1	0.1
S_X	6.7[7]	8.3[7]	3.7	3.3

[1] Data are from Tables 2 and 3 of the paper under review.

[2] Ministry of Economy and Finance, *Informe Económico—Resena Estadística,* 1981, Part I, Table 1.

[3] D. Heymann, "Alta Inflación y Estabilización de Choque en la Argentina" (mimeographed, 1986, Appendix, Table 1.

[4] As distinct from total gross investment and the other entries.

[5] M. A. Broda, *Política Monetaria y Fiscal desde el Plan Austral;* series of seminars of the Economic Research Center of the Torcuato Di Tella Institute, 1986, Statistical Appendix, Table I.

[6] Ibid., (3) Table 8.

[7] Own calculation.

A comparative study gives the impression that in both cases the same financial phenomena produced similar results, even though they did not occur at the same point in time. There are at least six phenomena that can be compared, and which are dealt with below.

The first comparison is the existence of a central monetary authority whose functions include administering the financial assets of society. In Argentina, the Central Bank was organized in 1935 and had already been through the phase of having its deposits nationalized (1946–57) before the creation of its counterpart in Brazil in 1964, although the process was completed only very recently, when the Banco do Brasil relinquished its money creation operations. Taking the last twenty years, the monetary authorities of the two countries do not seem to have exerted much influence on the public to adopt given financial assets and, more seriously, did not possess the political independence to stand up to requests for monetary financing of the public sector deficits and the granting of various subsidies not channeled through the government budget.

Second, in Brazil, the investment banks were institutionalized in 1964, as part of the financial reforms of that year, and soon after it became possible to undertake indexed operations (or operations with monetary correction, according to the Brazilian terminology). In Argentina, although this was provided for in the 1968 legislation, only in 1974 was this process regulated, and it did not in fact come into operation because in 1977 the principles of the system of financial universality were introduced, under which any (banking) institution can undertake whatever asset and liability operations it wishes.

Third, indexation of financial operations was introduced in Brazil in 1964 with satisfactory results that led to a growth in the financial assets/output ratio (p. 182; cf. table, above). In Argentina there have been minor and sporadic attempts at indexation. The most important took place at the same time as a substantial increase in the rate of inflation, and lent themselves to "speculation" (in the sense of the substitution of money in day-to-day transactions), so that their adoption acquired the unfavorable connotation that it still has.

Fourth, a massive housing financing program was begun in Argentina in 1946 and lasted almost a decade. It used loans from the monetary authority, taking advantage of the fact that there was no fiscal deficit because of higher rates of collection of tax from the recently expanded social security system. In Brazil, a similar experiment took place from 1964 onward with the SFH system. It provided special subsidized financing—for this is what it becomes when differential monetary correction indexes are used. With the present difficulties in the Brazilian system caused by the partial indexation of loans, it is not unusual that in the long run they should lead to the elimination of the system, as happened in Argentina in the mid-1950s.

Fifth, the systemic decline of money (M_1 = money in circulation + demand deposits) as part of financial assets is observable both in Argentina and Brazil, and is undoubtedly due to inflationary conditions, substitution by other assets with a positive (or less negative) yield, and technological innovations.

Sixth, also common to both countries is the coupling to the financial system of a complex mechanism for subsidizing borrowers, either in the form of interest rates set very much below the market rates—with the subsequent implicit tax on the depositor—or by rediscounts at preferential interest rates—financed by the monetary authority, and so on.

The usual method of measuring the degree of financial saving in an economy is the ratio between the aggregate of financial assets (stock) and the national product (flow). On the basis of this parameter—quite apart from the value it has in developed countries—Longo is a little pessimistic (p. 183), as in Table 1 he indicates that the value achieved in the decade after the financial reforms of 1964 remained stable from 1975 and, after deteriorating, "only recently returned" (ibid.). The desirable upward trend in private savings has not been maintained, especially now that the possibilities of government and foreign savings have been exhausted. The figures for Argentina would give an even more pessimistic impression: from values close to those Brazil had in 1965 and 1975, in recent years the figures amount to barely half of Brazil's.

However, in the present case, the ratio between a stock (financial assets) and a flow (national product) in an inflationary economy is affected by the presence of negative real interest rates, which means that the increase produced by new financial savings may be insufficient to restore the real value of already existing assets. This situation would not occur if all financial assets were indexed, because they would automatically be adjusted to a growing level of prices. Furthermore, the systemic decrease in M_1 in terms of the national product introduces a downward bias. These difficulties make an alternative measure advisable, such as the (annual) growth of financial assets—flow—in relation to the national product, and its separation into those that do not yield interest (M_1) and those that do (the difference between M_2, M_3 or whatever denomination is used, and M_1). This correction would be less indispensable in an economy in which indexed assets predominated (Brazil) than in one where they are virtually nonexistent (Argentina).

If it is postulated that for reasons of monetary illusion, indivisibilities, lack of other alternatives, or reasons as yet unclear, there is positive financial saving with reasonably negative real interest rates, the above pessimistic position should be altered. A careful examination of Argentine statistics, taking into account changes of financial assets over time, would indicate that financial saving can increase through the liberalization of the financial markets and a closer linkage between nominal interest rates and the pace of inflation.

There are two extreme solutions to the problem of increasing real interest rates: to liberalize the markets and allow them to fix the nominal interest rates, or to introduce indexation of financial assets. When the nominal prices of goods and services are fixed by credit-taking entrepreneurs according to the "full-cost" principle (fixed margin over variable costs) and the financial charges are part of the cost, the risk of future inflation remains with the creditors (depositors or holders of financial assets); the reverse is true when operations are indexed and subject to positive real interest rates.

On the basis of the Argentine experience, unrestricted liberalization of the financial markets at a time of high inflation has the following main effects: (a) it increases short-term financial assets; (b) they become the only placement; (c) the mechanisms for extending terms on the basis of use of short-term interest rates (floating rates) are disastrous; (d) it leads to greater discrepancies between lending and borrowing interest rates and growing inefficiency in the financial system. The current evolution of the Brazilian system toward (nonindexed) deposits at a maximum of 60 days and the introduction of charges on very short-term deposits as a means of discouraging them is probably analogous to the phenomena experienced in Argentina.

From the above discussion, it can be inferred that the indexation of financial assets is more beneficial than liberalizing the financial markets as the rule seems to be that the latter measure encourages short-term assets whereas the former encourages long-term assets. The most recent stabilization plans in both countries showed considerable aversion toward indexation, which was blamed for much of the inertial inflation. Even if we accept this diagnosis, the indexation of financial assets, as well as the development of institutions that undertake this kind of operation, is a vital condition for increasing long-term assets— or at least for keeping them at their present level—in countries with a long history of inflation.

The traditional argument between those who support the segmentation of the financial markets between long-term and short-term and those who support a unified market has not been resolved and is now coming up again. There is no reason to incline one way or the other without knowing the circumstances of each case. A certain degree of segmentation can be brought about through the institutions and regulations if it is desired to stimulate the long-term market, and consequently make economic development easier. Putting aside any more thorough consideration of the capital market, the existence of a secondary market in indexed assets would be a good complement to the measures mentioned.

Despite all this, it would be difficult to make the indexation of financial assets advantageous without any restrictions at all. The experience of Brazil and Argentina counsels certain conditions: (i) inflation should be relatively low (under 50 percent per annum, let us say) to prevent indexed assets being used as means of payment, (ii) the fiscal deficit should be low to avoid crowding out the private sector and because it is unlikely (as Friedman would have it) that indexation would act to reduce it, (iii) there would be just one correction index to avoid hidden subsidies that frequently occur when there are several of them.

Last but not least, the combination of a financial system and subsidy mechanism gives the worst of both worlds, a point that must be borne in mind in the future when contemplating any reform intended to modernize the financial system.

Pedro A. Palma

These comments will not be a criticism of Longo's paper but rather a supplement to it, trying to establish some similarities and differences between the case of Brazil and that of Venezuela in regard to the behavior of such variables as savings and private investment, fiscal deficit and its financing, interest rates, external debt service payment commitments, and so forth, which are analyzed in Longo's paper.

I believe that this comparative analysis should start by establishing some of the differences and similarities that exist between the two economies under review. One of the main differences lies in the behavior of inflation, which in the Venezuelan economy has traditionally been low. Indeed, during the period 1960–72, the average year-on-year increase in consumer prices was only 1.6 percent. While this situation changed during the years of the oil bonanza (1974–77), inflation still remained low during this period (8.5 percent per annum), partly owing to the price controls and abundant state subsidies but mainly to the massive increase in imports, which made it possible to keep under control the price increases on tradable goods, despite the sustained high growth of demand during those years.

In the second half of 1979 and during 1980, Venezuela suffered the highest inflation rate in its recent history, over 20 percent. This was due to price liberalization combined with speculation, deliberate wage increases, very low labor productivity, and external upward pressures created by high interest rates and higher international inflation. From 1981 onward, there was a deceleration in the pace of price increases, which was sustained for several years. Even after the progressive devaluation of the bolívar that took place once exchange controls were established in February 1983, inflation remained moderate, despite the fact that the official exchange rate underwent a devaluation of about 75 percent over a three-year period, and that the free rate has depreciated substantially more severely.

The table that follows shows the very different behavior of inflationary pressures in the two countries.

This modest inflation has meant that Venezuela has not experienced the indexation processes so typical of the Brazilian, and to a lesser extent, the Argentine and other Latin American economies.

Percentage Change in Consumer Prices in Brazil and Venezuela

Percentages

	Venezuela	Brazil
1969–73[1]	3.2	19.2
1974–78[1]	8.2	36.0
1979	12.3	52.8
1980	21.6	82.8
1981	16.0	105.6
1982	9.7	98.0
1983	6.3	142.0
1984	12.2	196.7
1985	12.0	227.0

Sources: Central Bank of Venezuela; and International Monetary Fund.
[1] Average year-on-year changes.

Turning now to an analysis of the similarities between the two economies, mention should first be made of the drop in savings, and above all in private investment, which have taken place in Venezuela as in Brazil, in the last few years. During the period of the oil bonanza, real expenditures in capital formation, both public and private, increased rapidly, with an average year-on-year growth rate between 1975 and 1977 of 36 percent for the former and 23 percent for the latter. However, since the end of the 1970s, a radical change has taken place in this trend in the case of real private investment, which did not grow in 1978, and then underwent a sustained and abrupt contraction. Indeed, in the period 1979–83, it fell to a year-on-year rate of 26 percent.

This decline was due to a series of events, both domestic and foreign. The former includes overinvestment during the oil boom period, when new centers of production were created and others expanded, in the belief that the growth in demand in those years would continue uninterrupted for a long period of time, and that consequently the private productive sector would have to prepare itself to meet this increased demand. However, the completion of these investments coincided with the stagnation and subsequent contraction of private consumption which followed the bonanza, causing many enterprises to have to work at 40 percent or 50 percent of their installed capacity. This contributed substantially to the abrupt contraction in investment.

Likewise, the high world interest rates in 1979 and the early 1980s, together with the expectations of devaluation in Venezuela in 1978 and the first half of 1979, and also in 1982 and early 1983, due to the weakening of the oil market, all had an adverse effect on investment and private savings. These circumstances stimulated the outflow of capital from Venezuela, a process that was unimpeded due to the lack of restrictions on foreign exchange and the overvalued fixed exchange rate, which existed at this time, contrasting with the exchange controls and the regular minidevaluation process that Brazil had adopted.

Private savings also underwent a sustained contraction once the oil boom was over. This applies particularly to personal savings, as a result of the drastic decline in real disposable personal income and in particular the real average wage, which amounted to somewhat more than 25 percent between 1979 and 1985. This has resulted in a reduction in the average propensity to save, to such an extent that by our own estimates, these savings could presently be equivalent to 2 percent of disposable personal income, which contrasts with the level reached by this ratio at the end of the oil boom period when it was about 14 percent.

The contraction of investment, combined with the decline in private consumption as a result of Venezuela's reduced purchasing power, generated an economic recession which lasted for the seven years 1979–85, during which period real non-oil gross domestic product contracted at a year-on-year average rate of 1.1 percent, and the level of unemployment increased substantially.

All this led the Venezuelan authorities to define growth as the principal objective, which is also the economic policy recently applied in Brazil. Thus, in 1985, the Government announced its intention of implementing an expansionary fiscal policy, in order to stimulate economic activity through additional spending plans for capital formation above the budgeted levels. This policy began to be implemented in the last quarter of 1985. It has produced the desired results in its initial phase, as we have seen some recovery in the level of economic activity during the months it has been in force.

Paradoxically, the start-up of this expansionary expenditure policy actually coincided with the collapse of prices and the decline in value of oil exports, which in Venezuela's case led to an equivalent contraction in public sector revenue, and in particular central government revenue, the main contributor to which is the oil industry itself.

The introduction of this fiscal policy, combined with the fall in oil revenues, will obviously generate a disequilibrium in the public budget that will have to be financed. In the first phase (1986) the main source of deficit financing was public savings previously accumulated during the adjustment period 1984–85, together with additional resources obtained and saved by some state enterprises, in particular the nationalized oil industry after an adjustment in the official exchange rate from Bs 4.30 per U.S. dollar to Bs 7.50 per U.S. dollar, which generated additional revenue in bolívares for this industry, thus improving its cash flow and allowing it substantially to increase its deposits in the Central Bank. These resources are now being used to finance the public deficit.

However, the fact that there is little likelihood of oil exports increasing significantly in the short run raises a number of questions regarding the possibility of maintaining this expansionary fiscal policy in the years to come.

In Venezuela, the origins of the current public deficit lie in the sudden reduction in export revenue, over which it had no control. This distinguishes it from Brazil and Argentina and from many other Latin American countries, where the budget disequilibria derive from the rigidity of ordinary revenues, traditionally of domestic origin, combined with a sustained expansion of expenditure.

The question is what to do in light of the above: the choice is between attacking this deficit generated by a sudden drop in external revenue by means of a contraction in domestic expenditure, thereby keeping the budget in equilibrium and living with the consequences, or alternatively, trying to keep the public sector in a deficit situation in order to limit the dampening effect of the reduction in export revenue, thus avoiding a recession even deeper than the one we have had over the past eight years.

I believe that in the case of Venezuela the more logical choice is the second, because when oil prices collapsed we had abundant reserves in the public sector, as well as a very high level of international reserves, equivalent to over 24 months of imports of goods. Likewise, the trade surplus was in excess of US$8 billion and the current account surplus exceeded US$3 billion. It is reasonable to hope that if world prices for hydrocarbons fluctuate between US$13 and US$15 per barrel during the next few years, it will still be possible to preserve favorable trade balances somewhat in excess of US$2 billion and manageable current account deficits.

At all events, a decision of this kind is no easy task, because apart from the economic complexities involved, there are political and social factors intimately related to the economic policy alternatives. Similarly, it should be emphasized that the decision taken in the fiscal and monetary sphere must be just one aspect of the overall economic policy to be defined and implemented.

The direction the Venezuelan Government has decided to take on the fiscal side is to pursue the expansionary expenditure policy within the appropriate limits, trying at least to stop any major decline in real domestic expenditure.

Because of this, it is necessary to estimate the deficit financing requirements that will arise in the next several years and on that basis to decide what action to take. In this regard, on the one hand, the fact that ordinary revenue has been limited by the decline in oil exports and, on the other, the growing needs of domestic expenditure, are evident. Hence the need to limit external expenditure to the extent possible by postponing external debt amortization payments and by reducing the differentials on interest, while at the same time making serious efforts to make best use of the depleted resources through reorganizing expenditure and increasing its efficiency. In other words, an overall fiscal reform similar to the one proposed by the Fiscal Study and Reform Commission should be introduced, covering not only tax issues but also expenditure, indebtedness, budget, planning, as well as administration, inspection, and control of the *res publica*.[1]

If the depressed oil price situation and the low level of savings in the public sector persist, it will become imperative to find alternative sources of financing to cover the deficits for the years to come. As regards next year, apart from some funds still available being transferred to the Treasury, approval has been given to some changes in tax laws such as the Income Tax Law and the Stamp Tax Law, which increase collections from these sources, and the possibility is being studied of amending the law on the Central Bank and the General Banking Law, in order to expand the capacity of the institute of issue and other financial institutions to purchase government obligations.

If oil export revenue does not show signs of an upturn by 1988, and if the decision not to change the present par value is still in force, thus preserving an overvalued exchange rate that does not correspond to any economic reality, then the pursuance of an expansionary public expenditure policy could generate undesirable competitive pressures on the financial market, which in turn would lead to a scarcity of borrowable resources, due to the public sector's need for resources to cover its deficit, given the limited access to foreign savings and the low level of domestic savings that would then be available to it.

---

[1] See Fiscal Study and Reform Commission, *La Reforma del Sistema Fiscal Venezolano* (Caracas, 1983).

This leads to the conclusion that in the current scenario, the public sector will not have sufficient resources to stimulate economic activity so as to beat the recession on its own. Hence the need to define and introduce without delay a coherent overall economic policy with a medium- and long-term horizon, that will not only improve the financial situation of the public sector but will also create the necessary circumstances for sectors other than the government sector to take the necessary action with a view to reaching the common goal of reviving the economy.

I have outlined below some of the most important variables or actions (apart from those already mentioned), that should shape such an economic policy, in an attempt to identify the ways in which they resemble, and differ from, Longo's proposals regarding Brazil. The first difference comes in the recommendations on fiscal and monetary policy, as Longo favors introduction of restrictive policies, making the possibility of stimulating economic activity wholly dependent on private investment. While this recommendation is made against a background of high levels of growth in the Brazilian economy, I believe we should not lose sight of the fact that implementation of such contractionary policies would have recessionary effects, or would at least lead to a slowdown, which could in turn limit the possibilities of private investment and consequently the growth potential of Brazil. However, this recommendation is made in a situation in which growth of private consumption is of such proportions that, apart from creating disequilibria in Brazil's external transactions, it is generating growing inflationary pressures, which are precisely the ones that they are seeking to control.

On the other hand, as I have already explained, I believe that in Venezuela's case, the implementation of moderately expansionary fiscal and monetary policies is justified, because they would at least avoid a sharp contraction of financial resources in light of the drastic decline in oil revenues, because otherwise recessionary pressures could return, and could reach unsustainable limits.

Turning now to the points on which the recommendations agree, I believe that in Venezuela it is becoming vital to introduce a dynamic exchange policy such as has been applied in Brazil for some time now, by means of which, after a devaluation of the commercial bolívar, regular adjustments of the exchange rate would be made to keep Venezuelan products competitive with foreign products. Furthermore, Longo's observation regarding Brazil does not apply to Venezuela, where there is a high import substitution potential which, if the conditions were right, could lead to considerable investment which would contribute not only to improving the balance of payments but also to stimulating economic activity.

Given that Venezuela is a country with no tradition or experience of exporting, I do not think that in the short run much hope can be placed in this area, particularly in the present world circumstances in which every country is seeking to export while at the same time keeping its imports down to a minimum. There is, nonetheless, a high export potential in some areas where there is an obvious comparative advantage and where results can be achieved in a relatively brief period of time. This applies to numerous primary products, such as petrochemicals, aluminum, steel, and so forth, and to tourism.

It is important to remember that the introduction of such an exchange policy would have significant repercussions on government finance in Venezuela. However, it would be a serious error if exchange decisions were taken to achieve this objective, rather than with a commercial purpose. Similarly, it must be borne in mind that, given the fact that the public sector is an exporter and the private sector is an importer, the devaluation of the bolívar would mean the transfer of resources from the private to the public sector, which would mean that these exchange adjustments would have a restrictive effect equivalent to that of an indirect tax. Hence the importance of the fiscal expenditure policy being very well planned, so that it can ensure that the additional resources obtained from the private sector can be channeled toward those activities that it is wished to stimulate.

Another essential aspect of this coherent overall policy that should be introduced in Venezuela, and one that fits in with Longo's recommendations for Brazil, is the fixing of positive and realistic real interest rates, which would stimulate domestic savings, thus generating a greater capacity for domestic financing. In this way, the pressures on the financial markets that would appear as a result of competition between the public sector and the private sector to capture resources would be reduced. Consequently, the very limited approach used so far in fixing interest rates, whereby they are established according to how world market interest rates behave, without taking into account domestic inflationary pressures, should be abandoned. This approach has led to negative real interest rates, which not only discourage domestic savings but also promote the outflow of capital.

Last—without intending to declare this comparative analysis complete, for it could be substantially expanded—I agree with Longo's recommendation that an extension of the amortization terms on external debt should be negotiated. In the specific case of Venezuela, this is of crucial importance, as apart from freeing resources for domestic expenditure, the contraction in oil exports, and their possible stabilization at current levels makes it necessary to increase efforts to reduce the deficit in the nonmonetary capital account, which would be the decisive factor regarding the size of the overall balance of payments deficit in the years to come. Hence the need to link foreign debt service to commitments to new lending by creditor banks, to be used to finance viable projects, and to make conditions suitable for stimulating foreign investment.